FAMILY IN INDIA

FAMILY IN INDIA

Krishna Chakrabortty

RAWAT PUBLICATIONS
Jaipur • New Delhi • Bangalore • Guwahati • Kolkata

ISBN 978-81-7033-710-2

Reprinted, 2023

Published by
Prem Rawat for **Rawat Publications**
Satyam Apts, Sector 3, Jawahar Nagar, Jaipur 302 004 (India)
Phone: 0141 265 1748 / 7006
E-mail: info@rawatbooks.com
Website: www.rawatbooks.com

New Delhi Office
4858/24, Ansari Road, Daryaganj, New Delhi 110 002
Phone: 011 2326 3290

Also at *Bangalore, Guwahati* and *Kolkata*

Typeset by Rawat Computers, Jaipur
Printed and bound in India

To my students
in the Department of Sociology, Calcutta University,
who always helped me in bearing the dual burden of
teaching and research

Contents

Acknowledgements

Any piece of research being a cooperative venture, is difficult to complete without the help of the others. This inquiry has also been possible through the kind cooperation of several well-wishers. It is not possible to name here all the kind souls, but a few of them deserve special mention.

I am thankful to the University of Calcutta which extended a grant for conducting this inquiry. I take this opportunity to acknowledge with thanks the valuable assistance and cooperation of Mrs. Ruma Banerjee, Mrs. Saswati Kar and Mrs. Asma Begum (Bangladesh) who shared with me the most hazardous and yet the most interesting part of this work, namely, the task of data collection. They worked with full devotion, attention, sincerity and responsibility. I am also thankful to Dr. S.K. Bhattacharyya who put some valuable suggestions.

Likewise, any inquiry, based on primary data, cannot be successfully conducted without the cooperation of the respondents. I am, therefore, profoundly indebted to my respondents without whose cooperation I could neither begin nor complete this work.

Finally, I owe thanks to my publishers.

1

Introduction

I

All of us know about marriage and families. Parents, siblings, spouses, children—these are not remote and academic subjects but virtually everyone's first-hand experiences. Family is a social unit of which almost everyone of us is a member. It is the most remarkable and one of the oldest of all our social institutions. In fact, no other social institution can transcend the family in the intensity of its sociological significance.

Family organisation, however, is not instinctive. Nevertheless, it is found everywhere. The fact of universality can be taken for its functionality or usefulness to the personal and social needs. It influences the whole life of a society in innumerable ways, and any change in it reverberates through the entire social structure. It is capable of endless variations, and yet reveals a remarkable continuity and persistence. Society depends on the institution of family for the reproduction, protection, socialisation and social placement of its members—functions through which its continuation as well as maintenance of social order is possible. In addition to these universal functions, the family performs important economic, social, educational, recreational and religious functions. For all these reasons family is called the 'cradle of human nature'.

Most of us can learn about family from our direct experiences as this institution is a part of our everyday life. In addition, we learn much about family life through observation of those who are around us, from mass media, from literature and from drama.

Many of our views about family life are shaped by religious and political traditions. Religious doctrines and state laws have sought to institutionalise the desired form of family behaviour in human societies everywhere. Doctrine and laws, for example, frequently prescribe and proscribe the choice of marriage partners by age and relatedness, confine sexual relations to marriage, limit the number of children permitted, specify the forms of inheritance and the rights of sustenance, and various other rights and obligations of the members of family. One can note what Goode (1965, pp. 1-2) most pertinently remarks: "Philosophers and social analysts have noted that society is a structure made up of families, and that the peculiarities of a given society can be described by outlining its family relations. The earliest moral and ethical writings suggest that a society loses the strength if people fail in their family obligations. Confucius thought, for example, that happiness and prosperity would prevail in the society if only everyone would behave 'correctly' as a family member—which primarily meant that no one should fail in his filial obligations."

However, traditions, religion and law generally underscore the normative aspects of marriage and family life. They address the question of 'should' and 'ought', and seek to differentiate what is wrong from what is right and what is good from what is bad. But families can be understood in yet another way. Many a time we feel interested in learning "What is it?" as distinguished from "What should it be?" But accurate answers to questions of the former type regarding family can hardly be obtained by our intuitions or by referring to normative prescriptions about what is right or good as distinguished from what is wrong or bad.

One may ponder over the following questions:

Is it at all meaningful to talk of a kinship or an extended family system in the modern Indian society? Or, conversely, does the relatively isolated nuclear family emerge as the typical family unit in the modern society?

Has it been empirically tested and confirmed that the central tendency of the Indian society remains in favour of continuing the joint family organisation?

How have the processes of industrialisation and urbanisation affected the family system in India?

Does the Indian joint family system help or hinder industrialisation?

Is the change in the family system a simple function of industrialisation and urbanisation? Or, is it more likely that changes in the ideological or value systems which are partially independent of the above changes, have some effect on the family changes?

Does the nuclear family tend to be an isolated unit relatively cut off from the extended kin network?

Does the transition from pre-urban to urban living necessarily involve stresses and strains, conflicts and socio-cultural maladjustments?

What was the base of emergence of the system of value which nurtured and stabilised the joint family organisation in the Indian society?

Whether and, if so, why is the previous set of values losing its influence in contemporary India?

Is there any evidence of a qualitative change in the value system of the people which will lead to a complete nuclearisation of the family structures of India? What is exactly the other set of values which confront the above values?

Is the course of change in values already expressed in the opinion of a substantial section of the people?

Has that attitude been translated into action and evidenced by a shift in the behaviour pattern of the people vis-a-vis their family life?

Are all the segments of the society affected by this shift of attitude and behaviour, if any, uniformly?

What is exactly meant by 'family solidarity' or 'functional jointness'?

What are the various ways of maintaining functional jointness among the component household units when they live in separate dwelling units?

Whether and how do the practices of maintaining functional jointness vary from family to family, or from society to society?

Is any change noticeable in the mode of performing functional jointness across different age-groups, geographical areas and socio-economic categories?

For addressing the above type of questions an empirical approach would be the most helpful. 'Empirical approach' means gathering of data from the real life situations and analysing and assessing the same in a systematic way. Evidences collected through carefully conducted empirical research can help us better understand the phenomena relating to the family and draw relatively reliable and precise conclusions about our family behaviour. Empirical studies would provide a counterbalance to our personal predilections and inferences drawn on the basis of our personal experiences or assertions made on the basis of the so-called common sense or legal assertions stressing the normative requirements.

II

'Family' is a word which is difficult to define, as a variety of definitions of the family have been provided to suit different purposes. There are legal and administrative definitions, there are statistical and demographic models and there are ideal-typical definitions of, for example, 'nuclear family'. There are actors' definition of their own and others' families and summations of typifications of these definitions. There are also idealistic models of what the family ought to be like, evaluations of the importance and meaning of family life in the context of society as a whole.

Often confusions over the definition of family arise from the differences between popular and academic uses of the term. Again, this popular usage itself is extremely complex. Frequently people are found to refer to their relatives as 'the family': "All the family turned up for the funeral." In the next breath they will say, "Of course, I knew *my* family would come, but I never expected all *my husband's* family to show up." Apparently we have one family which is simultaneously two families—his and hers. "But, of course, my brother didn't bring his family along; they are much too young." Here the reference is to the offspring. "The neighbours were very good too. Rambabu came with his wife and their two children. It was very nice that the whole family turned up like that." Here the use is more restricted than 'relative', or 'his relatives', but includes both the parents and the offspring. "Of course, the children will be leaving home soon. It's always sad to see the families break up like that." Here, the reference is not only to the parents and children, but to their co-residence, that is, to the household. "Anyhow they won't be living too far away—I always think it nice if you can keep the family together." Here the reference is to some sentimental ties among the members of separate dwelling units. Even though the members are spatially dispersed, they still do not cease to be members of the same family, whatever that means.

The academic use of the term 'family' is also no less confusing, particularly the use of the term 'joint family' in the Indian context, as it would be revealed in the next chapter.

Sociologists often define the family and distinguish among its different varieties in terms of its functions. The simplest statement about the functions of the family will be roughly that the family is a universal institution and must therefore perform some universal functions. This appears to be the position of Murdock (1949). A slightly more sophisticated version of this statement is that there are certain basic functional prerequisites that must be met if society is to survive, and the institution of family is unique or best able to meet these functions.

These rather simplistic perspectives are, however, opposed to another functionalist orientation which recognises that the family can lose some of its functions or that the functions can change. Thus, the institution of family is not invariably tied to some universal and necessary function. This is the approach of Talcott Parsons, and it is linked to an evolutionary perspective. Briefly, this assumes that as societies evolve they undergo a process of 'structural differentiation' whereby social institutions become differentiated from one another and develop some measure of autonomy in relation to the society as a whole. In this process the family becomes a more separate and more specialised institution, fulfilling more specialised functions. True, the family has lost some of its traditional functions—economic (in a productive sense), educational, religious and so on—but this does not mean that the family has become functionless or a more or less useless 'survival'. Instead, it has come to specialise in the function of 'socialisation' and the emotional support of adult members of the society. Here Parsons counters those critics who argue that the family is facing dissolution and a loss of function by arguing that we are witnessing a process of change rather than one of dissolution. By 'change' he means that the family is now relatively isolated and this relative isolation is functional for the demand of a modern industrial society.

III

One of the principal controversies in the study of family in India has been whether the joint family is incompatible with industrialisation and urbanisation—the famous 'joint family controversy' in short. Most of the family sociologists *believe* that the patrilineal-patrivirilocal joint family has been the 'desired norm' for the Hindus since the ancient times, and the norm continues through modern times. For example, Mukherjee (1977, p.168) holds that "the motif in West Bengal is thus to form the patrilineal joint family of procreation—presently, eventually or potentially". Other orthodox family sociologists also more or less share the same view, as we shall see in the following chapter.

One group of social scientists in India takes a position similar to the one held by Parsons (1949) and Goode (1963) whose observations are related to the family in industrially advanced countries. They argue that the joint family cannot be predominant in industrial societies because it is inconsistent with the changing economic and social patterns. The main contribution in this direction is from Morrison (1959), Nimcoff (1959), Kulkarni (1960), Ross (1961), Dube (1974), Kaldate (1961), Sarma (1964), Sen (1965) and Desai (1932). Scholars of the other group contend that the joint family has not disintegrated but has adapted itself to the modern industrial setting. They hold that though the joint family might have undergone some structural changes, it continues 'functionally' to remain the same. Although the family may no longer be a physical aggregation of lineal agnates and collaterals, they see it continuing to be a joint family 'in spirit'. Arguments supporting this position have been advanced by family sociologists like Kapadia (1956, 1959, 1966), Desai (1956, 1964), Gore (1968), Mukherjee (1977) and Madan (1989).

Authors, however, more or less, agree on two points: (1) Though the traditional norm of the Indian family has been that of the joint type, consisting of three or four generations of close kin related patrilineally or sometimes matrilineally, the family unit of husband-wife-children group has retained its parallel existence since long. (2) The small family consisting of husband, wife and children with or without some close relations like parents(s), unmarried brother(s) or sister(s) is nowadays becoming more and more popular.

The bone of contention among the authors is the prevalence and chance of survival of the joint family in the changing condition of India. Authors asserting the survival of the joint family argue that 'jointness' of the Indian family is displayed not so much by the outward symbols like co-residence or commensality, but by the sentimental bonds, sharing of privileges and obligations among the kin. This is often called 'functional solidarity' of the joint family, which does not disappear with occupational diversification and geographical dispersion of its members.

However, the problem is that, as has rightly been pointed out by Dube (1974, p.323), the functional jointness as it has been used so far, appears to be an elusive concept. She denotes, "To insist that nuclearisation of households caused by migrations, occupational diversification, and so forth, has not affected the joint family sentiment and joint family norms is to ignore the normal processes of social life. If this concept is to be used, clear-cut indicators will have to be evolved."

It is not wholly sensible to conclude that the economic development and the accompanying increased employment opportunities, accelerated process of urbanisation and migration from the rural to urban areas are bound to disintegrate the joint family norm; for, the bonds of jointness, privileges and obligations do not cease to operate with the establishment of separate dwelling units in the urban areas. Equally it would be a gross oversimplification to assume that geographical dispersion has no impact over the joint family structure and norm or that the behaviour and interpersonal relations in the family are not affected by the break-up of the family into several nuclear units, or that every nuclear family of today is a future or potential joint family.

True, the extent of nuclearisation and disintegration of the joint family cannot be directly measured simply from the relative incidence of nuclear and joint family structures at a certain point in time. It can be assumed, however, that sons and brothers who have departed from their families of orientation and started living in their own families of procreation will register some change in attitude and behaviour towards their 'kin'. Their kinship bonds, for instance, may be less strong now than in the earlier phase because they will be involved by this time in a new series of duties and obligations, new strains of psychological integration.

The three or four generation family, even when dispersed in more than one domestic group, is expected to have close contact in relation to affines and uterine kin and also in relation to agnatic kin outside the immediate household in the changed context. Generally, there may be obligations of rendering assistance and cooperation of various kinds in rituals and ceremonies. But should this group of individuals connected only by bonds of these types be still regarded as a joint family?

Another fact that deserves mention is that in many of the co-residential, commensal joint families, particularly in urban areas, which are forced to stay joint because it is the norm, or due to fear of gossip, or social disapprobation, or due to some advantages of remaining joint, or because of dearth of alternative accommodation or any such reason, there may be considerable internal separation in respect of style of living, socialisation and upbringing of children, entertainment, type of consumption, mental orientations, and so on. These differences may cast serious effects on the familial bonds and levels of familial integration. These internal arrangements, therefore, deserve to be inquired as a distinct category in a study of functional solidarity of the joint family.

One more fact needs to be specified. It may be presumed that the function of any social entity is closely related to its structural arrangements. The services which may be rendered by the members of a joint family when they live within the same compound, for example, looking after the ill, the aged, helping in baby-sitting, taking care of the house and belongings when some or other inmates of the household go out, cannot be performed when they lack geographical propinquity. Geographical dispersion does not, however, prevent the members from participation in and sharing certain other kinds of activities like rendering financial assistance or occasionally participating in family ceremonies and gatherings. But, the types, levels and degrees of these participations are bound to vary with geographical proximity and dispersion. The association between the physical proximity and functional jointness, therefore, deserves to be looked into.

Moreover, as there is a change in generation depth and collateral width of households, change can be expected in the structural and functional characteristics of the household too. The authority structure, division of labour in a lineal-collateral joint household, for instance, will be significantly different from those in a lineal joint or in a nuclear household. The supposition of the present study is that jointness of households is not only a matter of sharing of sentimental bonds and mutual privileges and obligations, kinship composition, jointness of property, largeness of size, but consists of certain interactions and role behaviours of the members of a family unit.

Studies on forms and types of the family, relative incidence of the nuclear and joint family structures, or mental orientation or sentimental solidarity among the break-away nuclear units cannot provide answer to whether the joint family solidarity remains intact or to which direction our family structure is moving. Unless we precisely study the interpersonal relations in the family we cannot refute the criticisms levelled against the Indian family sociologists by their western counterparts: The joint family, is the cultural ideal of most sectors of the Indian society but it is not, and probably never has been, the typical family organisation of any sector (cf. Goode, 1963; Straus, 1975).

For analysing what the emerging family type is—joint, nuclear or any combination of both—we have to define and specify, first, attributes of nuclearity and jointness and then search for the same in *both* types of family structures. Instead of searching for only jointness in nuclear households, inquiry is to be directed towards nuclearity in joint families as well. And, for realising the above purpose, namely, for looking into the dynamics of the family behaviour and interpersonal relationships among family members, a mere classification of families (on the basis of composition) into nuclear, supplemented nuclear, extended, joint (or whatever labels may be used) will not be useful. Such inquiries can at best indicate a residential pattern. But it will be worthwhile inquiring as well if the smallness of the residential group is associated with the closeness of distance in relationships.

In addition to observing interpersonal relationships among the family members, the role definitions of different persons in different relationships, the beliefs, values and attitudes also are to be investigated. They will indicate the cultural and psychological elements in the interactions between the members of the family, and will enable us to characterise the 'family sentiments' as joint or nuclear.

The study of beliefs and values in any sociological inquiry is pertinent. For, sociology is concerned with both 'culture' and 'structure'. Thus, it deals with both the beliefs, values and norms of behaviour that members of a society share, and the way in which they act in pursuance of those beliefs, values and norms.

Unfortunately, a survey of research on family studies in India indicates that the field has been more dominated by Indology and law than sociology. This tendency can be found in all stages of inquiry, namely, the selection of research issues, defining the concepts, drawing the samples or units of observation, and interpreting the data. One net result of this confusion is that we are yet to achieve a unanimous or a more or less agreed-upon definition of the concept of 'joint family'. We do not have, as yet, a precise knowledge as to what are the essential structural components or functional indices of a joint family, or, whether and how far it empirically differs from an 'extended family'—another concept commonly used in the parlour of family research. All these irregularities and confusions have led to the emergence of the popular 'joint family controversy'. The present venture is a very modest step towards the removal of some of these irregularities, confusions and ambiguities.

The present inquiry, instead of starting with any pre-formulated hypothesis that nuclearisation of the joint family is or is not taking place, seeks to discern and depict the mode of functioning of our present-day family system, the patterns of interactions among the kin. The family has been viewed here as an interactional unit with diverse and dynamic intra-family relationships.

The aim of the present venture is not just to add yet another volume to the famous and popular 'joint family controversy', namely, to search for any association between economic development and the survival of the traditional joint family of India. Nor is the intention here to find out the loopholes, inadequacies and logical irregularities in the existing literature on the Indian family. The job has already been done effectively (cf. Dube, 1974; Kolenda, 1987; Shah, 1964, 1973; Mukherjee, 1971, 1975; Hallen, 1982; Chakrabortty, 1982), and this author can do no better than refer the reader to these discussions.

The present inquiry intends to focus on a rather neglected but highly pertinent aspect of our family life—the nature and extent of family solidarity among the members of the household units. So, the point at issue here is not whether the members psychologically belong to one 'family' even when the co-residential, commensal joint family breaks up, but whether and how the familial bonds survive under such conditions. Rather than assuming 'jointness' as one and uniform entity, we propose to distinguish between the different levels of family solidarity by commensality, by co-residence, by the closer ties of cooperation and obligations, the distant ties of obligations, and the ties of recognition. Following Mukherjee (1975, p.47), a distinction can be made here between the 'familial bond' (bond shared by the members when they live in the same co-residential, commensal unit) and 'kinship bond' (bond of privileges and obligations maintained by the members when they break away from their families of orientation and live in their respective families of procreation).

Mukherjee, thus, admits the justifiability of distinguishing between these two types of bond and integration. Though he has also suggested some method of measuring this distinction (1975, 1982) he himself, however, has not tested or applied this method in his empirical studies on the family.

The present inquiry proposes to begin from the hunch of Desai (1975). In his later years, Desai realised the relevance of revising the orientation and approach of the conventional type of family studies made in general by the Indian scholars. He includes himself also in this list: "It will also not be necessary to go into any elaborate classification of families of different degrees of jointness or nuclearity as was done by this writer. It is not necessary to go into the proportion of joint and nuclear households" (p.67). A fruitful approach of family research would, as is suggested by Desai, be to study the dynamics of the family, that is, how the members bound by specific relationships interact with one another in definite situations and on definite occasions. Such inquiries into the joint households also will enable us to know the elements of nuclearity in them if there are any. Whether the nuclear households are joint in terms of rights, obligations and norms will be seen while observing the dynamics of nuclear households (ibid.).

Thus, Desai proposes to rectify one shortcoming in our family studies which is often pointed out by the western sociologists. Straus, for example, comments, "But almost none of the vast literature on the Indian joint family compares joint families with nuclear families. Typically, only joint families are studied and comparisons are made with characteristics *imputed* to nuclear families, or vice versa", and thus the mode of functioning of nuclear and joint families cannot be ascertained from these studies (1975, p.135).

It should be made clear at this point that the present venture is concerned not with the alleged decline in the importance of the joint family in the present-day Indian society. Hence, we shall not consider here the kind of family system we might desire, or analyse the way in which these desired ends might be achieved or some of the probable obstacles in the way of their realisation. Rather, the functions currently being performed by the family in the Indian society, the patterns of interactions as pursued among the members of the joint family, the family behaviour as is actually engaged in by the members of nuclear and joint families will be the focus of interest. More specifically, it will deal with the extent to which kinship network works outside the immediate nuclear household. It will be checked here whether relatives are the first ones most people turn to for fulfilling their needs.

An evaluation of the family *system* (relationships and interactions within and between the families) in India apart from the family size and structure is highly relevant for a proper and useful understanding of on-going changes. This will not be merely an academic exercise. It has implications for many aspects of social policy including housing, insurance, land ceiling, urban development, old age pensions and old age homes, and the re-location of industry. If it is found that the family is in decline (in terms of functions) and that is to the detriment of the society, it will bring a host of social evils such as violence in the family, delinquency, drug abuse, problem of the aged and the old, and the like.

2

Family in the Changing Society: Views of the Western Sociologists

Since the family patterns currently followed is the focus of the present inquiry, a brief discussion over its various aspects as viewed by the family sociologists, is presented in this chapter. The relevant portions of the observations of the western family sociologists will be discussed here and in the next chapter the observations of the family sociologists made particularly in the context of the Indian society will be offered.

I

The popular 'joint family controversy', the major preoccupation of the Indian family sociologists, owes its origin to the writings of the western family sociologists. One of the most popular debates in the sociology of family revolves around the alleged 'decline of the kinship'. The debate was originally initiated by Parsons. While discussing the structural correlates of the American occupational system he predicts that this system "places severe limitations on the kind of kinship structure which is compatible with such a system. Mobility on an individual basis is incompatible with such a kinship system as that of the Chinese, for example, which places a primary emphasis on the continuity of general social status through kinship from generation to generation" (1949, pp.191-92). Thus, Parsons has argued that the "relatively isolated nuclear family is the type of family which is most adapted to (i.e., fits best) the other institutions found in the industrial societies. By 'relative isolation' Parsons implies that obligations to the members of the nuclear family are more stringent than obligations to kin outside it, that is, ego's duties to his spouse and *immature* children are more stringent than his duties to parents.

According to Parsons, then, in industrial societies the kinship system makes no provision for the formation of household groups wider than the nuclear family, and that obligations between members of the nuclear family take precedence over those to kin outside it. He points out that any kin group wider than the nuclear family would inhibit geographical mobility of individuals and that the nuclear family is the unit of mobility. If it can be shown that an industrial economy can function only if there is a considerable movement of people between jobs and that such movements must involve frequent spatial mobility and that the age at marriage is such, and that the age of retirement is such, that fathers and married sons are working at the same time, then it follows that even extended stem family households will be impossible in a large number of cases. Though there may not be perfect correspondence between Parsons' assertions and any actually existing industrial system, it may be assumed that a high degree of spatial mobility must disperse the sibling group.

Industrial society is characterised by the existence of specific institutions set up to perform economic activities. From this it follows that in such societies the family cannot be in the majority of cases the unit of production, and the kin group is not required to co-ordinate economic activities. Instead, the process of industrialisation, among other things, leads to opening of new vistas for earning, resulting into that sons are not to depend on the ancestral familial property or traditional occupation of the forefathers. For availing themselves of these new opportunities of employment, men may have to leave their ancestral residence and be geographically mobile.

Next, industrialism leads to job differentiation and increase in the level of skill. The more the jobs are differentiated (that is to say, the more different types of job there are) and the higher is the level of skill required, the less substitutable one worker will be for another. When substitutability is low, it will be difficult to 'fit' men to jobs. The more difficult it is, the more necessary it will be to appoint them purely on merit and the more mobile the people will have to be. Such a society is different from the one where agricultural sector engages a great majority of (unskilled) workers, and skill required is rudimentary. In the latter type of society majority of the people need not be mobile between jobs. Here property and jobs are transmitted on the basis of ascribed status.

But the question is: Does this geographical dispersion associated with industrialisation amounts to lessening of dependence on the family of orientation and intra-family household ties? Or conversely, is it true that in the changed situation sons are still to depend on their fathers and brothers who provide economic support (if required), advice and information? Interactions may not cease to operate but may be channelled in separate ways. It is to be examined to what extent exchange of goods and services which are not tied to close physical proximity are still maintained in these mobile families.

One of the functions of the family is supposed to be placement of the new born. Class membership is in this sense ascriptive. It is determined in two ways. First, the family into which one is born affects one's life chances, i.e., the chance of becoming successful, etc., because of the control over resources commanded by the family and the wider kin. Secondly, because family members share prestige, a social relationship with a member of a family group involves an obligation to treat the other members of the group in the same way.

Now, the members of a nuclear family which has achieved an upward occupational mobility, may be unwilling to treat their immobile kinsmen as equal. Therefore, they may be eager to maintain social distance from these kin. Hence, kin groups wider than the nuclear family, under the impact of differential occupational mobility leading to social mobility, are disrupted. This is because of extreme differences in socialisation and life-style among the various occupational strata in which different units of the kindred (lying outside the pale of a particular nuclear family) may be distributed.

In the above argument a close relationship between geographical and social mobility (social mobility has been defined here as movement from a manual to a non-manual occupation intergenerationally) has been assumed. It has also been presumed that social mobility starts with geographical mobility and that geographical mobility is a necessary step in occupational and social mobility.

Parsons' main arguments, however, do not depend upon inconsistencies between rules governing the activities of economic and kinship institutions. Rather, they centre round the 'conflicts of values' which arise because of the difference in type of the much more general ideas upon which each institution depends, and which govern the way in which roles in the society are allocated.

Parsons sees the growth of successful industrial activity as associated with the adoption of values which he calls 'universalism' and 'achievement'. The belief that it is wrong to differentiate between people in the same category on the grounds of their relation to the ego is in Parsonian terms 'universalism'. The belief that we ought to differentiate between people in this way is its opposite, 'particularism'. It is obvious that kinship constitutes a set of particularistic relationships, while successful industrialisation requires universalistic values.

By 'achievement' Parsons means the belief in the rightness of varying one's behaviour towards other people on grounds other than their possession of inherent qualities, which he calls, in contrast, 'ascription'. Kin relationships depend on categorisation on the basis of inherent qualities (being born of...), and not upon achieved qualities. They are governed not by achievement values but by ascriptive values. According to Parsons, modern industrial enterprises are governed by the values of universalism and achievement. As a result individuals who are both members of families and workers in industrial enterprises will be required to hold two contradictory sets of values at the same time.

The industrial society, with its normative requirement of universalism and individual achievement, prevents a sharp antithesis to the 'ascriptive solidarity' of kinship groups. The solidarity of the kinship unit is of such a character that if certain facilities and rewards are available to one member, they will have to be 'shared' with other members. Extensive obligations to kin and membership in a kinship group as a basis for role allocation is dysfunctional for the demands of an industrial system with its stress on social and geographical mobility and individual achievement as a major culturally desired motivation.

In an industrial society, people will be confronted with difficulties in the economic sphere when a relative asks for help in getting a job, or comes to the shop where they work and asks for a special treatment. Within the family they may find that they have to suspend judgements on their kinsfolk. Parsons argues that this conflict of values makes life difficult, but it can be avoided if one restricts one's family group to the nuclear family.

If Parsons is the major theorist of the sociology of the family, Goode is its major craftsman, and no discredit to Goode is intended in the use of the label. Goode's analysis of the relationship between the family and the industrialisation process is perhaps most widely known as it has been respected and reprinted in several places. Stated very briefly, Goode argues that throughout the world there is a tendency for the process of industrialisation to be accompanied by the move towards what he calls the 'conjugal type of family'. He outlines the main features of this type of family, recognising that it is an ideal typical abstraction: "The most important characteristic of the ideal typical constitution of the conjugal family is the relative exclusion of a wide range of affinal and blood relatives from its everyday affairs" (1963, p.8). The tendency is towards neolocality; there is a freer choice of mate; the descent system is multilineal, and so on. This family system corresponds broadly with Parsons' 'relatively isolated nuclear family'. Goode, however, does not stress that this family system cannot be stripped right down to its nuclear bones but that grandparents will still have an important part to play.

Like Parsons, Goode also argues that there is a degree of congruence between this system of family and the process of industrialisation. While analysing it, he points out that under this economic system the individual is ideally given a job on the basis of his ability to fulfil its demands, and that this achievement is evaluated universalistically. The same standards apply to *all who hold the same job*. This link with the job is functionally specific. Further, being achievement-based, an industrial society is necessarily open-class, requiring both geographical and social mobility. Moreover, in the industrial system, jobs based on ownership and cultivation of land (and thus on inheritance) become numerically less significant and encourage considerable geographical mobility leading to neo-local residence.

Goode, however, adds several important modifications. In the first place, he is hesitant to assign any necessary causal priority to either the changes in the family or industrialisation. Instead, he points out that the relationship between the changes in the family system and economic and industrial systems has often been taken for granted, and has never been scientifically demonstrated. No specific family forms seem to be correlated with the specific 'stages' of the economic and technological evolution.

Secondly, he maintains that changes will take place at different paces and from different starting points. Thus, the process of industrialisation may not have uniform implications throughout the world but vary depending on the local situations. Thirdly, Goode assigns some importance to the impact of ideology which may have an independent and intervening effect.

Goode notes that under some circumstances the kin network actually contributes greatly to the individual's mobility. First, in the modern industrial system, the middle and upper strata are by definition more 'successful' in the obvious sense that they own it, dominate it, occupy its highest positions, and direct its future. The upper strata recognise the widest extension of kin, maintain most control over its ownership and marriage choices of their young, and are most likely to give and receive help from one another. In contrast, individuals from the lower class families are forced to enter into the labour market with far less family support. Because their kin are also in the lower strata, they have little to lose by relinquishing those ties. Thus, lower strata families are most likely to be 'conjugal' (1963, p.13).

Goode also indicates that the ideology of conjugal family has an appeal to people who remain exploited or suppressed under the older system, specially youngsters, and women (p.19). He finds an association between women's participation in the industry resulting into their economic contribution to the family and their increased bargaining power in the family: "....they would be better able to assert their own rights and wishes within the family" (1963, pp. 372-73).

Several other western family sociologists have also examined Parsons' theory on the family. In the writings of Harris (1969) and Morgan (1975) there is a good discussion of these works.

Perhaps not the first case study, but almost certainly one of the most cited ones to contradict the writings of Parsons was the First Bethnal Green Study by Young and Willmott (1957). They discovered a real reluctance on the part of their informants to leave the east end of London. They found that after marriage there was a strong tendency and indeed a desire to live close to (but not with) the wife's parents. The mother played a pivotal role in this kinship system through whom siblings maintained their contacts with each other. The bond was not merely based on emotion or simple sociability but consisted of a high degree of mutual aid and support. Respondents of this study, however, came mainly from the working class, and the findings are not, therefore, applicable to all the segments of the society.

The theory of Parsons has been tested by several other writers (cf. Litwak, 1960a, 1960b, 1965; Sussman, 1953, 1970; Bell, 1968; Blood, 1970; Bell and Bott, 1957) among the middle and upper strata of the American society. Their own findings and the findings of other researchers cited by them contradict Parsons' theoretical assumptions. That industrial society requires social and spatial mobility is not questioned; what is disputed is whether such mobility tends to weaken ties between the grown-up children and their parents. No association was found by these authors between mobility and strength of extra-familial kin ties. Indeed, such ties have been found to help rather than hinder spatial and social mobility. The authors have noticed the fact that the parental help to the grown-up children and their families often concealed in the form of loans, substantial gifts, wedding or birthday presents or a monthly supplement to income, is very useful particularly in the period of the upswing of the latter's career or during the early years of their married life. The critics of Parsons argue that it is not the isolated nuclear family, but the 'modified extended family' which is the characteristic family unit of the industrial society.

Litwark observes that between the nuclear family and the extended family structures is "the modified extended family structure which consists of a coalition of nuclear families in a state of partial dependence. Such partial dependence means that nuclear family members exchange significant services with each other, thus differing from the isolated nuclear family, as well as retain considerable autonomy (i.e., not bound economically or geographically); therefore, differing from the classical extended family" (1965, p.291). The 'classical extended family', in the words of Litwak is defined "in terms of geographical propinquity, occupational dependence and nepotism, a sense that extended family relations are most important, and an hierarchical authority structure based on a semi-biological criterion, i.e., the eldest male" (1960a, p.9; footnote). The concept of the modified extended family would suggest that the nuclear family may be housed independently but remains active in situations where extended family aid as well as institutional aid (aid given on institutionally approved occasions such as birthday celebrations, marriage anniversary) continues to flow.

Litwak, however, agrees with Parsons on the point that the classical extended family is antithetical to occupational mobility. But, he argues, modified extended family relation is consonant with occupational mobility and is more functional for it. However, the strength of kinship bonds and exchanges varies with the class status (1960a, p.18).

Litwak, however, is ready to accept Parsons' hypothesis to be applicable in the earlier stages of industrialisation where extended family relations are heavily influenced by the peasant farm family which strongly incorporates the values of geographic and occupational closeness (pp. 19-20). Also, Litwak accepts that Parsons' hypothesis may find evidence among the upwardly mobile individual at the bottom of the occupational ladder, i.e., unskilled labourers (p.21). He thus accepts that part of Parsons' hypothesis which points to the functional inadequacy of the classical extended family, but rejects that part which posits the isolated nuclear family as the most functional type for the contemporary industrial society.

Litwak also argues (1960b) that the modified extended family, instead of restricting geographical mobility, rather encourages the same for various reasons. It legitimises such movements and provides economic, social and psychological support to the migrants; the migrant becomes a communication outpost for those who remain behind, providing information on job, housing, local social customs and language. Moreover, extended family relations can be maintained over great geographical distances because modern advances in communication techniques have minimised the socially disruptive effects of geographic distance.

Bell, while inquiring into the social and geographical mobility among the middle class families in England, find no apparent correlation between these two types of mobility (1968, p.26). He concluded that actual geographical distance seems unimportant. Families are free to live where they choose and their relationship with their kin does not depend on frequency of contacts.

Researchers like Sussman (1953, 1970) and Blood (1970) discuss the types and patterns of aid flowing within the kin network. Axelrod (1956) and also Bell and Boat (1957) emphasise that kin are still considered to be the most useful source of help in an emergency.

What appears from the above discussion is that kinship ties appear to be a Durkheimian 'social fact', something unassailably real. The content of kinship ties may include common residence, concealed or open financial aid, assistance during crises, more regular patterns of assistance such as baby-sitting or shopping, exchange of visits, gossip or information. Whatever might be the form of interaction, kinship relates to fundamental 'natural' processes; in a sense it might be seen as looking beyond the purely 'social' and may reflect 'biological and psychological' parameters of human social existence. In kinship bonds the stress is on 'inescapable moral claims and obligations' and a degree of trust that is not automatically possible with non-kin. It is taken for granted or simply deemed natural and normal that people would first turn to kin in times of need, and any attempt to ask 'why' might be considered unnecessary.

Yet we are still faced with the problem of explaining why it is that kin are apparently chosen out of a wider set of possible relationships, as well as of explaining why some kin rather than others are chosen for more intimate ties. There are two sociological explanations largely in terms of the functions which these relationships perform for the members and, indirectly, for society as a whole. Some sociologists stress the institutional function, viz., the importance of reciprocity and mutual aid. Others give emphasis to the expressive functions, arguing that visiting and 'keeping in touch' are themselves the main rationale and that the mere instrumental considerations are secondary. The notion of obligation is a common feature to all these explanations.

Still we are to explain why kinship interactions vary in different sections of the society. At one extreme we have the working class community situation. Here, though lack of opportunities, education and finance, couples fail to move far away from the community in which they were brought up. Consequently, they live near one or both sets of parents and interact with these parents—and sometimes other kin also—frequently. An environment of relative or absolute poverty provides the background for a set of mutual exchanges and aid. Thus, we have a situation of low mobility opportunities, low income, proximity to kin and frequency of interaction—all reinforcing each other. This observation contradicts the supposition of Goode.

At the other extreme, we have a situation where both members of the couple have moved far, geographically and socially, from their families of origin, are relatively affluent and have no instrumental need for kin. Nor perhaps do they desire to associate regularly with their parents, their siblings and the families of their siblings. They have greater desire and scope for the exercise of choice in their personal relationships, and these relationships may not include kin. Yet this distance does not mean that they severed all ties with kin altogether.

These idealised extremes suggest that we should take account of the varying structures of resources, the varying balances and mixes of opportunities that exist in a variety of family situations. Such an approach would give recognition not only to the complexity and diversity of family situations but also to the possible built-in elements of contradiction and conflict in these relationships themselves.

Another point to be emphasised in the explanations is the greater degree of involvement of women in this modified extended family system. To be sure, the studies emphasise the fact that the woman usually has a greater store of kinship knowledge, that she is more likely than her husband to keep up these ties and that the tie between the mother and the married daughter is often of particular importance.

To what extent will greater societal change in the respective roles of men and women affect this modified extended family as well as the nuclear family? There is some evidence to suggest that, to a limited extent at least, the occupational involvement of women need not necessarily work against the traditional domestic role of women but may reinforce it.

The growing employment of women without adequate supply of institutional facilities for child care or without the possibility to hire paid help leads to a certain degree to the strengthening of the traditional family pattern in which three generations live together and the kinship in general plays a rather important role.

The main features of the findings relating to kinship interactions in the urban society as depicted by the western sociologists may be summarised thus:

1. The term 'isolated nuclear family' is misleading and inaccurate in relation to the modern urban family. A more appropriate term is the 'modified extended family'.
2. This modified extended family is not the special feature of the working class, rural or upper class segments of the society but is found among all sections including the mobile urban middle class. Indeed, perhaps because of the impersonal nature of urban life, people are more likely to turn to kin—even kin who live at a certain distance—for help and for social interaction.
3. The use of the term 'modified extended family' reminds us that we are not dealing with a bounded system. Out of the total possible number of persons in a kin universe only a few are 'selected' for more intimate relationships. This selection process is influenced by the degree of relationship, geographical distance and personal choice.
4. In the order of importance, a married ego generally maintains relationships with his parents and siblings (kin who are directly related to the ego or those with whom the ego has the

first degree consanguineal relations). Then come those kin with whom the ego has second degree consanguineal relations (father's father, father's brother or sister, mother's parents or sibs, i.e., those kin who are related to the ego's kin). Then come those kin with whom the ego has third degree consanguineal relations (those kin who are related to the ego's kin's kin), and so on.

5. In the maintenance of kinship ties and the handling of flows of aid, information and resources, women play the most important role.

II

The moot question is whether there is a necessary correlation between the mobility engendered through industrialisation on the one hand, and the weakening of kinship ties, weakening of controls between the grown-up children and their parents, declining of bonds among the close kin leading to the 'relatively isolated' nuclear family, on the other.

Several sources of ambiguity may be noted in the arguments of the participants in this debate: (1) ambiguities around the meaning and degree of 'isolation' and 'decline'; (2) ambiguities concerning the level of society involved; (3) ambiguities concerning the definition of 'kin'; and (4) ambiguities concerning the definition of the term 'extended family' (or joint family). Let us discuss these ambiguities in some detail.

1. The extreme case of 'isolated nuclear family' hypothesis would be where the Ego marries, moves away from areas where his and/or his wife's families of orientation live, and maintains no further contact of any kind with these families. Such a situation may not be impossible, but it is neither desired nor normative. Parsons, of course, has never proposed such an extreme version of his thesis and this is why his emphasis is on the 'relative isolation' of the nuclear family. The term 'relative', of course, implies some kind of comparison so that we must immediately ask 'relative to what?' This comparison of the 'relative isolation of the nuclear family, may be made in several contexts:

(a) Generational comparison, i.e., comparison between the Ego's generation and his father's generation and/or grandfather's generation.
(b) Longer-term historical comparisons, such as that between the pre-industrial and the industrial society. One variation of this may be the comparison between the urban and the rural family at a given point of time assuming that the direction of industrialism is towards greater urbanisation.
(c) Comparison between kin and various sets of non-kin such as work-mates, friends and neighbours.
(d) Comparison between a theoretically desired 'normal' level and certain actual levels.

Given that the basis for the comparison implied in the word 'relative' is not always specifically defined and that different writers may be using different standards of comparison, there remains an ample scope for misunderstanding and ambiguity in this controversy. What is, however, clear is that any evidence that ego and his spouse maintain some kind of relationship (through visits, telephone calls, correspondence, etc.) with their parents and siblings does not in itself prove or disprove Parsons' thesis. Such interactions neither verify nor nullify 'functional solidarity' of the kin group.

One more source of ambiguity arises from the fact that it is often difficult to apply any precise weighting to the various indicators of 'isolation of the nuclear family' or its opposite, i.e., 'integration of the extended family'. For example, all the following behaviours on the part of a household member may be counted as indicators of 'isolation': (a) when a person only knows the names and addresses of a relatively few of his kin; (b) when a person interacts with a few of his kin; (c) when a person interacts infrequently or irregularly with his kin; (d) when little or no assistance is given to or received from one's kin; (e) when a person does not like to interact with his kin; and (f) any combination of these and other indicators. What is clear from above is that geographical *separateness* is not the same as a *sense* of isolation and that a lack of regular face-to-face encounter does not necessarily mean isolation in any sense other than this. Hence, there is plenty of scope to argue for either in favour of the kin solidarity or its decline.

The very word 'decline' is a source of ambiguity. In one sense it is taken to mean a shrinkage in terms of the structure and function of the family. However, the alleged 'decline' is usually referred to in more moral terms, dealing with a decline in the quality of relationships within the family. This interpretation incurs a serious value-loaded statement which can neither be proved nor disproved unless stated specifically in concrete terms. This again shows that any fruitful inquiry into our family system requires to be conducted in line with what is actually happening to the family keeping aside questions as to whether it is beneficial or detrimental to the individual and society.

If we do not come out of the arguments demonstrating what 'should' or 'should not' happen, we cannot get rid of another source of ambiguity, namely, the question of for whom or for what a particular institution (here, the kin group) is functional.

Probably, the most serious ambiguity lurks over the use of the term 'kinship'. In anthropological literature this term usually refers to those relationships established by birth and descent (including fictitious relationships). Basically, we have two types of kin—consanguineal and affinal. Though kinship relations are deemed basically biological (i.e., relations that are concerned with biological activities of begetting and bearing children), when we refer to a kinship tie we do not indicate biological relation except indirectly.

Kinship is a *social institution.* Kinship denotes the existence of shared expectations of the others who constitute the group. A relationship or piece of behaviour can be said to be institutionalised when the relevant behaviour is recognised and expected throughout the group concerned. Within the 'kin universe', however, a distinction can be made between the kin who are merely recognised and those who are actually part of an effective network of exchange and reciprocity. And, the ambiguity lies in specifying which category of kin should be included within the 'effective' network of kinship.

Still another source of ambiguity lies with the imprecise definition of the term 'extended family' (in the Indian context, 'joint family'). There is probably no other term, except 'family' itself, about which there is more confusion than the 'extended family'. The term has been used by sociologists in the study of bilateral kinship in western society to describe European families which permitted patrilineal inheritance, which were characterised by the formation of composite households, and which performed the activities of productive economic groups. Such households were formed either of parents and one son (called 'stem family') or of all or some of the sons and their wives living and working together as a joint domestic and economic unit. 'Extended family' has also been used by anthropologists in connection with the 'joint family' which is found among the Indian Hindus. Ambiguities arise as it is not made clear whether co-residence in the same dwelling unit is an absolutely necessary precondition of forming an extended family. It does not specify the types of solidarity which characterise such a family and hence fails to precisely define the type of social relationships including authority structure found in it. It is not clear whether the extended family is a social group or a set of people who recognise relationships to one another. Consequently, it becomes extremely difficult to know, once the criterion of co-residence in the same dwelling unit disappears, whether the linked nuclear families concerned still constitute an extended family or not. If extended family is regarded as a social group, we must specify the features or 'properties' which the members of this group are expected to share, for when we speak of a group, we are always referring both to a set of persons and the things which they share.

Every society has some norms of behaviour governing how people should behave towards the others with whom they are related by some kinship bonds. To recognise that an 'ought' is involved here implies the recognition of an obligation independent of sentiment. Kinship ties impose some obligations, some socially desired sentiments, feelings, and socially desired course of action which may not be found in case of relations with persons outside the circle of kin (neighbours, friends, for example), however intimate that relation may be. In the latter case, any decision regarding whether or not to build or maintain any relationship depends on individuals, liking and convenience. But, in kinship relations, it is the society which governs the individual's behaviour, and the behaviour is expected to be uniform in relation to all persons in the same kinship position. Friendship ties tend to rest on free choice and affectivity; neighbourhood ties, on face-to-face contact; while kinship structures, on permanent relations. Hence, kinship obligations are of a public or institutionalised rather than a private nature. This feeling of obligation is then something that an individual shares with other members of the group because s/he belongs to that group.

Thus, in kinship relations, the stress is on inescapable moral claims and obligations and a degree of trust that does not automatically ensue in case of relations with the non-kin. Kinship bonds have an involuntary nature which can be distinguished from voluntary, optional and flexible non-kin ties. Hence, any inquiry into the nature of kinship interactions should also make a comparative estimate of the ego's interactions with the non-kin in comparable situations.

3

Indian Joint Family: Dimensions and Issues

I

Family sociologists of India mostly agree that joint family continues to be the norm but the range of kinship within it has narrowed. Various processes of change because of modernisation are at work apart from the normal demographic changes. Moreover, one cannot ignore the drastic changes in the status of today's women who have traditionally played a vital role in maintaining family jointness. Unlike the past, women from all segments of the society now more or less actively and directly share the men's (traditionally assigned to) burden of providing for the family. Many of them now participate in the family decision-making process as well. Men are no longer required to suppress their love and affection for their own wives and children, nor does the traditional relationship of domination-subordination between the mother-in-law and the daughter-in-law persist. With the increase of the women's voice in the family and the neo-local residence, the intensity and incidences of interaction with the affinal kin are also increasing. All these developments have tilted towards a sort of egalitarianism within the family whereas the traditional family authority structure was characterised by hierarchy on the basis of gender and age.

That the enhancement of the status of women is negatively correlated with ties among the patri-kin has been referred to by family sociologists both in India and abroad (cf. Bott, 1957; Goode,

1963; Harris, 1969; Kapadia, 1959, 1966; Gore, 1968; Ross, 1961; Kolenda, 1987; Dube, 1974).

In the perspective of all these changes, and overemphasis on sentiment and norms (that joint family is an unchanging entity for the Hindus) may make one ignore the impact of space and time on social system. Also, it may appear to be an over-statement that physical distance (caused by spatial mobility) and occupational differentiation (caused by social mobility and leading to change in social status and status disintegration for some of the brothers) do not at all affect family solidarity. Such types of statement lead one to believe that Indians are a unique and incomparable human group whose relationships are not affected by space and time and who live only by norms and values.

In this context, the observations of Goode (1963, pp. 238-247) may be quite pertinent. He has examined in some detail the so-called decline of the joint family system of India. He notes that as appears from the census data, most individuals in India half a century ago had been found to be living in the small- or medium-sized families; and this is the practice of the present-day society as well. No basic change in the living style of Indians has, therefore, occurred. Goode also goes through the literature on family studies in India. He finds the definition of the joint family given by Kapadia (1959, p.74) too general. He points out that such definition lacks precision. And, defined thus, almost all family systems in the major cultural areas of the world, including the West, become 'joint family'.

Next, the non-partitioning of the property does not prove jointness in itself. For, the reasoning for non-partitioning may be that the property is too small to yield any income for the distant brother; or the desire to maintain an emotional tie with the village; or to have a distant future claim on the produce. Again, in case most of these men are found to stay with their brothers when they return to the village, only proves that their relatives are friendly, and that men who have no residence in the village will stay with their brothers, if possible. Goode sees that all this is quite common in the western society as well. It is no evidence of the continued strength of the joint family organisation to show that even when there has been partition, the relations between two households are intact.

Again, as Goode notes, although some large families among the wealthy and powerful are retained intact over generations, most families go through a life-cycle in which they change composition to some extent. In one of its phases, it may be a joint family. If the separation comes late, for some time the ego's father's household constitutes a joint family, though temporarily. Hence, all nuclear households can be called 'temporarily nuclear' and a genuine joint household can be called 'temporarily joint' (1963, p. 244).

Still, Goode admits, there is no strong ideological attack on the joint family and no firm and active set of values asserting that the joint family should no longer exist. The Indian justifications for the joint family are many, besides that it is sanctioned by the tradition. Together with the caste organisation, it offers many of the services and advantages which an urban and industrial society offers through more impersonal, governmental, educational and financial agencies. Goode, thus, concludes that although majority of the Indians prefer the joint family, the pattern of fission which was common in the past comes to be utilised increasingly by those who for many years migrate to the cities and begin to take up modern occupations. Those who become highly educated can use this opportunity to set up an individual household. The physical separation of members of the family also decreases the intensity and frequency of social contact so that the integration begins to reduce after a period of time. Thus, according to Goode, although the changes are not as yet great, the direction of change is clear (p.247).

It is not all true, however, that the Indian family sociologists have failed to notice these events. That is why currently the nuclear family-joint family controversy is called a futile or sterile exercise. To our opinion, the best way for resolving this controversy, i.e., for deciding whether and how far our families are sticking to the joint family behaviour, or contrarily, are marching towards nuclearisation—should be an inquiry into the functional jointness among the household units. For, it is a dynamic approach and it tries to find out *what it is* rather *what it should be*. The actual patterns of interactions among the members of the joint family are stressed here.

II

A review of the literature on the Indian family shows that the discussion mostly centres round the structural changes in the institution of the joint family in consonance with the coming of modernising forces into India. Two viewpoints are prevalent in this regard. The first group mainly follows the stand taken by Parsons (1949) and Goode (1963). This group asserts that nuclearisation of the joint family structure is taking place in India in tune with the global trend, and that one of the inevitable consequences of industrialisation (whatever it may mean) and urbanisation is the transition of the family from the joint to the nuclear type. Another viewpoint is that nuclearisation of the joint family structure is not taking place as the Indian social and cultural conditions are very much different from those in the West, and there is no necessary correlation between industrialisation and nuclearisation of the family structure.

Both these viewpoints are supported by arguments and counter-arguments, by evidences and counter-evidences. And, the result has been the famous 'joint family controversy'. In India, only a few family sociologists are ready to accept the assertions of Parsons and Goode in this regard. However, instead of countering their assertions logico-empirically, most of the Indian writers prefer to base their arguments in terms of cultural uniqueness of India. According to them, the basic values of the Indian society and culture of which family is a part, are qualitatively different from that of the western societies. This is why the western social scientists have failed to comprehend this institution which is significantly different from what seems to be its counterpart in the western society.

The disagreements between the western and the Indian writers begin with the definition of the term 'family'. For instance, according to Burgess et al., "the family may be defined as a group of persons united by ties of marriage, blood and adoption; constituting a single household; interacting and communicating with each other in their respective social roles of husband and wife, mother and father, son and daughter, brother and sister, and creating and maintaining a common culture" (1963, p.7).

Most of the Indian writers will find this definition incomplete or inadequate since it stresses, at the first instance, the interactions among the husband-wife-children group mainly, and does not include any flavour of interaction among the wider kin; and secondly, it characterises the family as a co-residential and commensal unit. But, then, what should be a proper and comprehensive definition of the Indian family which would include all its qualities and characteristics and also would satisfy all the family sociologists? Perhaps there is no such definition as yet. The observation of Madan (1993, p.420) can be referred to in this context. He has remarked that the confusion between the lawyers' conception of joint family (co-parcenary limits) and the Indological definition of joint family (members of agnatically related kin-group who can perform *shraddha* ritual or offer food to manes), and between the two above definitions and the sociological definition of joint family (a grouping of households of agnatically related men, their wives and unmarried sisters and daughters commonly known in North India by such term as *parivar*) has made the situation complicated and ambiguous.

Madan, thus, admits that the Hindu joint family generally operates at four different levels: (1) as a household; (2) as a grouping of households constituting a property group; (3) as a still wider grouping of households incorporating the co-parcenary which defines the outer limits for allodial and obligatory ritual purposes; and (4) as an all-encompassing dispersed grouping defined genealogically rather than in terms of active interaction (1993, pp.420-21).

Joint family is often defined from still another dimension—the fulfilment of "mutual expectations and support and amity, and the associated effective dimension of kinship, which are most intensely experienced and explicitly acknowledged among primary kin, whether residing in the same household or not, [and which] become gradually diluted with the stretching of degree of kinship..." (Madan, 1993, p.421). Madan calls this dimension as the 'cultural ideal' of the joint family which does not dwindle with the partition of the large multi-generational joint family.

The root of the 'joint family controversy' lies, therefore, in the problem of defining the joint family which still generates many confusions and controversies. Defining the joint family is a real problem. It appears, each particular specialist defines it in terms of his/her own particular purpose. We may refer to in this context the experiences of those family sociologists who have tried to synthesise the literature in this context.

The following observation of Kolenda is really instinctive in this context: "It is not an exaggeration to say that no two used the same set of definitions of family types. There are two sides to the definitional problem. First, *what* is shared by the family unit referred to, and, second, *who* shares it, that is, what relatives compose the various types of families?" (1987, pp.8-9).

While preparing an extensive survey of literature on the sociology of family in India, Leela Dube also agrees with the above observation. She laments that different scholars have put emphasis on a variety of factors as the criteria of jointness. Further, there is no unanimity among the social scientists whether the "presence of two cohorts has been a minimum requirement for jointness in most classification of households..." (1974, p.320), leaving the compositional aspect of the joint family in an utterly chaotic state of affairs. Hallen, while overviewing family research in India, also notes the same type of irregularity as the family scholars "differ in respect of the valid indicators of jointness" (1982, p.15). Some other studies have also referred to such ambiguities, inconsistencies and confusions in specifying the criteria of jointness (cf. Shah, 1964; Madan, 1962a, 1962b; Chakrabortty, 1982).

One basic point needs to be clarified here. If it is assumed or taken for granted that the Indian family can be of the joint variety *only and necessarily*, i.e., all Indian families are joint families in one way or another, currently or potentially, and that nuclearity can neither be the norm nor the practice, then methodologically there is no point in undertaking any inquiry into the Indian family system. For, in that case jointness will not be, methodologically speaking, a *variable*, a topic for investigation, at all. From the point of view of scientific research, before undertaking an inquiry into any form of social reality it is to be ascertained first that social reality is a *variable*, i.e., "any object or event which can vary in successive observations either in quantity or in quality" (Mueller and Schuesler, 1961, p.12).

Two other basic assumptions of the scientific research are: (1) "anything that exists must exist in amounts of more or less, or with greater and lesser frequency" (ibid.); and (2) "we can measure anything that exists" (Babbie, 1992, p.114). Measurements, however, may be quantitative or qualitative.

Hence, while defining and clarifying the 'joint family', nothing should be taken for granted. 'Jointness' cannot be assumed to be a static concept. The features and indices of the joint family are to be such as empirically observable and measurable, and also meaningful for analysing our family system from the sociological point of view.

It is to be decided first *what* and *who* makes a joint family. Is it synonymous with co-parcenary and need not be necessarily a co-residential and commensal unit? Or, is the Indological definition of the joint family which disregards its compositional aspect still valid today? Is it relevant to distinguish between a 'joint family' and a 'joint household'? Should the terms 'joint family' and 'extended family' be used interchangeably in sociological analysis? Is it useful to distinguish between 'structural jointness' and 'functional jointness'? If so, then what should be the indices of these two varieties of jointness? Are these two types of jointness necessarily correlated with each other? Is jointness a one and universal quality, or, does it vary in terms of the degree of solidarity (jointness)?

III

It was almost a fashion among the family sociologists to define joint family in terms of the ancient Hindu legal and sacred texts (*sastras*). From the legal point of view, joint family has been compared with co-parcenary. The Hindu legal text, *Dayabhaga* (mostly operating in Bengal) and *Mitaksara* (prevailing in the rest of India), formulate rules about the co-parcenary rights. These legal arrangements, however, limit themselves to dealing with the legal aspect of succession and inheritance of the family property, and have nothing to say about the composition of the household. In *Mitaksara*, as each son acquires by birth an interest in the joint property, even a father and his unmarried son are sufficient to constitute a co-parcenary.

Several authors have advocated that the application of the term 'joint family' should be restricted to a group of relatives who form a property-owning group, the co-parcenary family (cf. Madan, 1962a, 1962b; Bailey, 1960; Mayer, 1960). Some other scholars have also considered co-parcenary as a characteristic feature of 'jointness' of the family but not as its only essence. They have coupled co-parcenary with other essential criteria (cf. Kapadia, 1966; Mandelbaum, 1970; Nicholas, 1961; Kulkarni, 1960; Desai, 1956).

Like the legal definition, the Indological definition is also no less ambiguous about the structural features of the joint family. This definition is derived from the Hindu legal texts and is concerned with defining co-parcenary property relations (who should hold and inherit the ancestral property) and regulating matters of ritual (who should perform *shraddha* ritual and offer *pinda* for whom). The legal definition of the constitution of the joint family tends to coincide with and is sanctioned by the Indological definition of the joint family, i.e., the circle of kin who is entitled to inherit property is also entitled to perform the *shraddha* ritual. In terms of its kinship composition, the joint family in this Indological sense need not live in a single household, nor is it required to include even a single married couple (it might comprise, for example, a widow and her son, a set of unmarried brothers, or an uncle and his nephew, and similar combinations of kin). Thus, we find a close analogy between the legal and Indological definitions of the joint family both of which disregard its structural aspect. Whether these definitions of the joint family would be helpful for sociological analysis is a matter of judgement.

Shah, for instance, is strongly against the use of such definitions in any sociological analysis. He states, "...it laid down only the definition of the ideal household, or in my terms, only the maximum extent of progression of the developmental process of households" (1968, p.131). Shah points out that the main points here are two: (1) The legal definition is a highly specialised one and has nothing to do with the sociological distinction between elementary family and joint family. (2) The law does not lay down the rule that the joint family of the legal conception should always be a joint household as well. In brief, the law is concerned primarily with the rights of constitution of the household group (1969, p.279). Elsewhere Shah draws: "It must be clear that there are basic differences between the meanings of the legal and the sociological 'joint family'. Sociologists would be perfectly justified in smiling at jurists if they talk about the sociological joint family without understanding its meanings" (1964, p.12).

Moreover, these legal definitions and state of affairs very often differ from the actual state of affairs. For example, often it is found that though the property has not been legally partitioned (as most people in our country do not like to take disputes about inheritance and succession to courts of law) it is *actually* divided among the heirs in all intents and purposes.

The situation becomes more complex as the legal position is not clear enough. The terms *Mistaksara* and *Dayabhaga* carry somewhat different meanings. Then, the implications of these terms are different from the meaning of joint property given in Income Tax Law, for instance, and all these again may be different from the conceptions of the joint property group in different sections of the Hindu society.

Perhaps, the reasons behind the high popularity of these legal and Indological definitions among the family sociologists lie in the fact that most of the early studies on our family system were carried out by the Indologists (including historians, sanskritists, and orientals) on the basis of sacred literature. And, as both Indologists and lawyers were predominant in the academic field of India, the Indological norm of the joint family earned a lot of weight and popularity.

So it can be argued that the legal rule and the social custom of joint family should be distinguished. In sociological analysis we should view joint family from the sociological perspective only.

In the broadest sense, 'sociological perspective' means a perspective which enables us to view events and activities in relation to their institutional structure. To put it in more concrete terms, this institutional structure comprises, first of all, the identification of the structure of enduring groups and categories, and secondly, the structure of values and norms in a society. Next, the sociological perspective will require the investigator to examine the social relations of individuals and groups with each other in terms of a series of socially defined rights and obligations, rather than simply in terms of what is prescribed in legal codes and moral texts. Thirdly, in examining the relations between persons in terms of a set of rights and obligations, we have to examine these rights and obligations *as they actually operate in reality* and not merely as they are defined in sacred texts and legal codes. A crucial aspect of the sociological perspective is that it guides our attention to the relationship between principle and practice in whatever sphere of social life we happen to be investigating. Finally, this perspective requires us to seek continually the interconnections among different institutional systems. Sociologists seek to disclose the relations among different aspects of the social life.

IV

While measuring family jointness, it is to be noted whether and how far our currently practised family behaviour sticks to or deviates from the 'ideal type joint family'. This notion of ideal type joint family has been compiled from the writings of our family sociologists. The present inquiry will try to measure changes in the present-day familial behaviour and practice from this ideal type or normative structure of the joint family.

Joint family as a social system has particular role relationships, authority structure, division of labour, bonds of duties and responsibilities, apart from the rules regarding common hearth, residence, property ownership, and joint performance of rites and rituals. Leela Dube observes: "Patrilineal, patrivirilocal, property-owning, co-residential and commensal joint family, comprising three or more generations, has been depicted as the ideal family unit of Hindu society..." (1974, p.298). According to Irawati Karve (1953) and Prabhu (1963), who provide the most comprehensive definition of the joint family from the social-anthropological and Indological point of view, a joint family is a group of people who generally live under one roof, eat food from one hearth, hold property in common, participate in common family worship, and are related to each other as some particular type of kindred. Other scholars have followed this definition but have dropped out or added some other characteristics to it. For example, Agarwala (1955), Gore (1968), Kapadia (1966), Mandelbaum (1970) include the quality of hierarchical authority structure; Desai (1956) adds common income and common purse, and also stresses the fulfilment of mutual institutionalised rights and obligations, as conditions of jointness.

What appears from all these definitions can be summarised in the following way:

Traditional large joint family should share a common dwelling place. Each family unit might have one or two rooms for worship, a common hearth, a common drawing room, a common entrance, and a common dining hall where meals are to be eaten together. When the large house becomes overcrowded, brothers with their families of procreation may set up separate establishments near to the great ancestral home, sometimes within the same compound, thus forming the nucleus of new joint families. If the members of the new dwelling units are to settle in different places, they would often feel so attached to this ancestral home that even after living away from it for many years they would regularly visit the home and meet the family members. This ancestral village would be referred to by them as 'Home'.

Commensality or sharing the same hearth is the next condition of joint family. The wife of the head of the family or the oldest woman, would supervise the work of the other (generally younger) women in the kitchen. Men and women would not eat together. The typical pattern is that the elderly woman would serve food to the men of the household and later would eat by themselves. Generally, this meal time was a very important and interesting time as it served the scope for an assemblage of the males of the household where they should discuss various issues in a leisurely mood. Elderly women would also participate in these discussions, and most of the family decisions are to be taken during this time. This habit of taking food jointly also enhances the family solidarity. If any member is late to arrive, others should wait for him for the dinner. In the writings of the Bengali novelist, Sarat Chandra Chattopadhyay, one would find a lively and vivid description of these meal hours of the joint family.

Co-parcenary is another condition. Traditional joint family was both a production and a consumption unit, for not only was the family property held in common, but there was also a 'common purse' into which all the members put their earnings and from which money was taken for the expenses of the earners and non-earners alike. The senior male member of the traditional joint family usually managed the family budget. His decision was seldom countermanded by others in the family. Legally, however, he acted only as a representative of the males of the family in the administration of the family property and his responsibility was that of the trustee. The other male members helped him in looking after the family property. If any member had any additional income from any other source, it was to be deposited in the common purse under the care of the head of the family for the use of the whole family. After the death of the father, his next brother or the eldest son, if there was no brother, took over the management of the property, who might be assisted by the mother.

Next, each family had its own gods who were regularly worshipped. The members of the joint family participated in these rituals. These rites and rituals acted as the bonds of solidarity among the family members and separated it from other families. Each family thus emerged as a distinct entity. Religion is an integral part of the life of the Hindus. All important family events and festivals are deeply steeped in religious rituals and ceremonies, and daily family worship had always been a part of the family routine. Religious and ceremonial rites were performed in the families when all the members of the family gathered together and the oldest man/woman (as the circumstances required) performed the sacred rites.

One of the main functions of the family rituals and ceremonies was to emphasise and renew the feeling of solidarity, for they were outward symbols of their unity. Kinship contacts probably lasted longer during these occasions than any other for they were the main channels of publicly demonstrating family identity. Cordial relations maintained between the component units of the joint family were both the basis and product of mutual participation on occasions of family rejoicings.

Often members of the family who partitioned from the family and moved to a city away from the ancestral home returned to participate in the worship of the family gods of the larger kinship unit. One may mention the *Durgapuja* festival in Bengal in this context.

The separation of family gods or the separate arrangement of worship and holding rites indicated the loss of close ties with the ancestral home.

Besides these outward symbols of the joint family, some subjective features were also there. The large joint family was family-centred, characterised by intimacy, mutuality of interest, strong primary group controls and mutual assistance in times of need. Members had a pride for their family tradition. Superiority of senior members to the younger ones and of men to women was also marked.

A joint family was always an exciting group to live in. All the time something of interest used to happen there. Now it is the marriage of a girl or a boy, now it is an initiation ceremony, the birth of a new baby, the purity rites of a daughter-in-law, some particular family rituals, a fast, a feast, sometimes a death. Besides, there were frequent visits of guests. The brothers of the bride may come to invite her to their parental home, the daughters of the house are being brought home for a family feast or wedding. There were always hustle and expectation, laughter and quarrels, discussions and plans.

The fact was that the men in the Indian society played a major role in the public life and the occupational system, and this automatically made them a focus of power in the family system as well. The oldest male member became the centre of authority in the joint family. When the father died, the next oldest male succeeded to this position.

Seniority determined the rank of all persons in the family. It applied within each gender group. Thus, relations between the elder and the younger generations were of subordination and superordination. Egalitarian values were totally antithetical to this system. The advice of the senior should be heard and followed, and it was regarded as a mark of deviation to talk back to them. Differences, if any, were to be conveyed through a third person who either because of his/her age or familiarity was competent to argue with the senior members. The elders were not only to be respected but also to be obeyed meekly. Not only was there no questioning of the orders and deeds of the elders, but they could also not be directly approached by the members of the younger generation. As for the women, they were imbued with the ideal of *pativratya* or sole and unquestioned devotion to their husband. Their life was devoted ideologically to the service of their husbands in particular and their families in general. As such they were always considered inferior to the males. Thus, joint family was necessarily linked with the subordinate status and powerlessness of women.

The head of the family, however, exercised his authority only over the major matters which affected the whole family life, whereas his wife or the eldest female member of the family held authority in her own domain and could control the minute details of the household. She administered the household, supervised or did the cooking, organised or coordinated the work of the women of the household, and saw that the children were properly nourished and cared for. In the close confinement of the house, from which women rarely escaped, her main task should have been that of a mediator, although this element of her role was hardly mentioned. If she had a strong personality, she could even wield great influence over the male head 'behind the scene'. Even when her husband died, her authority did not totally cease to exist. The next male head often used to consult with her.

Among the brothers, authority generally rested with the eldest. When the eldest brother succeeded as the head of the family, his younger brothers and their wives and children were supposed to give him the kind of allegiance and respect that the father commanded. With authority, responsibility was also linked. The superior, in turn, was obliged to look after the welfare of all the members of the family and protect them from any untoward circumstances. He should not make any discrimination against the children of his brothers or favour his own wife and kids.

In the joint family, the authority of the individual 'father' over his own children was subordinated to the overall authority of the eldest male. This latter authority in many cases might be only formal but it was always decisive when used. This was an important feature of the joint family because it discouraged the crystalisation of the nuclear family with the dominant 'father' as a separate unit.

The relationship between the father and his children was seldom completely free and easy, for as the chief family disciplinarian, the head of the family tended to maintain distance from his children. Husbands and wives had relatively little in common in the large joint family besides the interest of their children.

The relationship between the spouses might change as they grew into more responsible positions in the household and were advanced in age. The wife might become her husband's main adviser and consultant. The husband's emotional dependence on the wife grew strongly only after his mother's death.

No family structure could have lasted down through the centuries unless the relationship between the husband and his wife was established in a way which could give satisfaction to both. The binding elements in their relationship were: the acceptance of marriage as a 'natural' and inevitable part of life (sacrament); common interests and goals developed in working together for their family and children; clear-cut division of labour and authority between them, each having an essential role to play in the household; and the expected subordinate position of the wife which eliminated much conflict and tension.

In the joint family system men were responsible for the financial support and the general administration of the family. Women managed the household work and raised and trained the children. Brothers, sons, nephews and/or cousins assisted the eldest male member in providing the family income, which was typically jointly owned and spent. Daughters, sisters, aunts, and daughters-in-law were in charge of the household chores. Thus, kitchen work was the exclusive duty and privilege of the women. And, it was considered as below men's dignity to interfere in these tasks. Thus, a rigid specification and segregation of roles and responsibilities could have been maintained.

V

In the earlier section, we have presented the normative structure of the joint family. In this section changes therein brought about by what may be considered as the break-up of the joint family will be discussed.

Indian family sociologists often regard the joint family as a generic part of the Indian social structure, an unchanging, eternal institution. Madan, for instance, opines: "What breaks up is the co-parcenary unit; ties of kinship are immutable" (1962, p.89). But an extended family may result from the operation of the developmental cycle. The growth of a nuclear family into an extended family is viewed as a spontaneous and regular process.

The Hindu ethos that extols family life, emphasised *dharma* and the reciprocal obligation of father and son, and sees no particular merit in individual economic and social independence. These norms originated from economic reasons. Land which was the main source of living, was held in common, and this common source of living necessitated a joint family. But the important point is that what was originally a matter of expediency became, in course of time, a way of life—the breach of which constituted a sacrilege. The *Puranas* and the *Smritis* had created for each individual his or her respective status in the framework of the joint family. And an unquestioned allegiance to it was the only *dharma* and the surest way to *moksha*. In fact, a whole epic, the *Mahabharata,* had been written on it. These values had been transmitted from generation to generation and through their sacred nurturing these values of themselves became a great binding force on the Indians. Thus, even though the economic reasons which had once created the joint family were to diminish in importance, the force of tradition in its favour continues to stay. Even when the households split up, much of the traditional obligations tend to be honoured.

Following Fortes (1958), Mayer (1960) has lodged arguments against this static approach of those who analyse the compositional aspect of the Indian family organisation. Fortes stresses that a social system, by definition, has a life (1958, p.1). He emphasises: "The domestic group goes through a cycle of development analogous to the growth cycle of a living organism. The group as a unit retains the same form, but its members and the activities which unite them, go through a regular sequence of change during the cycle which culminates in the dissolution of the original unit and its replacement by one or more units of the same kind" (ibid.).

It is argued that any inquiry which analyses only the compositional aspects of the family is, by definition, governed by a static approach because it fails to take note of the family as a process, and does not look at the particular type of composition of a household as a phase in the developmental cycle. Shah (1998, p.82) has rightly put that the studies of the developmental process provide a dynamic view of the family. He also accepts that both the types of household—nuclear and joint—prevailed in the past and in this sense are historical realities (p.70). The presence of nuclear households should not be taken as an indication of change in the family structure; rather they should be viewed as units which will be growing into joint families when the sons grow up and marry.

It is true that not everyone finds joint family life congenial, and that many sons separate from their fathers. But such courses of action are viewed as a part of the normal development process; they come into existence because of a variety of demographic, psychological, social and economic reasons.

A family has to go through several stages of development like marriages, births and deaths, which influence its composition. Thus each family has to pass through several phases in the developmental process which is often called the family developmental cycle. Fortes, thus, distinguishes three main stages or phases in the developmental cycle of the domestic group. First, there is a phase of expansion that lasts from the marriage of two people until the completion of their family of procreation. Secondly, and often overlapping the first phase in time, there is the phase of dispersion or fission. This begins with the marriage of the oldest child and continues until all children are married. Where the custom by which the youngest child remains to take over the family estate is found, this commonly marks the beginning of the final phase. This is the phase of replacement, which ends with the death of the parents and replacement in the social structure of the family they founded by the families of their children(1958, p.4).

According to the family experts like Desai (1956, 1964), Goody (1958), Kapadia (1959, 1966), Madan (1962, 1989), Gore

(1968), Conklin (1968), Orenstein and Micklin (1966), Sengupta (1958), Mandelbaum (1970), Mukherjee (1977), the joint family is an eternal institution of India and the joint family values represent their family life. The size or the composition of the family is an unimportant factor in deciding the type of the family. They argue that even when some households may appear to be in the so-called nuclear form which are composed of only the husband, wife and unmarried children, they cannot be called nuclear families proper. The arguments follow two lines. First, structural nuclearity does not in itself indicate functional separation. Secondly, this phase is not a permanent feature in the developmental process of any family. Family being a dynamic institution, this is only a transitional phase. As the central tendency is towards jointness, all the families in normal situations are to be regarded as 'potentially joint'. Because of the operation mainly of the demographic factors like marriage, birth, death, families show a tendency to oscillate between the nuclear and joint families. With the death of the parents and separation of the brothers, a family may turn to a nuclear form, but this occurs only for a temporary period. Thus, with the marriage of sons, the family again turns to its joint form. Thus, the developmental process operates like a cycle having the phases of expansion, fission and replacement.

In the opinion of a few family sociologists, the above interpretation of the family developmental cycle is inadequate, incomplete and therefore, misrepresents the reality. Kolenda (1987), Shahani (1961), for example, argue that the family being a dynamic institution, it must be remembered that the cycle may not be repetitive, and that some of the families at least may not undergo this sort of cyclical (joint-nuclear-joint) changes. Thus, some of the sons may decide to establish their own family just after their marriage, and when this pattern will be widely practised (i.e., many families break up with the marriage of the sons), it cannot be ascertained that *all families are potentially joint families*. Kolenda (1987) affirms that the concept of the family developmental cycle is, therefore, not that simplistic, uniform or one-dimensional. There is more than one developmental cycle. Shah also accepts the above view and stresses that "there is always some pattern in the developmental process, but it is not cyclical in nature..." (1998, p.54). He even goes further to point out a bias in our family studies: "In the delineation of the developmental process of the Indian family so far, the phase of growth of the family has received much more attention than has the phase of dispersal. Concern for jointness of the proverbial joint family has overshadowed the reality of division, separation and partition..." (1998, p.83). It follows, therefore, that each phase of the family developmental process (*process* is a more appropriate expression than *cycle*) requires to be studied for unfolding how our domestic groups actually function.

VI

While talking about joint family norms and values, a discussion on the levels and phases of the family break-up in terms of hearth, productive activity, land, house or belonging is pertinent. Inter-household relations in a joint family are affected by the phase in which fission takes place as well as its manner. Also, a discussion on the phase of partition is useful for understanding the family developmental process. Division of any family is inevitable since the kinship unit would otherwise be simply unmanageable in size. There are both physical and social limitations to the continuation of a large joint family. The necessary growth through incoming brides, therefore, necessitates eventual dispersion, because there follows a time when the household becomes too cramped, psychologically and socially and also physically, to hold the brothers, their wives and children. Even if the brothers manage to stay together as one joint household as long as they live, their sons almost certainly grow restive when they, in turn, become fathers, and then they separate to establish families of their own. Brothers' sons (cousins) are, therefore, not under the same obligation to stay together as are 'true' (uterine) brothers. The fission of the larger family is, therefore, an inevitable phase in the cycle of the domestic group.

Herein lies an inevitable contradiction and continuing strain in the joint family. The partitioning of the joint family, typically the separation of brothers, is, in fact, inevitable. But the norm is in favour of pursuing the fraternal solidarity. Hence, an *institutionalised point of break-up time has to be* devised, or else every division will be attended with guilt on the part of individuals concerned, someone would be at fault and be blamed. Thus, any family separation might be disgraceful. It would be then difficult to differentiate between stormy partitions coming through quarrels and mutual accusations and those amicably reached through mutual understanding.

Orenstein and Micklin (1966) have discussed in detail how the partition of a large joint family has been viewed by our *dharmasastras*; what, according to our normative structure, should be the ideal time of separation. Other family scholars (cf. Kapadia, 1956, 1966; Mandelbaum, 1970; Gore, 1968; Kolenda, 1987; Ross, 1961; Madan,1989; Bailey, 1957; Sengupta, 1958; Sarma, 1964; Shahani, 1961; Mukherjee, 1982; Kumar, 1974) have also noted this phenomenon and have explained it according to their own paradigms. What appears from these discussions may be summarised as follows:

A relatively well-institutionalised point of family division is reached when the old parental couple—the first generation father and mother—die, and when the responsibilities for education and marriage for all members in the second generation—younger siblings of the adult brothers—have been achieved in accordance with the tradition of the family. At this stage, partition is permissible.

Yet, people still believe that it is desirable to live in the joint family, and whenever they separate, they try to justify their conduct as legitimate. The birth of a nuclear household has always been attended with a certain sense of incapacity, if not guilt. This sense would be greater if the brothers separate during the lifetime of either one of the parents. It would be less acute if the separation comes afterwards, and would be considerably lessened further if the separation could be attributed to some factors in the objective situations around. Often such 'excuses' are pleaded to justify the separation: job outside the village/town, change in climate, impossibility of the whole family living in the limited accommodation provided by the ancestral home, and the like. In any event, men like to suppress the fact that separation occurred owing to their inability to get along.

When separation cannot be legitimised, it leaves a bitterness which forces the separated parties to put the blame on each other. Often the onus is shifted to the wives when brothers plead that the decision to separate was due to the inevitable difficulties that arose between the women of the family. These difficulties do arise, but they also give support to the 'mature' decision of separation made by the brothers. It is most important that the brothers be not seen—even by themselves—as in disagreement. Thus, the disunion among the brothers has been considered as the estrangement of the wives.

Thus, the most important inherent factor leading to the break-up of a joint family is its growth in size. As the family size increases, the chances of stress, personality clashes also increase. Moreover, the growth of the family size in and of itself leads to a per capita deterioration of the family's economic condition and may make it necessary for some members to seek work outside the family occupation. This leads to occupational and income differentials between the earning members and creates tension. The other important influence is the social and economic environment within which the family lives. If employment opportunities are plentiful outside the family, there will be a greater tendency for the family to fall apart. Fathers are more likely to partition their property during their lifetime if such actions are accepted and practised by the community in many cases. Economic gains are the chief determinants for the continuity of the joint family. Hence, economic considerations and other tensions between the members of a joint family are the main causes of the disintegration.

Though kinsmen and village elders usually try to restore friendly relations among the brothers after a stormy partition, the more property there is to divide, the more bitter is the process of separation. Perhaps, this is so because people tend to remain in joint families longer when economic factors support such a living arrangement. This is why the poorest and low caste people tend to have fewer joint families than the families of landowners, businessmen and merchants. Nicholas (1961) and Cohn (1961), for example, have shown that in respect of organisation of labour or pooling of labour there is no advantage in the joint family for the very poor, but there is a distinct economic advantage in the joint family for artisans and the landed.

But even people belonging to low caste and economic standing think it prestigious to have longer duration of the joint family.

When the joint family does not seem to be economically viable, members often plead that in the interest of maintaining 'peace' it is wise to separate. Here, 'peace' is referred to a peaceful atmosphere and emotional satisfaction existing between the members of the joint family. However, peace may be deliberately disturbed to achieve economic gain of some members.

If all the earning members are engaged in a joint venture, the income differentials would not develop. But if one brother is engaged in an outside occupation and earning more than the others, it would be advantageous for him to seek separation. The couple then would find some pretext or excuse for separation from the joint family.

The joint family may break up purely due to economic reasons without disturbing its peace. Such a situation generally arises after the death of the parents (specially that of the father) and when the joint property is not large. Married brothers find no special advantage in living together, so they disperse peacefully. Friction arises when the property to be divided is sizeable.

Even when peace does not prevail, joint family may still be maintained if the married brothers see that living in the joint family is convenient to them (economically). Then they may tolerate some disturbance of peace or tensions (among the children and wives).

The joint family will disintegrate only when quarrels and tensions in the family assume such a proportion that economic considerations are no longer a significant factor. Thus, economic motives and peace are interrelated and the final lot of the family unit is the result of their delicate balance. There may be many other reasons for family disintegration, but they are either related to the above two reasons or they become insignificant when the final decision is taken.

What appears is that among the families of some substance, of the middle and higher echelons of social rank, the partition does not usually take place all at once. The strains mount, but at every stage there are countervailing forces and people asserting cohesion. Generally, the family does not disintegrate totally. There are different levels in the process. The first step towards family fission is usually that of establishing separate hearths within the house; all no longer take food from the common hearth; food stores are divided; cooking and eating are done separately.

In the next phase, new walls may be built inside the compound of the house. Thus, a physical separation precedes the legal partition, namely partition of the ancestral property. The heirs may then separate their farming or craft activities and thereafter formalise the split in a legal act of joint family partition.

The presence of the father tends to slow this process. The death of the father, and even more of both the parents, tends to hasten the legal partition. Under the traditional legal code of Bengal, *Dayabhaga,* a married son was not ordinarily entitled to claim his separate share in the ancestral property during the lifetime of his father. Among the wealthier families of Bengal, the possession of a substantial house delayed the family partition.

Besides social and economic loss, separation is regarded as unwelcome by the lineage elders on political grounds as well. In the village society, no man can hope to stand alone, or can defend himself singly. Large property coupled with large family size makes it a very influential group in the village power structure. Stormy separation among the brothers may damage the solidarity of the lineage group. Thus, the pride, strength and security of the lineage are at stake when small nuclear families replace a large joint family.

Authors suggest that there are several timings of family break-up. Kolenda (1987) and Mukherjee (1982) emphasise that for knowing the typical and desired times of break-up we need information on cultural ideals as well as statistical data on the actual timings of the break-up. Mukherjee suggests that while collecting data, two types of information are to be collected: (1) whether the joint structures are breaking into nuclear units, and (2) whether the nuclear units are pursuing the course of nuclearisation by not reverting back to *status quo ante* (p.91).

VII

For a proper comprehension of the functional dimension of the joint family and for holding comparisons of the types and degrees of jointness among different types of genealogical units, our first task is to prepare a category-set of the genealogical units from their structural or compositional aspect. Otherwise we shall make statements about joint family in general which are applicable to only one of its segments. However, as the term 'family' is vague we decide to use the tern 'household', a commensal and co-residential domestic group, and try to prepare a category-set of households from the structural aspect. Categorisation of households according to types of composition is not, however, an end in itself. This is done only to indicate that the structure of the household becomes more complex as more categories of relatives are included. And, accordingly, the role relationships among the members also will change.

Of all the category-sets used by our family sociologists, the one developed by Kolenda (1987) seems to us the most precise, comprehensive and distinct so far as the compositional aspect is concerned. We agree with her on the four principles upon which the classification rests. These are: First, a joint family *must* include two related married couples. Second, these couples may be related lineally or collaterally. Third, the unmarried relatives (including widowed and divorced) who are not children of any of the married couples in a household *supplement* the household. Fourth, where there is no married couple and the relatives were formerly part of the nuclear family, then it is a sub-nuclear household. On the basis of these four principles Kolenda developed a category-set of eleven types of households (1987, p.12). In the present inquiry, however, this category-set will be used in some modified form. To make the analysis of data a bit convenient, the categories of 'supplemented collateral joint', 'supplemented lineal joint' and 'supplemented lineal-collateral joint', households have been merged with the nearest categories.

Ultimately, our position is as follows: The joint household has been defined here as a group of relatives comprising at least two married couples living in the same house and taking food in a common hearth, and also who are related lineally and/or collaterally with each other. It may include one or more unmarried, separated and divorced relatives. This is contrasted with a 'nuclear household' which comprises the husband, wife and their unmarried children *only*.

The above is, no doubt, a structural definition, and the functional part of the family has not been incorporated here. Though the functional aspect of jointness is the focus of this inquiry, the structural aspect cannot be ignored since the composition of the household is most likely to have a considerable influence in the shaping of actions and interactions both within and between the household units. It will be a gross injustice to the reality if we simply categorise households (from the structural perspective) into several categories such as sub-nuclear, nuclear, supplemented nuclear, lineal joint, collateral joint, lineal-collateral joint, for instance, and treat these categories as homogeneous units from the perspective of their functions and intra-family interaction patterns.

Let us clarify the stance concretely. Suppose after a social survey we find that 5 per cent of the sample households are of the sub-nuclear type, 30 per cent are of the nuclear type, 30 per cent belong to what may be called as the supplemented nuclear, 15 per cent are lineally joint, 5 per cent are collaterally joint, 5 per cent are lineally-collaterally joint, and 10 per cent belong to the 'other' category. Now, what meaning does this information convey? In which way will these data help us to understand the complex relational problems within the households? Take, for instance, the case of these 30 per cent nuclear households in this hypothetical sample. Admitting the structural homogeneity of these household units, suppose that in some cases father is the only bread-winner and the mother is engaged in household duties, whereas in some cases both the parents are gainfully employed and thereby both of them share the economic responsibility of the household; in some other cases, the son and/or the daughter also may be the earner(s), may help the parents or may be the sole provider of the household (parents being non-earning dependants). This last category of household units will also be categorised as nuclear as until married, the kid's status of being economically self-sufficient does not alter the structural nature of the household. However, in all the cases referred to above, the intra-household interaction patterns, division of labour, authority structure and decision-making process will vary from each other to a significant extent. The point is that if the 'simple' nuclear households include so may diverse sorts (from the functional perspective), one can only imagine the variegated non-uniformities the 'complex' (different types of joint) households can bestow. With each addition of members, the intra-household arrangement of roles and responsibilities also vary. And all these consequences will affect the inter-household interaction patterns or functional bonds among the kindred. The question is: How far will it be either methodologically or conceptually legitimate to categorise all these household units having structural similarities as one 'homogeneous' household unit? Will it be helpful for understanding the reality?

Complexities will further aggravate when the household units do not take food from the same hearth, and/or do not live under one roof, though hold property jointly. Such eventualities are there as, according to many of our family sociologists, the joint family need not be a joint household, and co-residence is not a necessary condition for making a joint family. It seems to be a gross oversimplification to us if all these forms of genealogical units, whether they satisfy any one or two or more criteria of jointness, are treated as one homogeneous category. The *degree* of family jointness or solidarity, family authority structure, division of labour most probably will vary under each of these conditions. It is too optimistic to expect that the relation between the brothers who live in separate households will remain the same when they live under one roof or take food from the same hearth, whether or not they hold the ancestral property in common. Or, take the case of two sons—one remaining (with his wife and children) with the stem family (parents and their dependants) and the other residing elsewhere (with his wife and children) and occasionally visiting the stem family and/or regularly/occasionally sending some money to the stem family. Is it valid to hold that the functional relations between the parents and the sons in these two cases are qualitatively the same or comparable (though they hold property in common), and that physical distance is not a significant factor in affecting family jointness? Sibling relationships too cannot be expected to remain unaffected under such eventualities.

Hence, the exploration in the field of family studies should focus on the authority structure, role relationships, division of labour and responsibilities, cooperation in economic and ritual activities which may vary with levels and degree of separation among the genealogical units in terms of hearth, residence, productive activity, land or belongings. The simple categorisation of the households on the basis of compositional aspects will not help to understand the kinds of spiritual oneness or emotional attachment among the members of the kindred who claim themselves to belong to the stem family, whether residing jointly or separately.

We, therefore, follow Mayer who suggests, "It is not enough to know about territorial aspect of kin ties. A description of the attitudes, rights and duties which kinsmen have to one another, and the degree to which these are fulfilled will give us a picture of the constitution of the effective kin group. There are four rough classes of interpersonal kin relations—those between kin living in the same household, between agnates living outside the household though usually in the same village, between other cognates usually in different villages, and between affines" (1960, p.214).

It is then clear that to get an all-round and comprehensive understanding of the family system, the analysis is to be conducted from both structural and functional standpoints. A functional joint family lays stress on the fulfilment of obligations towards the kin (extra-familial obligations). Such a 'family' may consist of a number of households of male patri-kin; they may be situated at different distant places and may not hold property in common but may identify themselves as members of the particular 'family', cooperate in rituals and ceremonies, exchange financial and other kinds of help and assistance, and cherish joint family sentiments and norms.

A word of caution. Unless properly defined, the indiscriminate use of the term 'family' and 'household' may create confusions. Among the Indian scholars, Shah has strongly advocated for distinguishing between these two concepts (1964, p.32), and between 'household' and *kutumba* (1968, p.127). He suggests that "the household is one of the several dimensions of the family" (1973, p.3). He regards household as a residential unit as distinct from a family which may not be so. Thus, even when all the members of a genealogical unit do not share the same hearth and residence, they may still be bound by a number of activities and ties and hence may constitute a joint family, but not a joint household. In this sense, we make a distinction between the *household* and the *family*.

In the absence of a universally accepted definition of the 'joint family' and, consequently, a uniform manner of identification of the family units, we think it convenient to use the term 'household' in place of family. Households will be referred to here as the co-residential and commensal groups of patri-kin. This definition of the household is in tune with its popular and indigenous meaning. For example, the Bengali version of this concept is *ekannavarti parivar,* i.e., a household which shares a common hearth.

Making a distinction between *joint family* and *joint household* is necessary from another aspect too. Joint family is a multi-functional group. It can be viewed as a property-holding unit, a *shraddha* performing unit, a ritual or ceremonial unit performing domestic worships, and as a unit that also performs functions in a variety of other fields, such as production, reproduction, socialisation, care of the elderly people, and so on. Hence, when one speaks of change in or even disintegration of the household dimension of the joint family, it is not indicated thereby the change in or disintegration of the total institutional complex of the joint family. It can be expected, however, that change in one aspect will be followed by sooner or later changes in other aspects as well. The present inquiry confines itself to the household dimension of the joint family only.

VIII

In the opinion of most of the Indian family sociologists, structural jointness and functional solidarity are correlated and this is almost axiomatic. Let us see how the forerunners in our family sociology have treated this issue.

While collecting data on the opinion of graduate teachers of secondary schools towards the disintegration of the joint family, Kapadia (1955) focussed on the sentiments or interpersonal relationships in the family. He distinguishes between residential and functional joint families on the one hand and only functional joint families on the other. He advocates for looking at the family as a set of relationships where the family functions as a unit even though consisting of residentially separate households.

Non-partitioning of the property is, in the opinion of Kapadia, the most important indicator of jointness. Fulfilment of mutual rights and obligations (sentimental identification) is another indicator, though it is weaker than co-parcenary.

Elsewhere Kapadia argues that in spite of so many social legislations providing security to people "the joint family still continues to be by far the major provider of security to its members as a means of relief and refuge to orphans, widows, and the disabled; and as a resort in financial and social crises, in obtaining funds for marriage and education and to meet emergencies..." (1966, p.318). He asserts that the care and maintenance of dependants is viewed as a moral obligation, as with aged parents and young children, and is backed by the force of social prestige and the fear of opprobrium. In short, the individual looks to his family for help and shelter in all situations of crisis, such as unemployment, sickness and any natural calamities such as flood, famine or epidemics (1966, pp. 311-12). The point to be noted is that, as Kapadia admits, though with the various welfare measures pursued by our government reliance on the joint family is diminishing, it still stands as an organisation for social security, because the agencies and devices which have emerged recently to take up this primary function of the family are still limited and inadequate in their scope and extent.

Kapadia stresses that these joint family bonds are so strong and deeply entrenched in the Indian value structure that even in cases where the property is partitioned and the income of the members is not pooled, the constituent households still maintain their connections through mutual co-operation and rights and obligations other than those concerning property. Members of associated households are duty-bound to be present on the occasion of a death or serious illness. Such obligations keep feelings for the joint family alive. Monetary obligations on all such occasions are considered natural and just and are consequently met readily and without a murmur (1966, pp. 301-2).

As a mark of the joint family spirit, it is a common expectation among the Hindus that a son should look after his parent(s) who have grown old and/or are unable to earn. The performance of these duties was viewed not as burdens but as privileges. People should not feel proud if they do this duty, rather they should have a feeling of guilt in case they fail to abide by this norm. It is also considered a moral obligation for a person to support teen-aged brothers and sisters who are not married or have not yet started a career. However, as Kapadia admits, the economic obligations towards the collaterals and distant kin are not so strongly felt as they are felt for one's parents and children. Still the higher castes generally require their members to discharge social and economic obligations to near kin, specially widows.

It appears from above that the image Kapadia has of the joint family is almost like a mini-social service institution. It is not clear whether he refers to the ideal or normative structure of joint family, or people's actual practice in the domain of family.

While reiterating the relevance for the study for functional jointness, Desai pleads that

(1) co-residence and commensality are neither adequate nor reliable criteria for judging the type of family;
(2) the joint family sentiment does not vanish with the residential separation; and
(3) the jointness of the separated units consists in the rights and obligations of the members of different units towards one another and in the feeling of oneness (1955).

Desai is very emphatic on the criteria of co-residence, commensality and size, and the relations within the household are not very significant to him. What matters are the property, and the rights and obligations between persons within the households and the kin without it (1956, p.154).

In his later years, Desai attempted to develop certain indices with the help of which the degree of jointness among different household units can be measured. But being pioneering efforts in the field, his experiments, though sincere, did not prove to be precise and systematic enough. Still, his credit remains in that he is the first and one of the very few of the Indian family scholars who treated the *family jointness as a sociological variable*. He did not regard it as a uniform and stable entity but something the degree of which varies with situations. Thus, for proving family jointness he did not take the help of non-sociological (e.g., legal, Indological) criteria, but relied on sociological data.

Desai also brings the concept of 'radius of kinship relations' or circle of relatives within which such role relationships are to be searched: "The small circle or unit that can be conceived logically is the group of husband, wife and unmarried children. There can be no limit to the largest circle or unit" (1964, p.29). While analysing his data he has, however, kept himself limited to the relationship between father, son and son's son from the point of view of the lineal depth. The collateral relationships have been searched between a man and his father's brother and his own brother (1956, p.156).

Desai's treatment of the issue seems to be the most methodical and sociological compared to his contemporary family sociologists. But being pioneer in the field, he could not be very precise in his measurement technique and reasoning. A few deficiencies in his analysis may be mentioned here. For example, the two sets of classification of families—one from the structural and another from the functional angles—remain almost parallel to each other. While stressing the functional aspect he has often undermined the structural aspect of jointness. This confusion, however, can be observed among all the family sociologists of his time.

Next, he has felt the need for studying jointness within a 'radius of kinship relations' the smallest limit of which has been specified, but not the uppermost limit. Does this mean that *any* interaction outside the smallest circle of the husband-wife-children group be regarded as a mark of jointness? Is there no difference between father-son and uncle-nephew or brother-brother or cousin-cousin interactions? If any interaction outside the smallest circle is the criterion of jointness, the search for the nuclear family in the Indian soil would be almost futile since it is quite unusual and also impractical for any household unit to remain totally isolated under the prevailing social, economic and political situation (in his language, families having 'zero degree of jointness').

Moreover, Desai has not clarified whether by 'interaction' he means interaction with agnatic kin only or all sorts of interactions with relatives from wife's, married sisters' and married daughters' side as well.

Then, Desai has put great emphasis on the fulfilment of mutual institutionalised role obligations in determining jointness. Friends and neighbours also fulfil some of these functions. Desai has not clarified how to differentiate between the rendering of service and help by a kin and a friend.

In the writings of other sociologists having done field studies in India we get more or less similar views. Srinivas, for example, who too is against describing the Indian family on the basis of the kinship composition, remarks that "an urban household may be perfectly nuclear in composition while kinship duties, obligations, and privileges overflow it in many important ways. Many an Indian household is only the 'satellite' of a dominant kin group living in a village or town several miles away" (1966, p.138). Ross, while accepting the existence of functional jointness, stresses that mutual obligations and duties may not be verbally voiced or even explicitly acknowledged by persons, but underneath lies a shrewd estimation of what each family member has given and what he has received. Should a member refuse to carry out his obligations, he is open to the severe condemnation of the group (1961, p.82).

The concept of the ancestral home and the sentimental bond has echoed in the writings of Mandelbaum too when he says that a family system may be physically separated even when legally split, yet the brothers may continue to act as a functioning family. Even when a brother moves to a city with his wife and children, he may return to the village home as often as he can; he contributes to the income of the village family; he rallies to their help and they too his whenever there is emergency need or ceremonial occasion. Before arranging a marriage or taking any decisive measures affecting their careers or fortunes, the members consult with each other, giving due deference to the views of the elders among them. This traditional spirit of the family is frequently upheld in both village and city (1970, p.45).

Gore also observes that joint family provides social security to its members. The ill, the aged, the widowed and the orphaned are provided for within the family as a member of legal right but more significantly as a moral obligation imposed by the value system. This has always been, and continues to be, the important factor motivating individuals to participate in the joint family system. The significance of the sense of moral obligation lies in the fact that the benefits are often extended much beyond the circle of those who would have a legal right to claim them (1968, p.29).

Authors have pointed out another dimension of this issue. Any trend towards nuclear households does not establish that nuclearity or conjugal companionship has come to stay in India. It seems that there is a difference between the nuclear family and the nuclear household. A nuclear household is one which is only residentially separate but maintains functional ties and emotional links with the ancestral family. The nuclear family, on the other hand, involves the full acceptance of the conjugal ties as the primary relationship in the family. It lays high importance to the husband-wife and parent-child relationships. Negatively, it implies the limitation of the circle of relatives, whether of the husband or of the wife, who may normally be helped. A nuclear family in this sense has never been accepted in the Hindu social system (Ross, 1961, p.68; Gore, 1968, p. 30).

In rural West Bengal, the marriage of a boy or a girl is, Sengupta notes, never an exclusive concern for their parents. Grandparents, uncles and aunts effectively participate in different degrees in carrying out the negotiations. In most cases, the kitchen is separate but the house is common with a common wall as its boundary and a common entrance (1958, p.389). Sengupta concludes that except when there is a definite breach (leading to litigation, etc.) the brothers even though separate, would live in most amicable terms and the elder brother will continue to retain his superior position in all social functions.

As the main focus of Mukherjee's inquiry is to find out the 'structural arrangements of the families in West Bengal', he has not devoted much attention to the functional dimension of the family system (1965; 1977), except for enquiring into the 'mental make-up' or the 'orientation towards the joint family' of the respondents (the heads of households) and whether the respondents 'maintain contact' with their 'permanent residence' elsewhere. This mental make-up or orientation has been measured simply by asking the respondents "to enumerate who were their family members". Elsewhere he himself has, however, pointed out the inadequacy of such measurement process: "It is virtually confined to social psychology if the 'jointness' of a family is determined by the mental orientation of the people, viz., whom one considers to be his or her family members. It becomes a matter of interpretation in sociology if 'jointness' is determined in terms of a sharing of what are regarded as 'familial' privileges and obligations among a number persons related by blood or marriage" (1982, p.90).

As Mukherjee's findings are based on secondary data and survey data, he could not inquire into the various dimensions of the functional ties maintained among the geographically dispersed nuclear units. Information regarding this is primarily non-quantitative in nature and therefore cannot be collected in surveys where data are collected by the hired investigators. Surveys are generally specialised in quantitative treatment of data. And, therefore, complex relational matters which are not easily amenable to quantification and standardisation, cannot be effectively studied through large-scale survey research where data are collected by hired investigators. Intensive field studies where the presence of the researcher is a necessity are more suitable for this purpose.

Functional jointness of families, though not enquired in detail, has been referred to by some other family sociologists (cf. Agarwala, 1955; Orenstein and Micklin, 1966; Sinha, 1977; Sarma, 1964). Their treatment is, however, not very systematic or illuminating. The only exception is Chekki (1974) who has made a detailed and thorough analysis of this issue.

4

Measurement of the Functional Solidarity of the Joint Family and Description of the Sample

We have already specified the objective and focus of this inquiry. Now, the next task is to describe the steps followed in conducting this inquiry as well as the rationale behind their application.

I

'Functional solidarity' among the members of the household units being the major focus of our inquiry, our prime task is to conceptualise and operationalise this concept. On the basis of the existing literature, this concept has been defined as the extent to which people abide by or deviate from the normative structure of the ideal type joint family (vide pp. 49-54) in their actual familial behaviour and practice, fulfil the mutual rights and obligations, along with the attitude they hold towards family-related issues, and the justification they offer in defence of their behaviour and opinion.

The next, task is to *operationalise* this concept, i.e., devise ways and means for objectively, concretely and precisely measuring 'functional solidarity' in a specific empirical situation, namely, among the wives at present residing in different types of household structures in the villages and towns of West Bengal. Thus, though functional solidarity of the family is the *unit of our analysis*, we have selected the housewives as the *units of our observation.* In operationalising this concept, we faced a real problem. Though our family sociologists have often referred to this concept, very few of them took the pains of systematically *measuring* the same. Hence, little guideline has been obtained from the existing literature in this regard.

Measurement requires a careful, deliberate and systematic observation of a specific phenomenon in the real-life situations for the purpose of describing objects and events in terms of the attributes constituting a variable. We should, therefore, first describe the empirical indicators considered in this work for measuring the concept of functional solidarity or jointness of our family structure. Some of these indicators are applicable to respondents residing in all types of household structures, while some others are meant for respondents living in a particular type of household structure. We shall first present the indices which are applicable to all categories of respondents:

1. whether financial aid is exchanged among the relatives;
2. whether the help and assistance of relatives are taken during such occasions as child-rearing; children's education; pursuing a career or finding a job for any member of the household; starting business; occupational hazard or mishap or temporary unemployment of the husband; pregnancy and childbirth of the wife; constructing/purchasing a dwelling place; arranging, negotiating and solemnising a marriage in the family; cultivation of land; looking after children if the mother is gainfully employed; and the like;
3. whether respondents exchange gifts with relatives on occasions like festivals, birthday celebrations, new year's day, etc.;
4. whether the respondents' residence is used by their relatives as an occasional shelter or centre of refuse while they search a job or prepare themselves for a job, or for continuing education, medical treatment, pursuing business dealings, negotiating for and arranging son's /daughter's marriage, and the like;
5. whether there is any regular custom of familial get-together on any occasion; whether people get together more frequently with the kin than with the non-kin; and whether the family continues to be the most important place of informal association;

6. to whom respondents primarily approach for help—kin or non-kin;
7. what opinion respondents hold regarding extending aid and assistance to relatives, or seeking aid from relatives;
8. whether respondents are close and intimate with the kin who live in close physical proximity;
9. whether respondents opine that they have relatives who at present live separately but who should live jointly;
10. the ideal time of separation from husbands' family of orientation;
11. type of household structure where respondents prefer to live;
12. how much dutiful and affectionate the respondents' husbands are, in the opinion of the respondents, towards their parents and sibs;
13. whether the respondents and their husbands desire egalitarian or hierarchical role relationships between the marital partners;
14. whether the family acts as a political unit, i.e., whether the respondents, their husbands, children and other members in the household cast vote in consultation with the kin or, contrarily, take decision individually on which political party they would support.

Another set of indicators have been put to the respondents living in nuclear households:

15. distance of respondents' dwelling place from the residence of their husbands' paternal kin;
16. distance of respondents' dwelling place from the residence of their paternal kin;
17. whether respondents' husbands' ancestral property is held jointly or partitioned;
18. whether respondents perform rites and rituals with their husbands' patri-kin;
19. frequency of contacts and communication with relatives;
20. regularity of contacts and communication with relatives;
21. the time of break-up of respondents' husbands from their families of orientation—before or how many days after their marriage;
22. the time of break-up of husbands' brothers, if any;

23. whether respondents' husbands separated after the death of their parents, after the marriage of their sibs, after their brothers, getting established, that is, whether the separation took place in the natural course of the family developmental process;
24. whether the separation occurred amicably or out of serious differences of opinion—reasons behind separation;
25. type or depth of separation; whether it was the separation of hearth only, hearth plus residence, hearth plus residence plus property, etc.
26. whether respondents' husbands/the other brothers of respondents' husbands look(ed) after their parents after being separated.

In the third category for measuring the internal solidarity or cohesiveness of the joint households, we have included some more indicators specifically for respondents living in the joint households:

27. whether the income of different members of the household is pooled together in a common purse from which all major expenses of the members are met;
28. under whose supervision and control the common purse is deposited and who decides the budget of the household;
29. whether the members of the respondents' households have separate and individual consumption patterns, style of life, child-rearing; or, whether everything is controlled from a single source of authority;
30. pattern of the division of the household chores among the members;
31. whether, according to the respondents, any member of their households desires to separate or should separate; and
32. pattern of taking meal; whether any meal-time talk or chat takes place regularly among the members of the household.

Apart from the information regarding the above indices, some more evidences were collected specially to assess the attitudinal or subjective dimension of the family solidarity (spiritual oneness). They may be stated as follows:

One way of judging whether a member of a nuclear household has a sense of obligation towards his/her family of origin, even in case he/she fails to fulfil them, is to understand whether he/she has any *feeling of guilt* that generally arises when responsibilities are evaded or not carried out. Another method is to observe the manner in which individuals talk of their obligations to the relatives: whether they think it a mark of duty or generosity to help the relatives and whether they feel proud for being able to help the relatives. Further, attempt has been made here to understand whether the respondents help their relatives, if and when they do it, out of a sense of duty and responsibility, or out of sentiments of love and affection, or because of the fear of social censure and criticisms.

The present inquiry has examined while helping the relatives whether the respondents indulge in such attitude: "It is very difficult in these hard days to look after oneself and the family. We may manage to save a little for ourselves and our children, but if we have to spend it for others, then we will have to suffer in times of need. So we feel that each one of us should save something against the rainy days and as far as possible try to avoid troubling others"; or, "helping people with money makes them lazy and unenterprising."

The value of the joint family further requires that whenever any substantive decision is to be taken, all the significant members (particularly the seniors), whether residing in the same compound or separately, are consulted and attempt is taken for arriving at a decision based on consensus (in the traditional joint family, of course, in a number of cases the *karta* of the joint family has the final say). It symbolises the corporate authority of the joint family and reinforces the respected position of the elderly persons. The consultation with the kin particularly before settling the marriage of a member of the family is important because this facilitates acceptance of a new member by all concerned and forging of an intimate and permanent relationship with another family. An attempt has been made in this inquiry how far this norm is followed by the respondents and the families they live in.

Next, according to the joint family values, one's relationship with the mother or with the parents must be given priority over that with one's wife and children. Even when living separately, this bond does not cease to exist. This inquiry has sought to probe as to whom—the parents and siblings or the wife and children—the husbands are more responsive; and whether the desire to have a close relationship with the mother and performance of duties towards parents and sibs by the husbands of the respondents conflict with their performance of duties towards the wife and children, and whether the betrayal of this desire antagonises the respondents. It has been seen whether the romantic love between the husband and the wife—one of the accopaniments of the values supporting the nuclear family—tends to get upper-hand over loyalty to one's (the respondent's husband's) parents and sibs.

It has also been looked into as to whether and how far segregation between the genders—another norm of the joint family—is practised. For example, respondents were asked whether they were usually accompanied by their respective husbands or also by the husband's kin, on their visits to the market, cinema hall, fair, exhibition and similar other places of amusement and recreation.

The study has further investigated whether the respondents have been 'choosy' in maintaining intimate relation with the husbands' kin; whether they behave with discretion with kin having the same degree of kinship bond. Under the norm of the traditional joint family, extending help to the kin is binding on the member of the joint family and it should not depend on one's choice. Hence, an identical relationship is to be maintained with the brothers or the cousins having the same order of relationship. It is to be seen, therefore, whether the respondents and their husbands form their own circle, possibly with those having an identical status, and thus impose limits on obligations to the kin or define by self which obligations to be honoured. When this is done, i.e., people who have gained a higher position and prestige, tend to avoid and become indifferent in relation to some kinsmen lower in social ranking, self-interest of the individual members becomes more important than the welfare of the group.

The study seeks to examine whether with the establishment of smaller separate household units, one's contacts with the relatives become irregular and less frequent. Contacts may be kept alive for some time through correspondence and through gatherings on festivals, ceremonies, rituals and holiday-celebrations. Affection may still be there but the bonds of common interest weaken. Visits to relatives become more and more less frequent and irregular. Even if they may still have love and respect for each other, in the absence of common shared interests their interactions become irregular. It is true that the relatives living far away may become closer in certain ways than when they lived in the same household. For, here they are detached from the day-to-day frictions and bitterness which often interfere with the feelings of affection. But, on the whole, these emotions need to be constantly refuelled by actual contacts, or they gradually die. This may be called the impact of geographical separation on the joint family ties.

Spatial distance does not necessarily imply that family influence is not at work. But, on the other hand, absence of spatial proximity and contact among the members are very likely to result in weakening of the sense of family obligation and emotional attachment to family members. In such a situation, the authority of the former patriarch in all likelihood breaks down. When it happens, little will be left to nurture and nourish the feeling of, and desire for, identity with the larger kinship group. The fact of spatial distance can be used as an excuse by those who intend to escape close family contacts and the resultant obligations for their action. The gradual separation, thus, will lessen inter-household influences over the day-to-day affairs of the different household groups, so that even though they may continue to consult each other on the major issues of life, households will grow as more independent units and the control of the family 'trunk' will become minimal.

Finally, the inquiry has looked into whether some sort of bilateral kinship system, i.e., close ties with the wife's relatives as well, sometimes at the cost of relationships with the husband's kin, is developing. This criterion has been regarded as relevant for judging the joint family solidarity because such a development would indicate a decline of the joint family system which is supposed to be strictly patrilineal, patri-local and patriarchal (at least in the eastern and northern part of India).

Appropriate questions were put to measure the above feelings of the respondents. Though a few of them were framed in advance, many of them were left to the understanding of the interviewers.

II

The subject matter of the inquiry is such which cannot be totally quantified. Relational matters, i.e., the familial bonds in this case, are not subject to quantification. Further, in the absence of prior literature in the field of our proposed inquiry, we had been more inclined to *exploration* rather than *description* of a social reality. We, therefore, decided to emphasise the collection of respondents' experiences and expectations in detail. Respondents were encouraged to give their answers in their own words and from their own perspective with illustrations from their experiences. At the same time, objective and systematic analysis of data and the compulsion to arrive at some concrete and tangible conclusions required us to follow some 'structured' means in collecting and presenting data. As a compromise, we, therefore, decided to collect data from the respondents through the face-to-face interview with the help of an interview guide where the issues to be raised and points to be discussed were specified. Hence, in our interview, we combined an interview guide approach with a standardised open-ended interview format. For example, a number of basic questions were worded quite precisely in a predetermined fashion, while allowing the interviewers more flexibility in probing the unsatisfactory answers and considerable autonomy in determining when it is appropriate to explore a certain subject in greater depth, or even to undertake new areas of inquiry that were not originally included in the interview guide. Sometimes our technique was to apply the standardised open-ended interview format for the early part of an interview and then to leave it to the interviewer to pursue any topic of interest during the later parts.

A team of four lady interviewers, all of whom were alumni of the Department of Sociology and currently the research students doing work for the Ph.D. degree under the supervision of this researcher, helped in collecting data. A sum of Rs. 5,500 was granted by the University of Calcutta for meeting the expenses of this project. Obviously, there was no question of payment to the investigators who accepted this job as an opportunity for gathering some research experience. This researcher being a whole-time employee and there being no provision for sabbatical leave in the University of Calcutta for pursuing teachers' own research work, taking help from others in collecting data becomes almost imperative.

As a check on the intrusion of bias and also as a measure to remove any incompleteness and ambiguity in the answers obtained from the respondents, we regularly interviewed and probed the interviewers, checked the filled up schedules, and held weekly group discussions with the interviewers. The interviewers were asked to report the verbatim answers and reactions obtained from the respondents as fully as possible, exactly as given, without any attempt to summarise, paraphrase or correct or 'break up'. They were instructed to be as objective and concrete as possible, and, as and when necessary, to quote the respondents directly rather than abbreviating their statements and using any modifying adjective or adverb in reporting the observed materials. This was done to base the findings and conclusions on *facts* or actual observations rather than on *inferences* from what has been observed. The verbatim reporting has been used in the final report as illustrations of the nuances in attitude and behaviour. The interviewers being the advanced research students, could realise and follow the instructions correctly, and they did their assigned job with sincerity and responsibility.

III

The goal of the present inquiry being primarily exploration of a social reality rather than description of a specific *population*, we cared to make our 'sample' purposively chosen, that is, we deliberately and purposefully selected those units of observations who, we expected, would best serve our research purpose. The subject matter of our inquiry required us to deal with many intimate personal matters of the respondents, and it would have been difficult for us to have access to such information through the application of more conventional standardised survey methods.

The purposive sample which has been adopted here may prove perfectly adequate if the researcher has no intention to generalise her findings beyond the sample, or if the inquiry is merely a trial run for a larger, more systematic study. If it is carefully drawn, it might be quite representative also. It does not, however, allow to measure *sampling error* in making statistical inference from the findings. Hence, it is perfectly legitimate to apply this sampling technique if the researcher intends to *describe* some characteristics of a part of the society from which it is hoped that the generalisation to the whole society, or *people in general*, can be made. This sampling design can also be used when the researcher attempts to answer some questions about the relationship between the variables, the emphasis here being on the kind and quality of relationships rather than the frequency of occurrence of each type of relationship in the sample. This is so because the nature and mode of functioning of the variables is more or less durable, and does not vary from context to context. Thus, purposive sample is quite suitable when relationships between variables is the focus of inquiry, or any theoretical generalisation is aimed at.

The objective of this inquiry being the description of people's present-day familial behaviour and any difference in the same among rural and urban people and among the residents of different household structures, the use of this sampling design is methodologically legitimate.

Besides, the use of this sampling design was imperative too because of its feasibility. Here the study design was intensive type and the researcher has to manage all its aspects almost single-handedly.

Before drawing our sample we conducted pilot studies on several categories of women to assess from which category we could get the relevant data. The pilot study showed that for obtaining useful information we should include respondents from both the village and the town households since there are vast social, economic, ecological and demographic differences between these two milieux though inhabitants from both the regions share the same value and culture. Hence, we decided to draw samples from the village and town which are contiguous to each other and where there are regular and frequent communications between them.

It must be admitted, however, that it would have been better if we could draw more samples from the socially and geographically mobile people to assess the relation between mobility and familial behaviour. In the pilot study, we found that in the village, mobility is still not a regular and typical phenomenon and relative immobility is the distinctive feature of the rural society (cf. Larson, 1968, p. 586). Cases of mobility are very few and far between in the village. In the town also since we had to limit our sample to a few contiguous areas (this was done mainly to save time and money as we could not afford the travelling expenses of the interviewers in case the units of observation were to be selected from a wide region) we could not include many cases betraying significant social mobility. In the town also social mobility is not still a typical feature of our society. However, whenever cases of social mobility were available, we included them in our sample. For this reason, the number of cases betraying lack of mobility is higher in our sample, and this is more so in respect of the village sample significantly. If we could draw samples covering a wider region, we could find some more cases displaying varying degrees of social mobility.

The research purposes dictated drawing of samples from different types of household structures. Thus, ultimately we selected samples from 50 rural nuclear (Nu), 26 rural lineal joint (LJ), 16 rural collateral joint (CJ), 8 rural lineal-collateral joint (LCJ), 82 urban nuclear, 22 urban supplemented nuclear (SuNu), 42 urban LJ, 12 urban CJ and 16 urban LCJ households (total= 274).

A note of clarification is needed here. While analysing data, we categorised the urban SuNu households under the label of joint household. Strictly speaking, this category of households should not be treated as joint since they lack one necessary condition for being labelled as joint, namely, co-residence of at least two couples. But since it was decided to dichotomise the households into two categories only—nuclear and joint—and since the SuNu households are functionally nearer to joint than to nuclear households, a compromise had to be made on the issue of terminological accuracy. The step taken facilitated simplification in the analysis but did not result in factural inaccuracy. Shah (1998, p.21) supports this sort of categorisation: "If we add to an elementary family even one person not belonging to it, they should be considered, strictly speaking, as constituting a joint family." However, the separate and distinct entity of this category of households has been preserved, and in the tables, and when required, they have been presented as a separate category.

IV

The nature of this inquiry being primarily exploratory in nature, we do not aim at measuring any *population value* or making any kind of statistical generalisation. The study mainly aims at opening up new areas of inquiry into the familial behaviour and relationships of our people. Hence, this inquiry generates far more questions than what it can answer. We have tried here to pose the problem properly rather than answer all of them. We do not claim *statistical* validity for our findings. For example, it cannot be answered from the study *how many* of our nuclear households are functionally joint with, or independent of, their families of origin.

We have tried to conduct an intensive investigation into the inter-household and intra-household (when respondents live in a joint household structure) interaction patterns to assess functional and spiritual bonds among the kindred. Our goal is to describe the pattern or style of mutual exchange of aid, and, for this purpose, we have tried to ascertain in which category of kin exchange of aid and assistance occurs more often, or in which category of people (rural or urban, spatially close or apart, living in nuclear or joint household structures, having low or middle or upper-middle economic status, and the like) such exchanges occur more often, or which are the avenues or modes or styles through which contacts and communications are maintained among the kin and the occasions on which such contacts are made, and the like.

Moreover, as the subject matter of the study is familial bonds and relationships which are largely subjective in nature, an emphasis on the qualitative analysis of data has been laid, taking illustrations and explanations from what the respondents exactly said. At the same time, to meet the need for the systematic and precise organisation of data, we presented the same in a tabular form as well. But, it is to be pointed out, these tables have been constructed only for the summarisation of data and have been used only for depicting the data. The inferential value of these data cannot be specified if applied to a wider population.

However, the social variables and attributes being relatively stable in nature, the statement of relationships among the variables (e.g., relation between residence and exchange of aid, or between household structures and pattern of interactions among the members of the household) as has been drawn from our findings, will be helpful for providing a generalised understanding of the social structure, here the family structure.

V

Villages, having the small size of the community of inhabitants and low population density, have some features which create notable differences in the conditions of social action, social organisation and life styles of the villagers and the town-dwellers. For example, in a village the pattern of social interaction involves relatively few contacts per individual in a given unit of time, and provides little opportunity for personal anonymity.

Secondly, in a village there is relatively little division of labour, as there is a restricted range of occupations and a limited variety of social roles; and thus there is relatively little heterogeneity at the community level as compared to the urban world. Social roles tend to be more diffuse in the village. Moreover, social class identification is based more on ascribed and general attributes than on personal and achieved attributes. From these facts, viz., ascribed status and limited variety of occupational and social roles, it follows that social mobility is more restricted in the rural world.

Finally, because of less anonymity, normative deviance within the rural society tends to be less frequent.

At the same time, it must be mentioned, in the present era villages are coming closer to the urban institutions and life styles because of change factors like the frequent and regular interactions among people in rural and urban areas through large-scale migration, the influence of urban-centred mass media, greater interdependence of rural and urban economies, etc.

However, besides these ecological, economic, social and demographic features, in terms of the value configurations rural and urban areas cannot stand apart since whatever values and cultural attributes the people of a country possess, they are shared by all regions and segments of the population comprising the nation. Hence, within a country, village and town people do not pursue absolutely different value configurations though there may be differences in the degree and intensity of their belief-value matrix. Thus, the behavioural patterns of people in different segments of the population will not vary in kind, and any change noted therein will be in the same direction throughout the society.

Rural societies of today are so interlinked and integrated with their national systems that the changes in their social organisation are highly similar in many respects.

Thus, noting that there are both similarities and differences in the social organisation and action of the people in the village and town, we have decided to include respondents from both these areas in our study of the familial behaviour patterns and belief-value matrix of our people. The urban sample for this purpose was selected from within the areas under the Kolkata metropolis. Two villages within the district of Hooghly, contiguous to the city of Kolkata, were selected for the purpose of drawing the rural sample.

Let us present a brief profile of our sample.

As appears from Table 4.1, respondents in the urban sample are older than the rural sample by 8.5 years. The average age of the rural and urban sample is 30.5 years and 38.8 years, respectively.

In the village sample, respondents from the joint households (LJ, CJ, LCJ households in combination) are younger than those from the nuclear households by 3.5 years, and respondents from the rural CJ households are the youngest. In the urban sample no such difference in the age of the respondents belonging to different household structures has been noted.

Likewise, so far as the duration of the married life of the respondents is concerned, the urban respondents show a slightly higher limit. In the village, while the average years of married life of the respondents is 13, it is 15 years for the urban respondents. The relevant data have been presented in Table 4.2.

As expected, the urban household size is smaller than household size in the village. It appears from Table 4.3 that while

Table 4.1

Respondents, by Age, Residence and Household Structure

Residence	*Type of Household*	*Below 26 yrs*	*26-30*	*31-35*	*36-40*	*41-45*	*46-50*	*51-55*	*56-60*	*61 & above*	*Total*
Rural	Nu	7	11	20	5	4	-	2	1	-	50
	LJ	7	8	1	1	3	3	1	2	-	26
	CJ	4	8	2	2	-	-	-	-	-	16
	LCJ	1	4	-	-	1	-	-	-	2	8
Total		19	31	23	8	8	3	3	3	2	100
	Nu	1	10	19	17	11	7	7	3	7	82
	SuNu	-	2	3	2	7	6	1	-	1	22
Urban	LJ	6	9	5	5	4	1	3	4	5	42
	CJ	1	1	3	4	1	-	2	-	-	12
	LCJ	2	2	2	4	1	2	-	-	3	16
Total		10 (5.7%)	24 (13.8%)	32 18.4%)	32 (18.4%)	24 (13.8%)	16 (9.2%)	13 (7.5%)	7 (4.0%)	16 (9.2%)	174 (100%)

Rural Nu Mdn = 32.25 yrs; Rural Joint Mdn =28.75 yrs; Rural Mdn= 30.5 yrs.

Urban Nu Mdn = 38.74 yrs; Urban Joint Mdn = 38.83 yrs; Urban Mdn = 38.78 yrs.

Note: Nu = nuclear; SuNu = supplemented nuclear; LJ = lineal joint; CJ = collateral joint; LCJ = lineal-collateral joint households.

Table 4.2

Respondents, by Years Married, Residence and Household Structures

Residence	*Type of Houschold*	*1-4 yrs*	*5-8 yrs*	*9-12 yrs*	*13-16 yrs*	*17-20 yrs*	*21-24 yrs*	*25-28 yrs*	*29 yrs & above*	*Total*
Rural	Nu	1	5	11	9	14	1	4	5	50
	LJ	4	5	4	3	-	1	3	6	26
	CJ	5	2	6	2	1	-	-	-	16
	LCJ	-	3	2	-	-	-	-	3	8
Total		10	15	23	14	15	2	7	14	100
	Nu	2	18	12	14	3	8	6	19	82
	SuNu	2	3	1	1	5	4	3	3	22
	LJ	12	6	2	5	3	1	-	13	42
Urban	CJ	-	1	1	4	2	1	-	3	12
	LCJ	3	3	2	2	2	-	1	3	16
Total		19 (10.9%)	31 (17.8%)	18 (10.3%)	26 (15.0%)	15 (8.6%)	14 (8.0%)	10 (5.8%)	41 (23.6%)	174 (100%)

Table 4.3

Respondents, by Household Structure, Size of the Household and Residence

Residence	*Type of House-hold*	*No. of Members per Household*												*Total*
		2	*3*	*4*	*5*	*6*	*7*	*8*	*9-10*	*11-14*	*15-18*	*21*	*26*	
	Nu	2	7	18	16	6	1	-	-	-	-	-	-	50
	LJ	-	-	1	3	6	3	4	1	-	-	-	-	18
	SuLJ	-	-	-	-	3	-	4	1	-	-	-	-	8
Rural	CJ	-	-	-	-	1	-	-	-	-	-	-	-	1
	SuCJ	-	-	-	-	1	2	1	2	7	1	1	-	15
	LCJ	-	-	-	-	-	-	-	1	3	1	-	-	5
	SuLCJ	-	-	-	-	-	-	-	1	-	-	1	1	3
Total		2	7	19	19	17	6	9	6	10	2	2	1	100
	Nu	6	46	30	-	-	-	-	-	-	-	-	-	82
	SuNu	-	-	5	8	6	1	1	-	1	-	-	-	22
	LJ	-	-	1	19	8	-	1	-	-	-	-	-	29
	SuLJ	-	-	-	1	7	2	3	-	-	-	-	-	13
Urban	CJ	-	-	-	-	2	-	-	-	1	-	-	-	3
	SuCJ	-	-	-	-	-	1	3	1	3	1	-	-	9
	LCJ	-	-	-	-	-	4	3	1	3	1	-	-	12
	SuLCJ	-	-	-	-	-	-	-	-	2	2	-	-	4
Total		6	46	36	28	23	8	11	2	10	4	-	-	174
		(4%)	(26%)	(21%)	(16%)	(13%)	(5%)	(6%)	(1%)	(6%)	(2%)	-	-	(100)

in the village an average household comprises five members, in the town it is composed of four persons.

In Table 4.3, we have presented data showing the number of dependants/additional members in the joint households. It seems that the rural joint households contain more such persons than their urban counterparts. In the village sample, in at least 26 joint households out of the total of 50 (i.e., 52 per cent cases), there are one or more additional members; i.e., these households are supplemented by some relatives (the supplemented LJ, supplemented CJ and supplemented LCJ households). In the town, out of the 70 joint households (here we have kept aside 22 supplemented nuclear households), in only 26 or 37 per cent cases (the number of supplemented LJ, supplemented CJ and supplemented LCJ households), we find the existence of such relatives. It shows that a larger number of village people assume the responsibility of their dependent relatives than their urban counterparts.

In both the village and the town, the number of dependent relatives is the highest in the CJ households; i.e., the number of the supplemented CJ households is higher than that of the CJ households (households where brothers live with their wives and children *only*). In the village, in fact, excepting one CJ household the rest are supplemented by some kin. These additional members in the CJ households are mainly the widow mothers-in-law of the respondents.

Table 4.4 presents information relating to the level of education of the respondents. The corresponding information about their husbands has been shown in Tables 4.5 and 4.6. As expected, both the number of the literate and educated and the level or standard of education are much higher in the urban areas than in the village. In the village, while 24 per cent of the respondents ate illiterate or just literate, in the town 74 per cent of them are graduate at the minimum. In fact, many of them have some sort of higher degree, diploma, professional or specialised qualification above graduation (graduate plus). A fact worth noting is that in the urban sample the incidence of the highly qualified wives is higher in the nuclear than in the joint households.

Table 4.4

Respondents, by Level of Education, Residence and Household Structure

Residence	*Type of Household*	*Ill/ just lit.*	*Up to class IV*	*Up to class VI*	*Up to class VII*	*Up to S.F.*	*Under Graduate*	*Graduate*	*Graduate +*	*M. Phil/ Ph.D.*	*Doc./ Eng.*	*N*
	Nu	14	9	14	7	6	-	-	-	-	-	50
	LJ	6	5	4	4	4	1	2	-	-	-	26
Rural	CJ	1	1	-	7	6	1	-	-	-	-	16
	LCJ	3	-	1	2	2	-	-	-	-	-	8
	Total	24	15	19	20	18	2	2	-	-	-	100
	Nu	-	-	1	1	8	9	36	21	1	5	82
	SuNu	-	-	-	-	3	3	8	8	-	-	22
	LJ	-	-	-	1	5	6	17	12	1	-	42
Urban	CJ	1	-	-	-	2	3	5	1	-	-	12
	LCJ	-	-	-	-	3	-	6	7	-	-	16
	Total	1	-	1	2	21	21	72	49	2	5	174
		(0.6%)		(0.6%)	(1.1%)	12.0%)	12.0%)	(41.5%)	(28.2%)	(1.1%)	(2.9%)	(100)

Table 4.5

Rural Respondents' Husbands, by Level of Education and Household Structure

Type of house-hold	*Illiter-ate/ just lit.*	*Upto class IV*	*Up to class VI*	*Up to class VIII*	*Up to S.F.*	*Under-gradu-ate*	*Gradu-ate*	*Total*
Nu	12	5	11	11	9	1	1	50
LJ	3	5	6	3	4	4	1	26
CJ	2	1	1	2	5	3	2	16
LCJ	2	1	2	2	-	-	1	8
Total	19	12	20	18	18	8	5	100

Table 4.6

Urban Respondents' Husbands, by Level of Education and Household Structure

Type of House-hold	*S.F.*	*Under-gradu-ate*	*Gradu-ate*	*Gradu-ate+*	*Ph.D.*	*Doctor/ Engineer*	*Total*
Nu	-	1	21	33	1	26	82
SuNu	1	2	5	7	-	7	22
LJ	-	1	15	17	-	9	42
CJ	1	-	8	3	-	-	12
LCJ	1	-	5	5	-	5	16
Total	3	4	54	65	1	47	174
	(1.7%)	(2.3%)	(31.0%)	(37.4%)	(0.6%)	(27.0%)	(100)

In general, respondents' husbands (males) are qualified than respondents (females). However, there is a notable difference between the village husbands and the town husbands in this respect. In the village, for 51 per cent of the respondents' husbands the level of education is up to class VI, and only five cases have been found where the husband has a graduate degree. In contrast, in the town, 96 per cent of the respondents' husbands are graduate at the least. Out of these persons 28 per cent have still higher qualification such as degree in medicine, engineering, accountancy, business management, law, and the like.

It appears that in the village both respondents' and their husbands' educational standard in nuclear households is lower than that of their counterparts in joint households. The picture is opposite in the town. Urban nuclear households seems to contain more husbands and wives who surpass their counterparts living in joint households in the sphere of educational attainments. Here all the five respondents who hold any professional degree such as MBBS or BE are residents of the nuclear households. The same trend is noted in case of their husbands too since out of 47 persons holding any professional degree 26 (55%) belong to nuclear households.

Table 4.7

Respondents, by their Employment Status, Residence and Household Structure

Residence	*Type of household*	*Not employed*	*School teacher*	*Clerk/ Typist*	*Weaver*	*Shop-keeper/ Trader*	*Officer/ univ. teacher/ professional*	*Total*
	Nu	44	-	1	4	1	-	50
	LJ	24	-	1	1	-	-	26
Rural	CJ	14	1	1	-	-	-	16
	LCJ	8	-	-	-	-	-	8
	Total	90	1	3	5	1	-	100
	Nu	45	17	9	-	5	6	82
	SuNu	15	3	-	-	2	2	22
Urban	LJ	36	2	4	-	-	-	42
	CJ	11	1	-	-	-	-	12
	LCJ	12	2	1	-	-	1	16
	Total	119	25	14	-	7	9	174
		(68.4%)	(14.4%)	(8.0%)	-	(4.0%)	(5.2%)	(100)

Tables 4.7 and 4.8 present information relating to the respondents' and their husbands' occupational status. Here also a wide gulf between the rural and urban worlds has been noted. In

Table 4.8

Respondents' Husbands, by Employment Status, Residence and Household Structure

Residence	*Type of household*	*Cat.I*	*Cat.II*	*Cat.III*	*Cat.IV*	*Cat.V*	*Cat.VI*	*Cat.VII*	*Cat.VIII*	*Cat.IX*	*Cat.X*	*Cat.XI*	*Total*
	Nu	3	10	5	9	6	3	1	2	-	11	-	50
	LJ	-	2	2	3	5	3	-	7	-	4	-	26
Rural	CJ	-	-	3	-	5	4	1	1	-	2	-	16
	LCJ	-	1	1	-	2	-	-	1	-	3	-	8
	Total	3	13	11	12	18	10	2	11	-	20	-	100
	Nu	-	-	-	-	7	-	3	17	54	-	1	82
	SuNu	-	-	-	-	6	-	1	2	13	-	-	22
	LJ	-	-	-	-	7	-	2	10	23	-	-	42
Urban	CJ	-	-	-	-	7	-	-	2	3	-	-	12
	LCJ	-	-	-	-	7	-	-	3	6	-	-	16
	Total	-	-	-	-	34	-	6	34	99	-	1	174
						(19.5%)		(3.5%)	(19.5%)	(56.9%)		(.6%)	(100)

Note: Cat. I = manual, agricultural labourer; Cat. II = industrial labourer; Cat. III =artisan like carpenter, weaver, potter or person engaged in any cottage industry; Cat. IV = vendor; Cat. V = shop-keeper, businessmen; Cat. VI = Class IV staff in government & private offices; Cat. VII = clerk, typist, stenographer, telephone operator, newspaper reporter, etc.; Cat. IX = doctor, engineer, lawyer, advocate, college/univ. teacher, charted accountant, persons employed in the executive rank in any office; Cat. X = owner-cultivator; Cat. XI = rentier.

the village, whereas 90 per cent of the respondents are economically inactive, in the town this figure is 68 per cent. It is expected since urban ladies are relatively qualified and the prospect of job is higher in the town than in the village.

In both the village and the town, the trend noted is that employed women are found in higher number in nuclear than in joint households.

Another similarity noted is that the incidence of wives being economically inactive is highest in the LCJ households. Perhaps, employed wives face difficulty in making adjustments in large households and so they tend to avoid LCJ type of households which are the largest in size.

As expected, in the village people are mostly absorbed in the primary and secondary sectors. On the other hand, in the town, as people are more qualified, they are found mostly in the tertiary sector. The picture of the employment status of the respondents' husbands (Table 4.8) also reveals the same trend. Thus, a wide divergence is observed in the sphere of the occupational diversification of the rural and urban people.

Table 4.9

Village Respondents, by per capita Monthly Income (in Rs.) and Household Structure

Type of Household	*Below 200*	*201-300*	*301-400*	*401-500*	*501-600*	*601-700*	*701-800*	*801-900*	*901-1000*	*1001-1100*	*1001-1200*	*1201& above*	*N*
Nu	6	23	7	5	3	1	1	1	1	1	-	1	50
LJ	-	6	2	3	3	2	1	4	2	2	1	-	26
CJ	-	2	1	3	-	-	4	2	2	1	-	1	16
LCJ	-	2	-	2	-	1	-	2	-	-	-	1	8
Total	6	33	10	13	6	4	6	9	5	4	1	3	100

Village Nu Mdn = 283.11; Village Joint Mdn = 600.83; Village Mdn = 408.19.

The wide gulf between the rural and urban people in the sphere of educational standard and occupational attainment or status is reflected, quite naturally, in their economic status as well. As Tables 4.9 and 4.10 reveal, the economic status (monthly per

Table 4.10

Urban Respondents, by per capita Monthly Income (in Rs.) and Household Structure

Type of House-hold	*Below 1000*	*1001-1500*	*1501-2000*	*2001-2500*	*2501-3000*	*3001-3500*	*3501-4000*	*4001-4500*	*4501-5000*	*5001-5500*	*5501 & above*	*N*
Nu	1	7	12	13	18	8	3	5	4	4	7	82
SuNu	1	2	6	3	4	2	1	1	-	-	2	22
LJ	-	5	8	7	11	3	4	2	1	-	1	42
CJ	1	2	2	2	4	-	-	-	-	1	-	12
LCJ	-	1	5	-	5	2	2	-	1	-	-	16
Total	3	17	33	25	42	15	10	8	6	5	10	174
	(1.7%)	(9.8%)	(19.0%)	(14.4%)	(24.1%)	(8.6%)	(5.8%)	(4.6%)	(3.4%)	(2.9%)	(5.7%)	(100)

Urban Nuclear Mdn = 2722.72; Urban Joint Mdn = 2521.33; Urban Mdn = 2607.64.

capita income) of the sample households in the village and the town is, in fact, quite incomparable. In the village while the average per capita income is Rs. 408, in the town it is Rs. 2,608.

Another striking difference between the village and the town noted is that in the village poor people live in the nuclear households in higher number, while in the town the trend is in the opposite direction. The average monthly per capita income of the people in nuclear households in the village is only Rs. 283, and it is Rs. 601 for the residents of the rural joint households. The corresponding figures for the urban people are Rs. 2,723 and Rs. 2,521, respectively. The higher income holders in the town live in the nuclear households.

It seems that when people's economic status is either much below or much above the standard, they tend to live in nuclear households.

5

Functional Solidarity in Households in General

I

The findings of the inquiry may now be presented. The inquiry started with the supposition that though the normative structure of the Indian society might still be oriented towards the joint family values, under the pressure of modern developments people's familial behaviour deviates in various ways from the traditional family norms. That is to say, the traditional co-residential, commensal, co-parcenary, collaterally and/or lineally joint family with a depth of three or more generations, honouring the authority of the head of the family, worshipping the common family deity and family ancestors is increasingly on the wane. The change factors, however, may not uniformly influence all the segments of the society. For instance, the reactions of the ruralites and urbanites, of different income and occupational groups may vary in degree and kind. Hence, it is pertinent to compare the familial behaviours and opinions of individuals from different segments of the society. Data obtained from the rural and urban areas have, therefore, been separately organised in the present inquiry.

Further, it may be assumed that the loyalty towards the stem family (stem family means those households where the husband's parents and/or, in case the parents are dead, most of the brothers live) is higher among the residents of the joint households than among the residents of the nuclear households. Because by the very fact of sharing the common hearth and residence, they show allegiance to the joint family norm to a certain extent. One should not take it for granted, however, that the simple fact of living in a joint household is a sufficient proof that all obligations towards the husband's family of orientation are fully honoured by the respondent (wife) and her husband as well as by other members of the household. For, men may or may not be attentive, affectionate and dutiful towards their parents and siblings even when they eat and reside together and do not seek partition of the ancestral property. By the same token, one should not assume that separation from the stem family leads to the termination of all sorts of obligations towards it. This inquiry, therefore, feels the need for searching for the elements of functional jointness in both nuclear and joint households. The data gathered from these two types of households are, therefore, separately treated and compared with each other.

This and the following two chapters seek to throw light on the nature and degree of compactness or solidarity in nuclear and in joint households in rural and urban areas. In other words, they highlight how far loyalty is shown and obligations and duties are honoured and performed by the respondents and their husbands towards such members of the husband's stem family as their parents, brothers and sisters. They examine whether there is any difference in this respect between the nuclear and joint households in rural and urban areas. Thus, for the sake of analysis, the total sample (N) has been divided into four categories: urban joint (Cat. A), urban nuclear (Cat. B), rural joint (Cat. C) and rural nuclear (Cat. D). Attempt has been made here to see which one of these four categories most conform to, or deviate from, the traditional family norm and behaviour. The numerical strength of the above categories in the sample is 92, 82, 50 and 50, respectively. To facilitate a quick understanding, the percentage figures have been indicated in the tables, though in row and column totals frequency of the respondents also has been mentioned.

II

Table 5.1 shows the nature and dimension of exchange of goods and services and assistance among the relatives. The purpose here is

Table 5.1

Exchange of Aid among Relatives, by Residence, Households Structure and Circle of Relatives (in percentage)

Residence	Type of household	Circle of Relatives among Whom Aid is Exchanged											Total	Little Exchange of Aid
		Husband's Side					Wife's Side				Married			
		Par.	Bro.*	Sis.*	F.'s sibs*	M.'s sibs*	Par.	Bro.*	Sis.*	Par.'s sibs*	Son*	Dau.*		
Rural	Nu	14	18	12	3	3	24	13	8	2	1	2	100 (f=295)	6 (n=50)
	Joi	13	13	21	16	7	17	5	1	1	2	4	100 (f=249)	8 (n=50)
Total no. of Exchange		72	85	88	51	27	115	52	28	6	6	14	544	
Urban	Nu	13	17	6	13	8	26	6	6	2	1	2	100 (f=478)	15 (n=82)
	Joi	8	13	14	27	12	14	5	2	1	2	2	100 (f=525)	4 (n=92)
Total no. of Exchange		107	152	104	206	100	196	55	36	18	14	15	1003	

Note: *These categories include the persons mentioned and their relatives. For example, 'brothers' include brothers, their wives, children, etc.

to understand whether there is any variation in this regard among the respondents residing in nuclear and joint households and in the village and the town. Attempt has also been made to see whether any variation exists in this respect between the husband's relatives and the wife's relatives.

The exchange of aid with the husband's kin may be taken as an indicator of the functional solidarity of the members of joint family or among those who are said to be informed by the 'spirit of joint family'. It can be logically assumed that if there is the feeling of unity and solidarity among the members of a joint family, irrespective of their residence in joint or separate (nuclear) households, they will come forward to help one another in times of need. It is excepted, therefore, that the number of cases of exchange of mutual aid among the relatives will vary directly with the intensity of their feeling of solidarity. This study, therefore, proceeds with the supposition that those respondents whose cases evince a larger number of exchanges of aid with the husband's relatives than those with the wife's relatives would have a correspondingly higher degree of solidarity with the joint family, or in other words, a higher degree of 'joint family spirit', since in the northern part of India joint family is a patrilineal, patri-local and patriarchal institution. Concomitantly, the lower the number of such exchanges, the weaker would be the solidarity or jointness between the respondents and their husbands' kin.

What is meant by 'help or assistance' here? Mainly, three kinds of aid have been considered here:

1. Physical help: Manpower is a very important resource. In many cases, it appears to be the most important resource, e.g., where the members of a household are mostly aged and physically infirm or where the number of the members of the household is very small.
2. Financial help or assistance: It is a kind of aid which may be required as well as provided on many different occasions.
3. Mental support or help provided in the form of information, suggestions, etc.: This kind of assistance is given by one relative to another through the provision of psychological or emotional support at the time of any crisis or problem. The former can provide the latter with the needed mental strength through consolation, encouragement or with proper

suggestions and useful information. One may help a relative or his/her son or daughter in getting a placement in life, in getting a choice matrimonial connection with the right kind of information at the right moment. All these forms of aid have been categorised in the study under the rubric of *psychological or information-based help.*

Table 5.1 has been organised to provide information regarding the dimension of the exchange relationship, i.e., whether people exchange aid more with the husband's kin or with the wife's kin. It does not, however, provide information as to which kind of assistance has been exchanged by a respondent with which category of relatives (e.g., parents, brothers, sisters, uncles, cousins, etc.). The detail in this regard will be found in Chapter 8.

Table 5.1 records the cases of major exchange of help on the basis of the answers provided by the respondents. This fact merits special mention because here the veracity of the report made by a respondent has been taken on its face value. Further, it is at the same time true that a respondent might not have reported many other instances of exchange of aid in various day-to-day and minor matters which had actually taken place but did not seem to the respondent to be worth-mentioning. People may consider such instances to be so 'natural' or habitual or routine matters as they do not consider it important to talk about them. For example, the cases of parents' helping their sons and daughters in getting married or finding a decent placement in life, or those of sons' looking after their parents in old age or illness belong to this category. But when a married daughter looks after her parents, or a man takes care of his uncle or aunt, it is readily recognised as provision of help to the 'relatives' and the respondents do not forget to report such cases.

One should, therefore, not infer that only 1,547 (as has been shown in Table 5.1) cases of exchange of help or assistance between or among the respondents and their relatives have taken place. One should rather consider these cases to be indicating a certain kind of trend. From these cases one can form an idea as to the dimension of exchange of help between the respondents and their relatives. One may understand from the table which type of relatives of the respondents rank higher than which others in terms of interchange of goods and services.

A few other points may be mentioned. A quick glance at the table reveals that the cases of exchange of help between parents and married sons and daughters are very few. It does not indicate that the interchange of help between these parties are minimum. The finding may be explained by the fact that owing to the young age of the respondents in the sample, very few of them have married sons and/or daughters.

Finally, 33 respondents (12%) in the sample have told that they have very few cases of such exchange to report since they either do not like such interchange or do not have any relatives with whom such exchanges can be made or they do not have any need whatsoever for such exchange of help. The breakup of these 33 respondents is as follows: 4 in Cat. A; 15 in Cat. B; 8 in Cat. C; and 6 in Cat. D. As no positive response from these 33 respondents has been received, the percentage figures for the table have been computed putting them aside.

Let us enter into the table. First, incidence of exchange is a bit higher in urban than in rural households. This may seem somewhat queer since the rural respondents mostly have a close physical proximity with their husbands' patri-kin. Accordingly, the scope and occasion for interaction with the kin are expected to be larger in the village. On probing, however, the respondents have admitted that sometimes such interchanges are underreported because they do not bother to mention them. This occurs particularly in case of the exchange of physical help and help through furnishing appropriate information. In this regard, only those cases which occur regularly or continuously or involve substantial transactions are only reported. Exchange of financial help is, however, always viewed as important and the respondents do not forget to mention such incidents.

Secondly, the urban joint households rank first in terms of exchange of help among husbands' relatives. These households are mostly of the LJ type. Here, either the respondents' husbands are the 'only son' of their parents, or their brothers live outside (for spatial as well as social mobility is higher in towns). Hence, in times of needs and exigencies, these households depend on relatives. In the village, on the other hand, joint households, mostly CJ and LCJ type, are mostly self-sufficient in manpower and money. Here interactions are mostly limited to husbands' first and second degree kin (husbands' parents and brothers) who live with the respondents (and their husbands) in the same (joint) household, and generally do not involve third and fourth degree kin (husband's uncles, aunts and cousins). Hence, whatever help is interchanged it is done within the household. One fact is common among the joint households in villages and towns—they interact mostly with the husbands' relatives than with the wives' relatives.

Thirdly, though the difference in the behaviour of joint households in villages and towns is markedly visible, this is not so striking in case of behaviour of the nuclear households.

Lastly, it is clearly discernible from the table that in both villages and towns the frequency of interchange of help or aid with the wife's kin is high in the nuclear households. That is, while in case of joint households interchange of help or aid takes place between the husband or his household and the husband's kin, in case of nuclear households a substantial number of such exchanges takes place between the household and the householder's wife's kin. This trend is more prominent in villages than in towns. This finding confirms the supposition that in nuclear households the wife exercises more authority or effectively shares power with her husband, and accordingly, gets more opportunity to interact with her own relatives, i.e., relatives of her natal family. In fact, the financial transactions in rural nuclear households occur mostly with wives' relatives. Nuclearity and enhancement of the wife's status thus go hand in hand.

Table 5.2 shows the pattern and dimension of the exchange of gifts between the respondents and their relatives. Here, we are concerned with the exchange of gifts on occasions like the *Durgapuja* festival, *Bhatridwitiya* (a Bengali ritual celebrated by sisters for wishing their brothers, long life and happiness), *Jamaisasthi* (another Bengali ritual celebrated by mothers-in-law for wishing the long life and happiness of their sons-in-law, which ultimately benefits their daughters), birth anniversary, marriage anniversary, and so on. By 'exchange of gifts' only those occasions have been referred to here where there is no social or ritual

Table 5.2

Exchange of Gifts among Relatives, by Residence and Household Structure (in percentage)

Residence	*Type of Household*	*Only Hus.'s Relatives and/or grand-children*	*All/most Relatives of hus.+some/few Relatives of Wife*	*All/most Relatives of the Couple*	*Some/few Relatives of the Couple*	*All/most Relatives of Wife+some/few Relatives of Hus.*	*Only Wife's Relatives*	*Rare/no Exchange*	*Total*
Rural	Nu	-	4	10	10	28	20	28	100 (n=50)
	Joi	22	6	20	14	16	10	12	100 (n=50)
Total		11	5	15	12	22	15	20	100
Urban	Nu	4	11	61	4	14	2	4	100 (n=82)
	Joi	9	14	62	5	7	1	2	100 (n=92)
Total		11	22	107	8	18	3	5	174
		(6.3%)	(12.6%)	(61.5%)	(4.6%)	(10.4%)	(1.7%)	(2.9%)	(100)

compulsion and obligation, and it depends totally on the sweet will of the giver and the cordial relation between the parties concerned whether or not to offer any gifts. Thus, the exchanges of presentations on occasions like marriage ceremony, *annaprasana* (the ritual performed to celebrate the first feed of rice to a child), *upanayana* (the ritual of donning the sacred thread among the twice-born, particularly among the Brahmins), *shraddha* (the ritual of offering of rice balls to the soul of the deceased and the manes)—occasions where there is a certain kind of social compulsion to offer costly presentations—have been excluded. For, these transactions depend not so much on one's willingness to offer, spontaneity or feelings, economic status (sometimes one may have to borrow money to meet such obligations), and cordiality or mutual relation between the parties concerned.

For measuring the joint family solidarity exchange of gifts among the relatives has been taken as an indicator. It has been assumed that such exchanges are directly related to the warmth of relationship, and closer the relationship the more frequent would be such cases of exchange. If it is found that cases of such exchange are more common with the husband's patri-kin than those with the wife's, it may be inferred that solidarity with the husband's kin is higher than that with the wife's. One should not overlook the economic factor here because financial capacity to exchange such gifts is a major consideration, and it may work as a serious constraint limiting such exchanges even when the parties are willing to offer. However, if it is found that a respondent having a certain economic standing exchanges gifts more often with her own relatives (parents, brothers, sisters or their kids) than she does with her husband's relatives, it can be assumed that she is more tied with the relatives of her natal family than with those of her husband's. Her feeling of solidarity with her husband's joint family is considered weaker than another respondent who belongs to the same economic category and yet does not discriminate in offering gifts to her own relatives and to those of her husband's.

One finds in Table 5.2 that the practice of exchanging gifts among relatives is more common among the urbanites than among the ruralites. Poverty of the villagers is mainly responsible for this.

Further, while the difference between the urban respondents living in nuclear and joint households is not very striking in the realm of exchanging gifts with husbands' relatives and wives' relatives, the case is not the same with the rural respondents. In general, the urban respondents prefer not to discriminate between these two categories of relatives in this regard, and the fact of living in nuclear or joint households does not significantly influence this behaviour.

In villages, in contrast, the general trend is that a substantial section of the nuclear households generally interchanges gifts with wives' relatives. Joint households, however, generally emphasise exchanges more with husbands' relatives or equally with relatives of both the spouses.

The economic status of the village nuclear households in the sample is poor indeed. On probing it has been observed that instead of offering gifts, they mainly receive gifts and they are almost unable to reciprocate the same. And, they mainly receive gifts from the end of the wives' relatives (wives' parents, brothers, sisters) who want to help their poor daughter/sister and do not expect any return of gifts. These relatives send dress and clothings on various occasions like *puja*, birthday, etc. But if husbands' relatives send any gifts, they expect gifts in return and would criticise the householder(s) and his/their wife (wives) if the latter fail to reciprocate. Hence, it is observed that people whose economic condition is poor and precarious, interact with and depend on relatives on the wife's side more in comparison with husbands' relatives. Accordingly, the joint family ties become weaker among this segment of the village society.

Table 5.3 depicts whether the relatives of the respondents and their husbands come to stay with them and treat the latter's residence as a temporary resort or consider it a second home where they can live, if necessary, for some length of time. It is particularly important for those relatives who live at a distance or in interior villages from where they cannot contact specialist doctors for treatment in critical illness and have to come up to the town/city, or have to send their children to modern institutes of education and so on. Sometimes persons may have to come to any stay in the house of a relative for making negotiations for their son's/

Table 5.3

Whether Respondents' Relatives Come to Stay with Respondents, by Residence, Household Structure and Type of Kin

Residence	*Type of Household*	*Husband's Side*					*Wife's Side*				*Married*		*Total*
		Par.	*Bro.**	*Sis.**	*F.'s sibs**	*M's sibs*	*Par.**	*Bro.**	*Sis.**	*Par.'s sibs**	*Son**	*Dau.**	
Rural	Nu	6	2	7	-	-	1	2	2	1	-	-	21
	Joi	-	2	21	4	2	-	-	1	-	-	5	35
Total		6	4	28	4	2	1	2	3	1	-	5	56
Urban	Nu	12	21	5	7	3	9	7	10	4	2	2	82
	Joi	1	10	30	27	31	4	2	8	1	1	1	116
Total		13	31	35	34	34	13	9	18	5	3	3	198

Note: * These categories include the persons mentioned and their relatives. For example, `brothers' include brothers, their wives, children, etc.

daughter's marriage, or for appearing at the interview of a job, or for holding discussions with business partners. On such and many other similar occasions, people would, generally, feel comfortable and secure to stay in the residence of a relative. It has been inquired whether the residence of the respondents is considered by their relatives to be places where they do not hesitate to stay on such and similar occasions.

The above information has been included here as an indicator of the functional solidarity of the joint family under the supposition that stronger the solidarity, the greater would be the frequency of visits to the household by the relatives from the husband's end. On the contrary, low frequency of such visits to the household by the relatives or shortness of the duration of their stay there would indicate a corresponding weakness of joint family or kinship ties of the relatives with the householder(s). Also, the higher frequency of visits of the wife's relatives will indicate the weaker feeling of solidarity with the husband's joint family. For, it is to be noted that in the patriarchal, patri-local joint family the husband's parents, siblings and their relations should consider the respondent's husband's home as a place where they have a right to stay, whereas the wife's relatives should be considered as *kutumba* who will be treated as honoured guests to the householder (the respondent's husband). Their stay would be short and would be, generally, ceremonial in nature. The wife's parents and relatives should not count upon the help of their son-in-law. Any parent who comes to stay with or depend on his/her son-in-law on a permanent or regular basis becomes a subject of gossip.

The construction of Table 5.3 needs some explanation. Here, the goal is to show in how many cases the relatives of the sample (N) taken as a whole has viewed their residence as a temporary shelter, and not to count how many of such cases have occurred for each individual respondent. That is the reason why the total number of visits surpasses the number of sample in Cat. A, where the number of visits has been found to be 116 though the number of respondents is 92.

An analysis of the data presented in the table shows that, first, the relatives of the urban respondents come to stay with them more often in comparison with the relatives of the rural respondents. The reason is clear. Geographical dispersion of the husband's patri-kin being minimal in the village, they generally do not feel the need to stay in the respondent's house. The urban respondents on the contrary, have many relatives who live in villages or other towns or even outside the state, and therefore, have the need for the respondents' home as their temporary resort whenever they have any business in Kolkata.

On the whole, so far as this indicator conveys, the finding is not at all encouraging. Respondents' relatives, in general, do not seem comfortable to stay in the former's residence for some length of time. Even for the urban sample, we find that only 198 such cases of relatives' staying with them have been reported by 174 respondents.

Further, in both villages and towns, the common trend noticed is that compared to the nuclear households, the rate of relatives' staying is higher in the joint households. It can be drawn, then, that with the replacement of the joint households by the nuclear ones, the concept of the 'home' where relatives could freely come and stay would also be on the wane.

Another common trend noted is that generally relatives from the husband's end come to stay more often than those from the wife's end. In both villages and towns, the relatives from the wife's natal family do not feel comfortable to stay with their daughter/ sister when she lives with her husband's stem family. As she separates from this stem family, the rate of her relatives' staying also increases. The trend is more visible in the urban sample than in the rural sample.

On further analysis of the table it can be seen that of all the types of relatives, husbands' sisters constitute the single largest category of 'visitors'. The trend is more noteworthy in villages than in towns and in joint households than in nuclear ones. This suggests that sisters do not feel at ease to stay in their brother's house in the absence of their parents.

In the joint households, husbands' parents, if they are alive, are regarded as permanent or regular members of the household, and hence their staying is not separately reported. This is otherwise for the nuclear households where these persons are viewed as temporary members of the household and hence their staying with the respondents has been separately mentioned.

A notable feature for the urban joint households is the relative frequency of visits by the respondents' mothers-in-law's natal family and their staying with the family of the respondents' households. In fact, these relatives constitute the single largest category of visitors (27%). It indicates the high leverage of the mother-in-law in such households. Relatives of the father-in-law also come and stay but their number is comparatively low (23%). This trend is not visible in the village joint households. So, it can be drawn that the wife (when her husband is the head of the household) enjoys a real power in the urban households compared to their rural counterparts.

Table 5.4 depicts whether the patri-kin of the respondents' husbands regularly/occasionally get together on the occasion of the performance of some particular rites and rituals or social ceremony or festival. It does not include, however, any information regarding participation of relatives in ceremonies or institutions like marriage or *shraddha* since the presence of relatives in these ceremonies is relatively obligatory, and these do not occur regularly.

The information has been collected on the supposition that higher the degree of solidarity among the members of the joint family, more frequent and regular would be the occurrence of such gatherings. Under the pressure of various factors like social and spatial mobility, lack of space in the ancestral home and such other factors, members of the joint family may at present be forced to live apart. But if the ties among the members of the joint family are, indeed, intimate and durable, they would utilise any opportunity of assembling in a common place at a regular interval to rejoice over or celebrate some common ceremony or festival and, thus, to renew and revitalise their mutual ties. Their participation in such gatherings would indicate their willingness to get together, to meet each other, to exchange and share each other's experiences, views and problems. Any relation, however close it might be, is bound to weaken and become redundant in the long run, if the parties do not regularly meet each other. Remaining out of sight means slipping out of mind. On the other

Table 5.4

Responses to the Question: "Whether there is any custom in your husband's family of origin that all/most of the agnatic kin should assemble at one place on some occasion.", by Residence and Household Structure (in percentage)

Residence	Type of Household	No such Gathering is Held	Occasion of such Gatherings				At Present no such Gathering Occurs	Total
			Performance of Rites & Rituals	Any Social Occasion	No Fixed Occasion	Kin Reside Nearby & Always Meet		
Rural	Nu	80	20	-	-	-	-	100(n=50)
	Joi	88	12	-	-	-	-	100 (n=50)
Total		84	16	-	-	-	-	100
Urban	Nu	63	15	6	5	2	9	100 (n=82)
	Joi	63	22	9	4	-	2	100(n=92)
Total		110	32	13	8	2	9	174
		(63%)	(18%)	(8%)	(5%)	(1%)	(5%)	(100)

hand, frequent visits and gatherings reinforce the mutual bonds. Another important function of these gatherings is to make the younger generations aware and familiar with each other. In such gatherings they will come to know of their cousins, uncles and aunts, whom they otherwise seldom meet and become conscious of their family heritage. This is particularly important when the younger generations are more interested in passing time in the company of their friends rather than their relatives. The above purpose may, of course, be realised through mutual visits by the members of the joint family to each other's house, e.g., when a brother goes to another brother's place. But in this way only two parties become involved. The purpose served by such visits is qualitatively different from the occasions like 'family get together' referred to above where a big gathering is held including the third and fourth generation members, and the whole family, not a fraction of it, is brought to one place and participates in a common function.

Let us see how our respondents have reacted to this query. It appears from Table 5.4 that the frequency of such gatherings is not at all encouraging. However, the frequency is higher in the town than in the village. In most of the village households (84%) no such gathering takes place. The corresponding figure for the urban households is 63 per cent. One major reason behind this difference may be that most of the village households live in close proximity with the patri-kin and they can meet and talk to each other almost everyday at any time if they like, and do not, therefore, have to wait for any special occasion. It is not so for their urban counterparts whose kin are scattered in many places. Moreover, compared to an urban family, a rural family is generally bigger and comprises more members. Therefore, such social occasions as marriage, *annaprasana, shraddha,* etc., where relatives are obliged to participate, occur more frequently, almost regularly, in the village families. This is also one reason why villagers are not required to 'create' occasions like birthday, marriage anniversary and the like for family get-togethers. Sheer demographic factors thus make family gatherings regular and/or frequent for the villagers. Their economic condition is also another bar.

The situation of the urbanites is different. The formal, institutionalised occasions for family gatherings are relatively few here because of the smaller size of the family. Also, as the relatives are scattered, they often feel the need for renewing their ties, which strengthens their sense of security.

It has been observed in course of the fieldwork that the elderly people evince greater eagerness to participate in such gatherings than the younger generations. The latter take more interest in and feel more comfortable with the company of their friends and peers. Frustrations of a sort have been noticed among 5 per cent urban respondents who have fondly recalled the days gone by, when such gatherings were regularly held. Those were the golden days and the modern times are, they lament, marked by lack of warmth of relationships among the kin. In this respect there is no significant difference between the feelings of the residents of the nuclear and joint households.

One may inquire as to whether the joint family functions as a solid political unit influencing effectively the formation of political opinion of its members as well as the manner in which they cast their votes. It may be assumed that the more its members consult each other in the matter of casting their votes, the more the family displays its solidarity and its character as a solid political unit. On the other hand, the more the members independently cast their votes, or the couples cast their votes independently, or the more the couple is influenced by the wife's relatives in this matter, the weaker will be the control of the joint family over the household units comprising it.

Our observations in this regard have been presented in Table 5.5. The first thing to be noted in the table is that the difference in this matter between the nuclear and joint households in both villages and towns is quite prominent. Also, the behaviour of urban respondents differs from that of their rural counterparts to some extent.

The behaviour of the urban joint households in this regard matches more or less with the commonsense expectations that the formation of the political opinion of the members of the joint

Table 5.5

Influence of Kin in the Formation of Political Opinion, by Residence and Household Structure (in percentage)

Residence	*Type of Household*	*Pattern of Exercising Voting Right by Respondents*								*Total*
		Couple + all members of both families	*Couple + H.'s family of origin*	*Couple + offspring*	*Only couple*	*Couple + W.'s family of origin*	*Wife + her kin*	*Independent & individual choice*	*Others*	
Rural	Nu	26	20	-	16	12	12	14	-	100 (n=50)
	Joi	14	12	4	20	-	8	42	-	100 (n=50)
Total		20	16	2	18	6	10	28	-	100
Urban	Nu	17	11	6	18	17	12	16	3	100 (n=82)
	Joi	44	5	7	15	2	9	14	4	100(n =92)
Total		54 (31%)	14 (8%)	11 (6%)	29 (17%)	16 (9%)	18 (10%)	26 (15%)	6 (4%)	174 (100)

Note: *Others* include those who do not exercise their voting right/do not know what their kin do/decline to answer the question.
Couple + all members of both families includes those cases where the political choice of the couple, of all or most members of the families of origin of both the spouses and their offspring (if any) is identical.

households will be influenced by the others in the household. While casting their vote, members will take account of other members' choice, rather than act independently. Like many other matters, in this respect also they would take the decision through a process of mutual discussions and understanding.

On the other hand, it may be assumed that living in separate households will generate a sense of independence in the minds of the members of these households. While exercising the voting right, wives in the nuclear households, therefore, will feel free from the control of their husbands' kin and will cast vote independently or in consultation with their respective husbands or grown-up children, or their relatives of their natal families .

Observations in this inquiry partially supports this assumption. The influence of husbands' relatives is quite weak in case of the urban nuclear households where the respondents prefer to behave independently or act in consultation with the relatives on the side cf their natal family. The behaviour of the respondents from the rural nuclear households, however, is not in tune with the above supposition. Rather than acting independently, they prefer to act in consultation with the relatives, and the influence of husbands' relatives and that of their (e.g., wives') own relatives is more or less equal in this regard. Thus, a difference is noted in the behaviour of the respondents in urban and rural nuclear households.

It seems, therefore, that living in separate dwelling units does not necessarily make women independent in the exercise of their political rights.

The behaviour of women in this sphere in rural joint households seems queer and deserves special mention. Contrary to popular conceptions, a sizeable section (42%) of these women have reported that they cast their vote out of their individual and independent choice, and are not influenced even by their husbands or their own relatives. It seems that these women are sufficiently alert and mature in exercising their political right. This observation refutes the popular notion that rural women, having little education and exposure to the external world, are mostly politically inert and inept, and therefore, incapable of properly exercising their voting right. However, the fact that a sizeable section of women cast their votes independently has been noted in respect of women living in joint households only, and this is more or less absent in case of the women belonging to nuclear households. One can then legitimately seek an explanation of this rather unexpected phenomenon.

On probing, respondents in this category (i.e., rural joint households) have reported that today's women are politically conscious and while exercising their voting right they depend on their own experiences, analyses and perceptions. They are, of course, chiefly concerned with the activities of the panchayat. They assess different political parties and candidates fielded or supported by them on the basis of the treatment they receive from them through or in connection with this institution.

The above observation is applicable to rural women in general. One may then ask: why does the behaviour of wives in nuclear households not confirm it? For this, one should look into the environment of the nuclear and joint households. Compared to the former, the latter generally have a larger number of members. So, here, the couple gets little privacy or leisure to chat or converse between themselves. Moreover, larger number of members in the household incurs larger number of problems for the members who come to interact with one another in a larger number of spheres. After the whole day's work when the husband and the wife meet each other, they have many things to discuss relating to household matters and, therefore, find little time to discuss such distant matters as political issues or elections—distant from the manifold problems of the day-to-day family life. Husbands also have little motivation and patience to persuade their wives to any particular political ideology or stand of any particular political party. Thus, wives act according to their own experiences and perceptions. Moreover, in joint households, generally the menfolk meet the political workers who come to campaign from door to door. And, it is the men of a household who discuss these matters mainly among themselves. Women are only passive listeners and they rarely join these discussions, which facts lead them to form their opinion by themselves.

One may turn to a more internal and more important aspect of life in the family. It relates to the fact of marriage. Marriage is one of the 16 classical *sanskaras* (stages) in the life of the Hindus and is by far the most important in its economic and social implications. Economically, a wedding ceremony involves for most people the occasion for the largest single expenditure in their lives. Socially, it inaugurates a new series of relations, and it also reflects and reinforces the existing ties through the interaction with the guests who come to attend the ceremony. Ritually, it is a desideratum for a son who will propitiate agnatic ascendants and thereby prevent their being denied the world beyond, as well as making major changes in the ritual status of the partners.

The occasion of wedding provides a series of gatherings, discussions, consultations, visits and correspondence among the relatives, which ultimately culminate into a complex of rites and feasts, lasting for a week or more. Hence, the occurrence of a marriage offers a chance of reinforcing and revitalising the ties among the relatives. It also dramatically reveals the kind and levels of interactions among the different types of kin. Family sociologists, therefore, put emphasis on the study of marriage ceremony in the analysis of joint family solidarity.

Table 5.6 has been constructed to display the extent of participation of different types of kin in solemnising a marriage ceremony in the respondents' family. Here the goal is to show: (1) the extent of authority exercised by the elderly people in materialising this event; (2) forms and levels of participation of kin in the event; and (3) a comparative picture of the roles played by agnatic kin, and non-kin, e.g., friends and neighbours, in the event.

On the basis of the above criteria data have been arranged under seven categories. In the first category those respondents have been placed who report adherence to the traditional norm. Here, the decision-making lies with the eldest male of the undivided joint family, even though he lives in a separate dwelling unit. All the relatives placed in this category think it their duty to participate. They regularly maintain contact over the progress of the ceremony. They are not formally invited; in fact, they do not wait for the formal invitation to join the event. Rather they think that it is a matter of prestige of their entire family to ensure smooth performance of the ceremony. Here their participation starts from

Table 5.6

Level and Kind of Kin's Participation in Solemnising Marriage Ceremonies of the Members of the Family, by Residence and Household Structure (in percentage)

Residence	*Type of Household*	*Cat.1*	*Cat.2*	*Cat.3*	*Cat.4*	*Cat.5*	*Cat.6*	*Cat.7*	*Cat.8*	*Total*
Rural	Nu	6	14	16	18	10	20	16	-	100(n=50)
	Joi	-	24	20	6	4	36	10	-	100(n=50)
Total		3	19	18	12	7	28	13	-	100(n=100)
Urban	Nu	4	14	24	14	12	24	7	1	100(n=82)
	Joi	25	13	17	12	13	19	-	1	100(n=92)
Total		26	23	36	22	22	37	6	2	100(n=174)
		(15%)	(13%)	(21%)	(13%)	(13%)	(21%)	(3%)	(1%)	(100)

Note: Cat. 1 = full-fledged participation of all relatives; authority lies with the head of the undivided family; Cat. 2 = full-fledged participation of all relatives; parents' decision is final; others are consulted at every stage; Cat. 3 = relatives are only informed; they participate and do the assigned job; responsibility lies with the members of the household; Cat. 4= son's/daughter's decision is final; relatives are informed and they participate if required; Cat. 5 = responsibility lies with the members of the household; help comes from affinal kin only; agnatic kin are only guests and their participation is minimum; Cat. 6 = responsibility lies with the members of the household; relatives' help is not available; they either do not participate or come only as guests; Cat. 7 = relatives are not often informed; or, no ceremony is held; bride/groom decides everything; Cat. 8 = respondents are unable to answer.

the very beginning of marriage negotiations and continues even weeks after the ceremony.

The second category comprises those cases who report the above kind of full-fledged participation by the relatives, but here decision-making lies with the parents of the brides/grooms. Relatives are informed and consulted at every point, and their advice, suggestions are honoured. Relatives also whole-heartedly participate in the event.

The third category consists of those respondents who report that in their families relatives are informed whenever any marriage ceremony is held. Particular relatives are assigned specific tasks like inviting the relatives, shopping, contacting the decorators, caterers, entertaining the guests on the ceremony-day, supervising of cooking, serving of food in the marriage feast, and many other jobs necessary for the smooth performance of the ritual and the ceremony. However, the decisions regarding the division of labour and the responsibility for successful completion of the ceremony lie with the parents of the bride/groom.

The fourth category contains those who report that generally the son or the daughter of their families selects his/her marriage partner. Relatives are then informed. They come mostly on the day of the ceremony and help the parents of the son/daughter to complete the ceremony smoothly. Though it is a love or romantic marriage, the event ultimately gets the form of a social marriage or a social gathering of the relatives indicating their approval and acceptance of the decision of the bride and the groom.

The fifth category is comprised of those who report that in their family the role and participation of husbands' fathers' relatives is minimum. They mainly depend on the affinal kin—mother-in-law's relatives, husband's sister and her husband, the relatives of their end (wives' parents, brothers and sisters), and their married daughter and son-in-law, if any. Other kinds of relatives come only as guests on the day of the ceremony. Here the responsibility lies with the members of the household in holding the ceremony.

The sixth category comprises those respondents who report that all the responsibility of arranging the ceremony lies with themselves—the respondent, her husband and their sons and daughters. Whatever help they require, they prefer to depend on friends and neighbours rather than relatives. Relatives, however, come and attend the ceremony as guests. These respondents either do not have any relative from whom help can be expected, or they do not have cordial relation with the relatives, or they have sufficient manpower of their own and do not require any help from relatives.

Category seven includes those cases who report that there is no custom of informing all the relatives during the marriage in the family. A few of them with whom intimate relation is maintained may be informed sometimes. Or, sometimes no marriage ceremony is held at all; sons or daughters marry by registration, celebrate the institution with their friends in hotels or restaurants, and no social ceremony with relatives is held.

It appears from Table 5.6 that the conformity to the traditional norm where authority lies with the elderly members of the undivided joint family and full-fledged participation obtains (Cat. 1 and 2) is highest among the urban joint households and lowest among the urban nuclear households. Rural joint households come next to the urban joint ones. Though small in number, cases of instances of conformity to the traditional norm are not totally absent in nuclear households also. It can be drawn, then, that in spite of the nuclear pattern of dwelling, adherence to the traditional norm of joint family behaviour exists among one-fourth of cases in the sample.

At the same time, it is to be pointed out, almost an equal number of households do not depend on relatives for solemnising the wedding. Either they manage by themselves or they invite help from non-kin (Cat. 6). Relatives in such cases attend the ceremony simply as guests. They do not share any responsibility for the ceremony. Marriage in such cases is not treated as a concern of the joint family. In fact, the concept of joint family is lacking here. This trend is discerned in both rural and urban types of households, though, interestingly, villages present more such cases than towns. Incidence of 'love marriage' where the son or the daughter settles everything (Cat. 7) is more common in rural and in nuclear households. Poverty may be the reason for such behaviour which prevents people from holding a grand feast or prolonging the ceremony.

Dependence on the affinal kin to the neglect of the agnatic kin (Cat. 5) is more discernible in urban areas and in nuclear households. This trend has also been noted in the urban joint households where generally it is the relatives of the mother-in-law who play the pivotal role; and, in a few rural joint households which show this tendency, the help of the sons-in-law of the household is taken for this purpose. Obviously, this trend somewhat undermines the traditional joint family spirit and norm in which the patri-kin are required to be most closely involved in the wedding since marriage is always a matter of family tradition. Apart from its economic and social implications, the phenomenon has great ritual implications as well. A bride is always an addition to the patri-kin who must accept her in their lineage through the marriage ritual (the institution of *bou-bhat* where the patri-kin receive for the first time boiled rice served by the newly wed bride). In fact, the wedding ceremony, along with the *shraddha* ceremony, is a most important event in the life cycle of a family which reinforces the joint family authority structure and thus revitalises the joint family solidarity. Thus, lack of active participation of the patri-kin or dependence on the affinal kin or non-kin in the marriage ceremony may be viewed as weakening of the functional solidarity of the traditional joint family. Instances of deviations from this norm have been found to be more common in the present sample than cases of conformity towards it.

An important indicator for measuring the joint family solidarity may be found in the fact as to whom the incumbents generally approach for help whenever any such exigency calling for others' help or assistance arises. Obviously, people will solicit aid from those persons with whom they have intimacy and cordial relation. Hence, an inquiry into the nature or status of individuals or families whose help or assistance is sought by the respondents in times of difficulties is regarded as pertinent for the present purpose. It has been assumed that people will approach their relatives when they receive a sympathetic understanding of their problems from them and, on the other hand, dependence on friends and neighbours or colleagues indicates absence of such reliable relatives.

Table 5.7

When Required, to Whom Respondents Approach for Help, and Do They Justify Their Behaviour?, by Residence and Household Structure (in percentage)

Residence	*Type of Household*	*Cat.1*	*Cat.2*	*Cat.3*	*Cat.4*	Cat.5	*Cat.6*	*Cat.7*	*Total*
Rural	Nu	46	30	10	10	2	2	-	100(n=50)
	Joi	78	4	4	8	2	-	4	100(n=50)
Total		62	17	7	9	2	1	2	100(n=100)
Urban	Nu	61	13	17	9	-	-	-	100(n=82)
	Joi	76	8	10	4	1	-	1	100(n=92)
Total		120	18	23	11	1	-	1	174
		(69%)	(10%)	(13%)	(6%)	(1%)		(1%)	100

Note: Cat. 1= approach relatives and think this is right; Cat. 2=approach relatives but think one should take care of oneself; Cat.3= approach non-kin and think this is right; Cat. 4=approach non-kin but think one should take care of oneself; Cat. 5= approach relative but think it is better to seek aid from non-kin; Cat. 6= approach non-kin but think that it is better to seek aid from kin; Cat. 7= should approach none; one should take care of oneself.

Observations on the above query have been presented in Table 5.7. It appears that still most people approach their relatives when they require any help or assistance, and also expect and urge that relatives should be the major source of aid. It also appears that the extent of dependence on relatives is more or less equal in both villages and towns. However, while urbanites see no wrong in such dependence, to many ruralites "self help should be the best help". They depend on relatives as they have no better alternatives, but they think that it would have been better if they were not to accept help from anybody—relatives, neighbours or friends (one should take care of oneself). This study, however, does not evince that relations with relatives are more cordial in towns than those in villages, since dependence on non-relatives, friends, etc., is almost equal at both the places. Sometimes villagers are not willing to disturb their relatives because of the latter's incapability and helplessness. Most of them are so much preoccupied with making their both ends meet that helping others is an unwanted botheration or unpleasant or difficult obligation to them. It does not mean that they are less hospitable or sympathetic to each other.

One should note that the respondents who legitimise their dependence on relatives are found in a larger number in urban nuclear households than in village nuclear households. The behaviour and attitude of the respondents from joint households in villages and towns is more or less similar.

Table 5.8 depicts respondents' opinion regarding extension of help or assistance—physical, financial, emotional or intellectual—towards their relatives. Though it is related to a query about the respondents, opinion and not behaviour, it may reasonably be assumed that attitude and opinion are indicators of behaviour. Therefore, respondents' views about providing help to relatives at least suggest their actual behaviour in this regard.

In all, 40 per cent of the respondents have opined that to help relatives is a duty to be performed by all, and no difference in this regard has been found between the rural and urban respondents. Not a single respondent has said that one should not help one's relatives lest this action indulges in the latter idleness, inertia or inaction.

Table 5.8

Respondents' Opinion about Helping Relatives, by Residence and Household Structure (in percentage)

Residence	*Type of Household*	*Opinion towards Helping or Looking after Relatives*						*Total*
		Cat.1	*Cat.2*	*Cat.3*	*Cat.4*	*Cat.5*	*Cat.6*	
Rural	Nu	28	-	12	30	8	22	100(n=50)
	Joi	52	-	4	14	26	4	100(n=50)
Total		40	-	8	22	17	13	100(n=100)
Urban	Nu	37	11	12	2	36	2	100(n=82)
	Joi	42	11	16	8	22	1	100(n=92)
Total		69	19	25	9	49	3	174
		(40%)	(11%)	(14%)	(5%)	(28%)	(2%)	(100)

Note: Cat. 1= helping relatives is our duty for this is our noble tradition; Cat. 2= helping relatives is not our duty, but it is good to do so for it enhances one's prestige and honour; Cat. 3= it is good to help relatives for it ensures reciprocal behaviour from the recipients in similar situations; Cat.4= there is a social compulsion to help relatives; otherwise one has to face criticisms and gossips; Cat.5= helping all relatives is not desirable; before helping relatives one must assess whether the need is genuine; Cat. 6= people today are so much preoccupied or engrossed with the problem of meeting their own needs that they cannot even think of helping others.

The congruence between the urban and rural respondents, however, ends here. While 22 per cent of the village respondents help relatives because of the fear of social criticism, 25 per cent of their urban counterparts do the same because they think that this action would enhance their prestige or would ensure reciprocal behaviour from the recipients when they themselves are in need. A total of 17 per cent of the rural respondents think that before helping anybody, one must assess whether the need is genuine, and the corresponding figure for the urban respondents is 28 per cent. Only 13 per cent of the rural and 2 per cent of the urban respondents have confided that they themselves are so much preoccupied or engrossed with the problem of meeting their own needs that they cannot even think of helping others. Those who have expressed such opinion are really poor.

As most of the rural nuclear households in the sample live at barely the subsistence level, the percentage of persons who regard that helping others is a 'duty' is the lowest (28%) in this group. The highest percentage (52%) of the rural joint households, however, nurture this idea. In town also, the positive attitude towards helping others is higher in persons living in joint than in nuclear households. This seems natural since an essential condition for the survival of the joint households is the mutual understanding, tolerance, dutifulness, sacrifice and sympathy. Accordingly, people living in joint households are generally more helping in their attitude and believe in reciprocity or mutual give-and-take.

Table 5.9 narrates respondents' mental image about the desired form of the household to which they wish they should belong. Respondents were asked whether they could remember any of their relatives who had not stayed with them but whose stay was desirable. An attempt was made to inquire whether the respondents, particularly those who live in nuclear households, were willing to take responsibility of any of their relatives who did not live with them, or alternatively, they thought that the present form of their household was satisfactory. We did not deliberately specify the circle of 'relatives' to be included here just to test the respondents' perception of the ideal or right form of the household regarding which relatives they thought should be included in their

Table 5.9

Responses to the Question: "Do you have any relative who, you think, should stay with you, but he/she does not live with you?, By Residence and Household Structure (in percentage)

Residence	*Type of Household*	*No such living relative exists*	*Mother-in-law*	*Parents-in-law*	*Hus.'s any near kin**	*Married son/ daughter-in-law*	*Hus.'s parents & bro.*	*Hus.'s married bro.*	*Wife's parents*	O.K.**	*Total*
Rural	Nu	40	28	4	-	-	-	-	-	28	100(n=50)
	Joi	-	-	-	-	2	-	-	-	98	100(n=50)
Total		20	14	2	-	1	-	-	-	63	100
Urban	Nu	4	13	7	4	4	4	4	2	57	99#(n=82)
	Joi	-	-	-	9	-	6	-	1	84	100(n=92)
Total		3	11	6	11	3	9	3	3	124	173
		(2%)	(6%)	(3%)	(6%)	(2%)	(5%)	(2%)	(2%)	(71%)	

Note: * such type of kin as the respondent's husband's uncle, aunt, sister, brother's wife, grandmother, and the like.
** opines that the present system is satisfactory.
# 1 respondent from the urban nuclear households has expressed her desire to jointly live with her married daughter.

households. Nowadays, under the pressure of various unavoidable circumstances, people may be compelled to live separately from their kin. However, this is to be seen whether this separation is forced or imposed or unwanted, or, desired by the parties concerned. In the former case, it can be expected, the person should interpret this absence as a vacuum or loss of the relatives from the household. In other words, we have attempted to see whether the respondents living in nuclear households, desire to live, if it were possible, in joint or supplemented nuclear households (for the addition of any relative will alter the structure of their nuclear household), and the respondents living in joint households desire to include any other non-living relatives and thus expand the present structure of their households. For measuring functional solidarity of the joint family the above information is regarded as a relevant indicator.

Respondents have been categorised into three sections. The first section comprises those respondents who have no living relative, according to their own perception, to be included in their household. The second section contains those respondents who have mentioned any of their relatives who should join them. The third section is composed of those respondents who have stated that the present arrangement is satisfactory, and those relatives from whom they are separated should not joint them.

The first feature of Table 5.9 which merits our attention is that there are striking differences between the four categories of households in this sphere.

Almost all the respondents (98%) in the village joint households are in favour of maintaining the status quo. By 'relative' they have meant their husband's living parents who are already with them. Though a similar tendency has been noted among their urban counterparts as well, these persons have interpreted the term 'relative' a bit broadly and have included such kin as husbands' married brothers who live separately, husbands' unmarried/widower/widow uncle, aunt, grandmother, sister, sister-in-law who live alone and the respondents (or their husbands) are there to look after them. Thus, 16 per cent of these respondents are in favour of extending the structure of their household. It also shows that more urban than rural people think of extending resort to kin. This practice has been noted in joint households only.

The picture is quite different for the respondents in nuclear households. Though by 'relatives' rural respondents have meant their living parents-in-law whom they are ready to include in their household, the urban respondents, however, (like urban joint) have referred to various types of kin under the rubric of 'relative' with whom they should live together. A notable feature is that a few urban respondents (3%) have expressed their desire to stay with their married daughter or their own parents.

Another important point of difference between urban and rural nuclear households is that 40 per cent of the respondents in the latter group have said that they have no possibility of extending the existing structure of their households since their parents-in-law are dead and another 28 per cent have said that though their father-in-law and/or mother-in-law are alive, their presence as members of the household is unsolicited. The corresponding figure for the urban people are 4 per cent and 57 per cent respectively. These observations indicate that the number of respondents who do not like to include their parents-in-law in their households is much higher in urban nuclear than in rural nuclear households. It means that the desire to live separately from the husband's near patri-kin is much stronger in urban than in rural women. This is also a pointer to the gravity of the problem of old age, particularly in the coming days. However, some (8%) of these urban respondents have expressed their desire to include such members as husband's married brother also. This feature is totally absent in rural nuclear households.

A further feature noted here is that of all the categories of relatives, it is the mother-in-law who is desired, if at all, by the respondents in their nuclear households. The trend is more prominent in the village than in the town. It means that next to one's husband and children, the kind of relative with whom women choose to live together is their husband's mother. From a deeper analysis of data, however, it appears that respondents' own interest or convenience rather than dutifulness to their mother-in-law lies behind this desire. Mother-in-law means a helping hand, and then the respondent can get relative relief from the household chores, or need not worry for her husband and children when she becomes ill or goes to her parental home for some days. Of the 28 per cent respondents in the village who have reported that they like to stay with their mother-in-law, 14 per cent have fathers-in-law who are still alive. These respondents, however, have not expressed the desire to include their living father-in-law in their household.

We have inquired the reasons as to why a substantial section of the respondents from nuclear households do not like to stay with their husband's near-kin, particularly parents. In general, these respondents have reported that as they have a bitter experience of living in a joint household, they do not like to continue or return to the same experiences any more, particularly when they have got the opportunity of living apart. Mainly they have accused their mothers-in-law for creating an unbearable situation in the pre-partition days. Sometimes, of course, the hostile and jealous behaviour of the other members of the husband's family of origin such as husband's brother, his wife, sister also was responsible for expediting respondents' separation from the stem family. It must be noted, however, that this is the opinion of those respondents only who do not like to expand the existing structure of their present household. On the whole, the picture that emerges is that most of the respondents from nuclear households like to continue the present arrangement, i.e., living separately from their husband's kin.

Table 5.10 provides some complementary information in addition to what has been presented in Table 5.9. While organising the table, we have thought it better to break up the frequencies of the joint households of different varieties, as respondents belonging to different varieties have reacted differently to this query. It shows which form of the household respondents prefer to live in—the type they are currently in or any other type. In other words, here our goal is to see whether respondents living in the nuclear households have any desire to return to the joint type, and alternatively, whether respondents belonging to the joint type like to change their present household pattern, for instance, have any plan to separate from the present household, if circumstances permit. The information has been assumed to be relevant to assess

Table 5.10

Household Structures Respondents Prefer to Live In, by Residence and the Present Household Structure (in percentage)

Residence	*Type of Household*	*Present Form*	*Nuclear Type*	*Any Form of Joint Household*	*LJ Type Household*	*Su.Nu.Type with Hus.'s Mother Only*	*Nuclear Household with Separate Residence*	*Total*
Rural	Nu	90	-	4	2	-	4	100(n=50)
Joint	LJ	85	15	-	-	-	-	100(n=26)
	CJ	81	19	-	-	-	-	100(16)
	LCJ	75	25	-	-	-	-	100(n=8)
Total		86	9	2	1	-	2	100(n=100)
Urban	Nu	66	-	17	12	5	-	100(n=82)
Joint	SuNu	82	14	-	4	-	-	100(n=22)
	LJ	74	26	-	-	-	-	100(n=42)
	CJ	67	17	-	8	8	-	100(n=12)
	LCJ	75	25	-	-	-	-	100(n=16)
Total		123	20	14	12	5	-	174
		(71%)	(11%)	(8%)	(7%)	(3%)		(100%)

how much deep-rooted is the respondents' attachment to the joint family structure.

What appears at first glance from the table is that the respondents mostly have expressed their overall satisfaction with their present household type and have opted for continuation of the same. They have said that they have been somehow habituated with the present type, and hence in spite of some inconveniences it seems more or less workable. Advantages outweigh inconveniences which, they think, are tolerable or can be corrected anyway. This attitude is most prominent among the respondents living in the rural nuclear households (94%). Of these, 4 per cent who still share their husband's ancestral home, have even expressed their desire to separate their residence too. This leaning towards the present form of household is not, however, that much clear-cut among their urban counterparts, and one-third of these women like to practise one or another variety of the joint type. While 18 per cent of the respondents in rural joint households prefer to shift to the nuclear household, the corresponding figure for their urban counterparts is 22 per cent.

What is to be noted here is that the desire to maintain the status quo is stronger among the respondents from the village nuclear households than that from the village joint households. Again, though this desire has been noted to some extent in urban joint households, the attitude of the urban nuclear households is somewhat ambiguous. Though a substantial portion of them do not like to include even their parents-in-law in their household (Table 5.9), many of them are willing to expand their present household structure.

These respondents who are in favour of joint households however, have clarified that they prefer small joint households containing the parents-in-law or the mother-in-law only (LJ or SuNu type of households) to the traditional pattern comprising three or four generations (CJ or LCJ type of households). Some residents of the large joint households in the sample also have, in fact, expressed their liking for smaller joint type (LJ or SuNu type of households.

On further analysis of data it appears that respondents who are at present living in nuclear households but have a leaning for the non-nuclear pattern, are of two types. The elderly women whose married sons live separately with their families of procreation comprise one category. They report that the usefulness of the joint household is specially felt in the old age when people are in need of emotional security and physical safety which can be provided only by the joint household. Nuclear households breed a sense of helplessness and insecurity.

Another category is constituted by those young women who are gainfully employed and are in need of some helping hand which may be available from the mother-in-law. However, they have asserted, they would choose LJ or SuNu type of households only. Large joint households are totally unsuitable to them.

To conclude, though the majority of the respondents of the urban nuclear households are in favour of continuing their present household pattern, the popularity or suitability of the joint households is also notable. Next, majority of the respondents who are habituated with living in joint households, are not thinking in terms of separating from it. Thus, it can be said that in the near future there is no possibility of total disintegration of the joint households or its replacement by the nuclear type of households.

Most of our family sociologists, particularly the male ones, believe that all Indian families are potential or future joint families, whatever might be their present structure. For empirically substantiating these beliefs, one is required to systematically collect data relating to the family developmental process, i.e., information on the actual and desired time of break-up of the joint families. Family sociologists, however, have shown little interest in gathering the relevant data.

The present inquiry has tried to fill in this gap and therefore has collected data relating to what is, in the opinion of the respondents, the ideal or desired time of break-up of the joint family. Table 5.11 contains this information.

Only one respondent has been found in the sample who has asserted that the question of 'ideal' time of break-up is redundant since at no stage members should think in terms of being separate from the stem family. Excepting this person, from the analysis of the opinions of the remaining 273 respondents several points emerge. First, the opinions of the rural and urban respondents are

Table 5.11

In Respondents' Opinion, What should be the Ideal Time of Separation from the Husband's Family of Orientation, by Residence and Household Structure (in percentage)

Residence	Type of Household	Just after Marriage	After Hus.'s Parents' Death	After Hus.'s Sisters' Marriage	When Hus.'s Brothers are Financially Self-sufficient	When the Feeling of Solidarity is Lacking	Total
Rural	Nu	2	42	32	6	18	100(n=50)
	Joi	-	72	10	14	4	100(n=50)
Total		1	57	21	10	11	100(n=100)
Urban	Nu	37	12	6	11	34	100(n=82)
	Joi	14	32	2	3	49	100(n=90*)
Total		42	39	7	12	72	172*
		(24%)	(23%)	(4%)	(7%)	(42%)	100

Note: * One respondent said that one should never separate from the joint family. Another respondent said that sons should separate whenever they become financially independent.

strikingly different in this matter. Rural respondents have mentioned some specific stages or conditions which should be fulfilled before the sons separate from the stem family. These are: death of the parents (57%), marriage of all the sisters (21%), and attainment of economic self-sufficiency by the brothers (10%), and only 1 per cent of them hold the view that the ideal time of break-up should be just after the marriage.

The opinion of urban respondents is strikingly different. About one-fourth of them (24%) assert that sons should separate just after their marriage and a substantial section (42%) of them have opined that members should remain joint so long they have a feeling of solidarity, unity, mutual understanding, readiness to sacrifice for each other. At the same time they have expressed the apprehension that under the present circumstances it is difficult to cherish this feeling. But if it can be done, it will benefit all. In its absence, however, the mere sharing of the hearth will only intensify the member's bitterness and unhappiness and vitiate the family atmosphere. It is better to disjoin under such circumstances. This feeling of solidarity, which is, of course, a subjective condition, does not depend on any specific material factor but on the member's mentality and mental make-up, early socialisation pattern, and the family environment, particularly the environment of the family of origin of the incoming wives.

Only one-third of the urban respondents (34%) agree with their rural counterparts that certain events like parents' death, sisters' marriage, etc., should occur before separation.

Thus, while the reasons behind remaining joint for the rural respondents are fulfilment of some concrete needs or the fear of being criticised or censured or blamed by others, urban respondents do not in general care for being reprimanded. This is quite natural since social pressure would be weak in an urban environment. They do not care much what others say.

Secondly, differences have been observed between the respondents from the nuclear and joint households too. The dictum that "sons should not separate during the lifetime of their parents" is followed by the highest number (72%) of respondents in rural joint households, and the condition of 'solidarity among members' is not at all appealing to them. The opinion of the respondents in rural nuclear households is, however, much diversified.

As expected, the opinion that the ideal time of break-up should be just after the marriage is most prevalent (37%) among the urban nuclear households. In all, 49 per cent of the dwellers of the urban joint households believe in mutual understanding and solidarity among the members. On further analysis of data it has been observed that this view is shared by respondents mostly from the CJ households (75%). This is quite natural. For, the basis of these households is mutual understanding and convenience. In the Indian society separation between the brothers after the death of the parents is socially approved and tolerated. Thus, whether or not to continue a CJ household, depends mainly on the consideration and choice of the members rather than on any social pressure. Hence, the prevalence of solidarity among the members is required by them.

To summarise, this table shows that, in general, village women think that so long parents are alive or sisters are not married, sons or brothers should remain in the stem family. Thus, they accept that to this extent at least functions of the joint family should be honoured. Also, they reject the view that sons may separate just after their marriage. It can be drawn, then, that in the village each household should remain joint at least for some period. It should also be noted that the monthly per capita income of these households is only Rs. 478, and that is also uncertain and irregular. Most of them are landless and live on physical toil. It shows that the joint family values are present in this class of people also. In contrast, the appeal of these values is weak to the urban women who are economically well-off, educated and culturally enlightened. To the majority of them, while deciding upon the form of household, personal happiness, satisfaction and convenience get primacy over the performance of duties to the husband's parents and siblings. In other words, any supposition that all families should remain joint at least for some period (say, so long parents are alive) is absent in majority of the urban women. They would desire to live in the husband's stem family so long this is satisfactory and convenient to them.

However, this is about the opinions expressed by the respondents. Their actual behaviour, that is to say, which stage in the family developmental process they chose to part with will be presented in Chapter 6.

Next, this inquiry assumes that there is a contradictory relationship between romantic feeling between the husband and the wife and the husband's being loyal to his consanguineal kin. In other words, the more the husband is attached to his family of procreation, the weaker will be his ties with his family of orientation. For this reason, the Indian value system, which perpetuates the joint family norms and values, never gives indulgence to or permit's husband's being close to his wife. Such behaviour has been regarded as a mark of lack of vigour, manliness and personality on the part of the husband. An ideal wife should, as has been asserted by our scriptures and illuminated by many folktales, be servile and obedient to her husband's elderly kin, regard her husband as her *guru*. But such an attitude and behaviour on the part of the husband towards his wife is totally disgraceful and lamentable. Egalitarianism has never been accepted or even tolerated by the Indian value structure and that is why here the social structure is hierarchical. Joint family, one of the main pillars of the Indian social structure, is no exception and it has been advised that for the purpose of maintaining its solidarity and continuity a hierarchical authority structure along gender and age is a necessity. The head, the oldest male in the household, is required to look after the well-being of each and every member. Following him, other male members also should learn not to treat their wives and children as separate units which are to be specially nurtured and cared for. In fact, the joint family concept does not accept the separate existence of a man's family of procreation as a distinct entity within the joint family.

Accordingly, a son's becoming more attentive, dutiful and attached towards his wife and children will undermine his loyalty towards the others, which action, in turn, will definitely affect the joint family solidarity. Hence, a question was put to the respondents as to whether their husbands were equally attached to both their families of orientation and procreation, or alternatively, leaned towards either of them. In case husbands have reported by the respondents to be tilted towards their wives and/or children, the assumption is that the trend is towards the weakening of the joint family solidarity.

We have compared here the allegiance of the respondents' husbands towards his wife and/or children with that towards his parents and siblings. We have tried to see whether there is a contradiction or conflict between these two loyalties and whether separation from the stem family (i.e., when the husband lives in a nuclear household) affects in any way these two loyalties. In other words, we have tried to see whether a man may be equally dutiful, intimate and loving towards his parents and siblings when he lives separately with his wife and children rather than when he lives with these kin in the same household. Findings in this regard have been presented in Table 5.12.

It appears from the table that still, on the whole, men are dutiful and attached to their consanguineal kin (parents and siblings) whether or not they live with these kin. It also appears that malefolk in urban areas are more conscious of their duties and responsibilities towards their parents, brothers and sisters than their rural counterparts.

A feature which is noticeable in the townsmen but almost absent among the ruralites is that a portion (17%) of the former is more attentive to their wives than to their mothers, another portion (14%) is equally dutiful to both mothers and wives, and still another portion (8%) is more attentive to mothers than to wives, as has been reported by the respondents. It seems that compared to their rural counterparts, urban men are conscious of the potential conflict between their mothers and wives both of whom compete for winning their attention. Urban wives are not that much concerned with their husbands' allegiance to other kin like their father, brother and sister as with the husband's allegiance towards their mothers. And, that is why they have separately mentioned whether or not their husbands are more attached to them or their mother-in-law.

To the rural men, however, this is not an important event. Here they have to balance their allegiance towards all the members

Table 5.12

Husband's Attitude towards his Mother, Father, Siblings, Wife and Children as Perceived by the Wife, by Residence and Household Structure (in percentage)

Residence	*Type of Household*	*Hus. is Most Attentive to his Parents & Sibs*	*Hus. is more Attentive to his Mother than Wife*	*Hus. is Equally Attentive to Each & Everybody*	*Hus. is Equally Attentive to Mother & Wife*	*His. is more Attentive to Wife than Mother*	*Hus. is More Attentive to Wife & Children than to Parents & Sibs*	*Total*
Rural	Nu	2	4	28	-	2	62	98* (n=49)
	Joi	4	4	60	-	-	32	100 (n=50)
Total		3	4	44	-	1	47	(99*)
Urban	Nu	1	5	32	18	29	12	97# (n=80)
	Joi	1	11	67	10	6	4	99*(n=91)
Total		2	14	88	24	29	14	171#
		(1%)	(8%)	(50.5%)	(14%)	(17%)	(8%)	(98.5)

Note: * 2 respondents have reported that their husbands love the children only.
2 respondents have reported that their husbands love none in the family.

of the stem family in which their wives and children also are included, and that towards their wives and children only. The question of satisfying specially and separately their 'mother' and 'wife' does not have much relevance to them.

The above difference between the urban and rural men is noteworthy as it has a special importance in causing disintegration of the stem family. The clash of personality and the rivalry between the mother-in-law and the daughter-in-law is a more powerful factor in bringing about family disintegration in the town than in the village. For this reason, the LJ type of households in the town, even when the husband is the 'only son', sometimes are to face problem of disintegration (if there is a serious personality clash between the daughter-in-law and the mother-in-law). This problem is not still that acute in case of the rural households which also separate but for different reasons.

For measuring husband's attachment to their wives, i.e., to assess which type of emotion is more prevalent in the husband-wife relationship—romantic love or affection—another question was put before the respondents: which type of role relationship they most expect from their husbands—that of a friend or the one of guardian, and whether there is a parity between their expectation and that of their husbands. Maybe, both the partners may choose to be each other's friend or each other's guardian, or one party may prefer to be the other's friend, while his/her partner may like to see him/her in the role of the guardian, etc. The supposition is that a friendly relation between the marriage partners is helpful to the development of romantic love and egalitarian relationship. This egalitarian relationship between the genders is an important step towards the formation of the nuclear household replacing the joint one. On the other hand, the more the husband will be preferred in the role of the wife's guardian, the more will be reinforced the hierarchical role relation between the spouses. The observations in this regard have been presented in Table 5.13.

The table shows, that still most of the husbands prefer to remain their wives' guardian or, at the most, simultaneously guardian and friend. However, a striking difference in this regard has been noted between the urban and the rural respondents.

Table 5.13

Whether the Respondent Likes to See her Husband as her Friend or Guardian, and how far Husband Reciprocates, as Perceived by the Respondent, by Residence and Household Structure (in percentage)

Residence	*Type of Household*	*Both like that hus. should be wife's friend*	*Both like that hus. should be wife's guar.*	*Both like that hus. should be both friend & guar.*	*Hus. likes to be guar. while wife likes to be friend*	*Hus. likes to be wife's both Gr. & Fr. but wife likes him to be fr. only*	*Hus. likes to be wife's Gr. but wife likes him to be both Fr. & Gr.*	*Hus . likes to be wife's Fr., wife likes him to be her Gr.*	*Hus. likes to be Fr. only; wife likes him to be both Fr. & Gr.*	*Total*
Rural	Nu	12	86	-	-	-	-	2	-	100(n=50)
	Joi	4	96	-	-	-	-	-	-	100(n=50)
Total		8	91	-	-	-	-	1	-	100
Urban	Nu	46	6	12	15	16	3	1	1	100(n=82)
	Joi	28	12	29	11	15	4	-	-	100(n=92)
Total		64	16	37	22	27	5	1	2	174
		(37%)	(9%)	(21%)	(13%)	(15.5%)	(3%)	(.5%)	(1%)	(100)

In the village a clear trend has emerged indicating that women like to see their husbands as their guardians, and their husbands also are ready to oblige them. Hence, there is no incompatibility between the choice of the husband and the wife. Respondents from both types of households show the same trend.

The picture is, however, a bit anomalous and varied in the town. The percentage of women (9.5%) who like to see their husbands in the guardian's role is not at all significant here, whereas the highest number of wives (65.5%) want to see their husbands in the role of a friend. There are 25 per cent of the respondents who have desired that their husbands should be their guardian and friend simultaneously.

Another point to be noted is that while in the village sample there is almost a nearly perfect total consistency between the wives' choice and that of their husbands, in the urban sample the consistency exists in case of 67 per cent respondents only.

One more fact to be noted is that though less in number than their rural counterparts, many urban husbands (52.5%) also, according to the rating of their wives, prefer to remain both guardian and friend of their wives and 25 per cent like to be their wives' guardian, whatever might be their wives' choice. This inquiry, therefore, does not evince that egalitarian values have been strong in our country (so far as male attitude is concerned) or hierarchical role relationships and gender-based authority structure have weakened, or that our malefolk have been in general liberal and appreciative of women's freedom. In the village, the survival of the traditional values is clearly prominent. The urban picture is a bit promising as here the women are educated, sometimes economically self-sufficient, conscious and assertive of their rights. Most of them demand an egalitarian relationship with their husbands, whether or not this is liked by their husbands.

More respondents from the nuclear households are in favour of egalitarian relationship with their husbands compared to those from the joint households. A relationship is , therefore, noted among women's urge for egalitarian role relationship, urbanisation and nuclearisation of households.

Let us try to summarise what has been described above. The goal of this inquiry is to explain the nature and measure the degree of functional solidarity or the compactness of the household units belonging to a joint family, which may or may not share a common hearth. We have tried to see whether the solidarity of the household units is affected by the fact of their separation from the stem family; that is to say, whether any difference is observable in their mode of functioning when the household units belonging to a joint family share a common hearth (thus forming a joint household) and when they form separate co-residential, commensal units (thus forming several nuclear households), and whether this difference goes to such an extent as the spirit of the joint family is injured. Next, assuming that the location of the incumbents is a vital factor in influencing their familial behaviour, we have compared the mode of functioning of nuclear and joint households separately in the rural and urban contexts.

In this chapter, the functional solidarity of the households in general has been measured with the help of thirteen indices (the relevant information has been presented in Tables 5.1 to 5.13). It appears that the household units display some amount of functional solidarity or compactness in terms of such criteria as the exchange of aid and assistance among the members (Table 5.1), the exchange of gifts among the members (Table 5.2), role of the joint family influencing the formation of members' political opinion (Table 5.5), members' attitude towards approaching relatives for aid (Table 5.7), members' opinion about extending aid to relatives (Table 5.8), and the husbands' attachment to their patri-kin (Table 5.12). In other words, as has been reported by the majority of the respondents, the spirit of the joint family has been found to operate among the members, irrespective of their sharing the common hearth and residence, in the matter of extending and accepting help or assistance of various kinds (financial, physical, emotional), and the functioning of the joint family as a solid political unit. Men still regard that they have some duty to perform towards their family of orientation. And, when some exigency or need arises, people mostly approach their kin rather than non-kin (like friends and neighbours) for help. People also accept that one should help one's relatives. Also, if economic condition permits, people tend to exchange gifts with their relatives, which action reinforces the ties of the joint family.

In contrast, the spirit and the unity of the joint family has been found to be somewhat lacking when measured in terms of several other criteria. For example, the concept of the ancestral home where the joint family should be situated and which acts as the centre of attraction and meeting ground as well as resting place, if need arises, of members scattered over different places, is on the wane (Table 5.3). The members no longer feel interest in regularly arranging and participating in family get-togethers (Table 5.4). Moreover, the authority of the head of the family, and the full-fledged spontaneous participation of the members in arranging and solemnising a marriage ceremony of the family is diminishing day by day (Table 5.6). The decline of the role and importance of the joint family in this matter is both symbolic and substantial since the team spirit of the kin group is overly manifested on such occasions.

Still, in some other spheres, no clear-cut specific trend is discernible. The, behaviour and attitude mostly vary here in terms of the residence and the type of household which the respondents belong to. For instance, in expressing opinion about which should be the ideal time of separation from the stem family, the opinion of the rural and urban respondents highly vary (Table 5.11). While the rural wives, particularly those from the joint households, are clearly of the opinion that so long as parents are alive or the marriage of the sisters cannot be arranged, sons or brothers should not separate from the stem family. The urban respondents, on the other hand, believe that whether or not to remain in the husband's family of origin should depend on a subjective condition, i.e., so long as members can maintain a sympathetic understanding and a spirit of oneness among themselves. A substantial portion of them, specially those belonging to nuclear households, also is of the opinion that it is better for sons to separate just after their marriage or when they attain the economic self-sufficiency. Clearly, the opinion of the urban respondents in this regard goes against the spirit of the joint family.

In another respect also the somewhat greater devotion to the spirit of the joint family is displayed by the rural respondents than by their urban counterparts. Rural wives, and also their husbands, think that husbands should be their wives' guardian. Urban wives, in contrast, like to see their husbands in the role of their friends, while the urban husbands eulogise the role of their wives' both guardian and friend (Table 5.13). The authority structure and the division of labour within the household will be significantly contingent on this factor.

Still in another field the opinion of the respondents has been found to be highly diverse depending on the household type they belong to (Table 5.10). Majority of the respondents of both the joint and nuclear households express their satisfaction with their present household type. However, while one-third of the urban respondents living in nuclear households express a mild preference for small-sized joint households, their rural counterparts are strongly against any such move. It shows that the utility of the joint households is felt more by the urban women, particularly a section of them, than the rural women. Another observation (Table 5.9) is also quite consistent with the above. Though in general respondents are not willing to extend the present structure of their households by including therein any members from their husbands' kin, a section of urban respondents have expressed their desire to accommodate such persons as husband's parents, particularly mothers, under certain conditions. This shows that the utility of the joint household is not totally absent from the case of the urban people.

6

Functional Solidarity in Nuclear Households

The previous chapter made a comparative assessment of the solidarity of households with their respective stem families in terms of such behavioural traits and mental preoccupations of the respondents (evinced, of course, in their verbal responses) as were relevant, for the purpose, to both the types of households. In this chapter, the focus is on the nuclear households solely and the goal is to highlight the kind of ties and degree of solidarity and attachment exhibited by the respondents living in nuclear households toward their husbands' families of orientation. In other words, it will show whether and to what extent the nuclear households are functionally and spiritually related to their respective stem families. Some queries relate to the respondents' behaviour and experiences and the others, to their attitudes and opinions. We have tried to compare the answers provided by the rural and urban respondents with a view to estimating whether the village nuclear or the urban nuclear household are more functionally related to their respective families of orientation.

Next to commensality, co-residence is an important feature indicating closeness of ties with the stem family (Shah, 1998, p.5). That is to say, sharing a common residence with the husband's patri-kin, even when the hearth is separate, indicates a certain degree of closeness of the respondents and their husbands with the latter's family of origin. Hence co-residence has been regarded as an indicator for measuring a nuclear household's solidarity with its stem family. By 'co-residence' here we mean where the nuclear units share the same ancestral home which has not yet been legally partitioned among the heirs.

Data as to how many nuclear households in the present sample share their residence with the respondents' husbands' patri-kin have been presented in Table 6.3. It appears from the table that in the urban sample out of 82 respondents from nuclear households, 11 per cent have no such permanent place of dwelling where their husbands' patri-kin reside in a close proximity with them. They did not, or do not have any ancestral house. The parents of the respondents' husbands used to reside in the quarters provided by their employers or in apartments rented temporarily. When the sons, i.e., the respondents, husbands and brothers-in-law, grew up and secured jobs or independent source or earning, they separated and arranged their respective places of dwelling according to their taste and means. After retirement, so long as the parents were alive, they used to stay with one of their sons either permanently or with each son by rotation. After their death, when all the brothers of the husband are settled in their respective places of dwelling, the concept of the husband's ancestral home no longer exists, in fact, it never existed at all. Those husbands who lost their parents at an early age and were brought up either by any relative or in hostel also do not have any ancestral home to be shared with their patri-kin. The corresponding figure of such households in the village sample is only 4 per cent.

Excluding households without ancestral home, out of the remaining 73 urban nuclear households only 8 (11%) live in the ancestral home, whereas 79 per cent of the village nuclear households having an ancestral home live in close physical proximity with the respondents' husbands' patri-kin. It seems that an overwhelming majority of the village nuclear households are at least physically attached to each other. Here, the general trend is that when the sons (or brothers) separate from the stem family, they do not immediately leave the ancestral home as well. Rather they somehow manage to stay within the same compound. In the town, however, this pattern of living is almost an exception and here the separation of hearth and residence occurs in most cases simultaneously. Sometimes, of course, urbanites are forced to separate their residence for some extraneous factors, For example, when a son gets a good employment or is transferred to some other place lying outside the town or city, he has to leave the parents' residence. Inadequacy of space in the place of dwelling is another major factor forcing sons to make new living arrangements, when they get married. A substantial section of the urban people lives in rented house or apartments. So, whenever a brother (or son) purchases or acquires a house of his own, he leaves the residence where the remaining members of his stem family reside. Anyway, spatial dispersion of the household units belonging to a stem family is a common phenomenon in the town rather than in the village.

Hence, as appears, the dwelling pattern of the villagers is mostly clustered as they generally share their respective ancestral homes. Even when they construct new houses, they do it within the same compound or adjacent to the place where their patri-kin live. This high incidence of close physical proximity is as accountable by economic factors (villagers' inability to buy land or house elsewhere leaving behind the ancestral property however meagre it may be) and social factors (lack of economic, educational and occupational mobility) as by emotional factors (villagers' high degree of attachment towards the primordial ties). Anyway, if living in the close physical proximity with the husbands' patri-kin becomes an indicator for measuring the solidarity of the joint family, villagers decidedly rank higher than the urbanites.

Many of our family sociologists attach a great deal of importance to co-parcenary as an evidence for joint family solidarity (for detail, cf. Ch. 3). One can assume, therefore, that if co-parcenary is regarded as a pillar or evidence of the spirit of the joint family, its absence will indicate the lack of the same. In other words, the more it can be found that households possess property in common, the stronger will be the spirit of the joint family, and conversely, the more people divide the property, the weaker will be the spiritual and functional solidarity of the joint family. We, however, regard co-parcenary as merely one of the indicators of jointness, and do not propose to place any additional importance on it. Anyway, the findings relating to the prevalence of co-parcenary among the nuclear households have been presented in Table 6.1 where we have tried to show how far the nuclear households in villages and towns still hold property in common with the husband's patri-kin.

It appears that in the context of the total sample of nuclear households, full-fledged co-parcenary is maintained in only 21 per cent of the cases. Besides, in another 30 per cent cases (columns 6 and 7) also co-parcenary is somehow maintained as here either the husbands have been denied any share to the property (as they separated during the lifetime of parents and against their permission) or they have not put their claim (husbands live in their office quarters or rented house or house purchased by themselves). This latter case is particularly a feature of the urban men who being separate from the stem family make living arrangements of their own, whereas the stem family continues to reside in the ancestral home. Neither party demands formal partition, nor feels its need. In another 6 per cent cases (columns 3, 4 and 5) also co-parcenary is at least partially maintained as here a portion of the property is partitioned and some other portions remain joint.

In case of about one-third of the households (33%) there is no existence of co-parcenary, and in case of 9 per cent cases, mostly urban households, the issue is redundant as here there is no property to be divided or jointly owned.

From the religious point of view there is no restriction on dividing the property after the death of the father (Kapadia, 1966, pp. 220-21). The present trend, however, is that property may also be divided before the father's death or after the establishment of collateral joint households through mutual agreement.

It seems that a substantial number of the nuclear households, particularly in the urban areas, those which have separated their hearths and in many cases also their residence, tend to hold property in common. That is to say, though from the social point of view as well as the members' perception and experience and to all intents and purposes, these households form separate 'families', from the legal point of view they are 'joint'.

The difference between the village and the town is distinct in this matter. In case of 69 per cent of the urban households, it

Table 6.1

Whether Ancestral Property (Land, House, Garden, Pond, etc.) is Held in Common with Husband's Father and/or Brothers, by Residence (in percentage)

Residence	*Property is held jointly*	*Only house is joint*	*Only house is sep.*	*Only business is joint*	*Hus. has not been given any share*	*Hus. lives in his own house. Ancestral home is joint*	*Ancestral property is amicably, not legally separated*	*Property is separate*	*No property worth separation*	*Total*
(1)	*(2)*	*(3)*	*(4)*	*(5)*	*(6)*	*(7)*	*(8)*	*(9)*	*(10)*	*(11)*
Rural	18	6	4	-	6	2	4	58	2	100(n=50)
Urban	22	2	-	2	2	41	-	17	14	100(n=82)
Total	21	4	1	1	4	26	1	33	9	100(n=132)

seems, property is held in common either fully of partly, and it has been divided in case of 17 per cent cases only. The corresponding figures for the village households are 32 per cent and 62 per cent respectively. It seems, then, that in terms of co-parcenary urban households reveal a higher incidence of joint-type households than their rural counterparts.

What to be pointed out in this context is that, in majority of the cases in the urban areas, 'ancestral property' in effect means a house or a portion of a house only, whereas in the village context, in addition to house other forms of immovable assets like arable land, garden, pond, shops and establishments, business, etc., also are included under the title 'ancestral property'. Another fact is that in the urban context in most cases the living space is already too small to accommodate all the members of the stem family when the children are grown up and sons get married. Only those people who are absolutely helpless will remain in this too crowded and congeted condition of the ancestral home, and those who can afford, will try to shift to any other place and make any alternative provision. Under such circumstances, in the ancestral home the parents would live with one or more sons who take the responsibility of looking after the parents and other dependent relatives, if any. Besides, married daughters and kin related to parents would visit and come to stay in the place where the parents reside. Thus, the son who stays with parents in the ancestral home takes the charge of the parents, kin related to parents and all sorts of social and ritual obligations in lieu of the facility of staying in the ancestral home. On the other hand, the son who does not claim the share of this home and moves elsewhere also foregoes, along with this claim, all the above responsibilities. Co-parcenary here means a quoting of the relinquishment of responsibilities towards parents and patri-kin. And, this is the nature of functional jointness that emerges from the single fact of co-parcenary when other dimensions of this complex issue are ignored, overlooked or bypassed.

In the village the condition is a bit different. Most of the villagers do not have that much of economic solvency which is required by them for shifting to elsewhere whenever any differences of opinion arise with the parents. They can at best separate the hearth and somehow manage to stay in a portion of the home. Only in case of the extreme differences of the opinion sons are forced to leave the ancestral house. Thus, in general, with their separation from the stem family, villagers cannot afford the cost of leaving the ancestral house or eschewing their claim on it. Under such circumstances, they manage the situation by separating the ancestral property through mutual understanding. Though these are not legally registered, respondents have reported these events as ones where property is owned by the respective heads of the household.

Moreover, villagers in general are dependent on land either exclusively or partially. Their income from other sources, if any, is not sufficient and regular as most of them join the secondary sector as unskilled industrial labourers. So they cannot easily forgo their claim on the ancestral property however meagre its quantity might be, like their urban counterparts who have a relatively steady and secure source of income. Instead, they insist on an amicable division of their ancestral property. This is why the number of co-parcenary is fewer in villages than that in towns.

To make the story complete another fact deserves mention. Villagers need not depend on the help of kin for cultivating their share of the ancestral land like their urban counterparts having some landed property in the village. The latter themselves are employed in the urban tertiary sector. So they find little time for visiting the village to take care of their portion of the property. Rather, it would be convenient for them not to claim any formal or legal partition of the property. They instead maintain an amicable relationship with their kin in the village who are entrusted with the task of looking after the property. They occasionally visit the village, are treated as honoured guests by the kin who mainly enjoy the property, and come back to the city with some produce of the land, though not the share exactly due to them. Their kin in the village who are not that well-off, also feel obliged to them as they do not seek formal partition of the land. Instead, if these townsmen sought partition of the land, it would become difficult for them to keep this land under control as in that case they would have to arrange for regular cultivation of the land, failing which the land may be vested with the state or occupied by the *bargadars*. Hence, if the amount of the ancestral property is small, it is uncongenial for urban men to seek legal partition of it.

What we are trying to highlight is that it will be misleading if the mere fact of co-parcenary is regarded as the only or even a sufficient proof in favour of jointness of the family, nor is it true that absence of co-parcenary amounts to loss of ties with kin. One should rather want to know why and when people seek and do not seek partition of the property. Also, the above descriptions show that co-parcenary in itself cannot be a sufficient proof of functional jointness for the measurement of which the help of other indicators is required.

To meet the above requirement, we have inquired, among other things, whether respondents in the nuclear households perform rites and rituals separately in their own house, or jointly with their husbands' kin. Joint family, being a social organisation, has got a religious dimension too, and hence like commensality, co-residence and co-parcenary, one should assume the joint performance or rites and rituals also as one of the indicators of jointness. Hence, we include performance of a variety of rites and rituals like ancestor worship and the worshipping of various Hindu gods and goddesses like Shiva, Laxmi, Bipattarini, and the like. According to the Indologists, our joint family system is an important carrier of the tradition of the Indian way of life, the continuance of which depends a great deal on the performance of various rites and rituals. And, the nature of many of these rites and rituals is such that they are to be performed by a person along with others, sometimes with the husband's patri-kin who share the same *gotra* or lineage. Thus, joint performance of rites with the husband's parti-kin often is a religious requirement through which both the purposes—social (reinforcement and revitalisation of solidarity among kin) and religious (correct performance of rites)—will be realised.

In Table 6.2 data have been presented in relation to the above matter. It has been assumed that the higher the incidence of performance of rites by the respondents and their husbands along with the latter's patri-kin, the stronger will be the indication of the solidarity of the joint family; and, on the other hand, the more they do it separately by themselves or with their (respondents')

Table 6.2

Whether Respondents Perform Rites and Rituals in their Own House with their Husband's Kin or elsewhere, by Residence (in percentage)

Residence	*Perform with husband's kin*	*Have separate arrangement in own house*	*Perform with mother*	*Perform with non-kin*	*No fixed pattern*	*Do not perform rituals*	*Total*
Rural	24	76	-	-	-	-	100(n=50)
Urban	28	51	2	4	1	14	100(n=82)
Total	27	61	1	2	1	8	100(n=132)

own kin or with non-kin (neighbours, friends), the less will be the solidarity of the joint family. This latter type of behaviour marks distance from their husbands' kin.

Looking at the table, one finds, in general, the solidarity of the joint family is poor in this respect. While 27 per cent of the respondents perform rites with their husband's kin, 8 per cent of the respondents, all of whom are from the town, however, do not perform any such rituals at all. Most of the respondents (61%), have separate arrangements in their homes. And, this trend is more prominent among the rural women (76%) than among their urban counterparts (51%). This shows that physical distance or proximity is not a factor influencing this behaviour. For, rural women, though have physical proximity with their husbands' kin, show little interest in joint performance of rituals. In the town, leaving aside 11 respondents who have informed that they do not find time for or have faith in such circumstances, out of the remaining 71 respondents 48 (more than two-thirds) have reported the same, i.e., independent performance of rituals.

For measuring intimacy and closeness of relationship among the relatives a dependable instrument is the measurement of the regularity and frequency of contact and communication among the persons concerned. The affectionate feelings and emotional bonds amongst kin need to be constantly reinforced by contacts. Otherwise, they gradually weaken and die ultimately. 'Communication' here includes any type of contact—visit, correspondence or contact over telephone. Here our assumption is: the closer the ties among the kin, the more frequent and regular will be the contacts among them. When our purpose is to measure solidarity among the members of the joint family, we should emphasise the contacts between respondents and/or their husbands with the husbands' kin. Our supposition is: more frequent and regular contacts of the wives (and/or their husbands) with husbands' kin rather than with wives' kin are an indicator of closeness of ties with the former. On the other hand, if contacts with wives' kin surpass in regularity and frequency those with husbands' kin, closeness of ties with wives' relatives is thereby evinced, which somewhat negatively affects joint family spirit and solidarity.

In general, a regularity in the maintenance of contacts between the respondents (and their husbands) and their primary kin such as the parents, brothers and sisters of the couple has been noted, and this is done more or less frequently. One can draw, therefore, that in respect of maintenance of contact and communication, the behaviour of respondents (and/or their husbands) in general indicates close ties with such members of the joint family as husbands' parents and siblings. However, from this perspective ties with husbands' third and fourth degree kin such as husband's father's brothers and sisters and their children seem quite infrequent for the urban nuclear households. In most of the cases the contacts have become only rare and ritualistic, i.e., they meet each other only in ceremonies and festivals such as a marriage ceremony which is generally and customarily attended by the relatives. Often even such infrequent and irregular contact is terminated or not continued, which is revealed from respondents' submission that they cannot remember when they last met such relatives. From the information presented above one may infer that the phenomenon of the traditional three- or four-generational joint family is few and far among the urbanites. Even the first condition in making a relationship viable—regular communication— does not work here. Hence other conditions and evidences of functional jointness—coming to each other's help in times of exigency or nurturing a feeling of solidarity—can hardly be expected from such kin. In the village, however, this problem is not that much acute. This shrinkage of the circle of family relationships has been noted by Shah (1998, p. 106) too.

Data further reveal that compared to their urban counterparts, village households are more regular in maintaining contacts with the kin. One reason for this is the close physical proximity among the patri-kin in the village. Here it is convenient, if the parties are willing, to meet each other even daily. However, this is not the only reason. Village respondents have shown more regularity and frequency of contact with their husbands' married sisters also, who must live at a certain distance (because of the general practice of village exogamy). Still, this distance does not obstruct the maintenance of ties. It shows that villagers are more eager to maintain ties with the relatives, particularly those from husbands' side, than the urbanites.

Our observations show that the urban respondents put more emphasis on maintaining ties with relatives on the side of their natal family than with those of their husbands, and here the physical distance is no bar. The village women also do not neglect their contact with their parents, brothers and sisters, but contacts with them are not more frequent or more regular than those with their husbands' relatives. They generally meet their parents or siblings once or more than once a month. On the contrary, a substantial section of wives from urban nuclear households meet their parents and siblings at least once or more than once in a week and that too when these relatives live in some distance. These women (and/or their husbands) are not so prompt and eager in meeting the husbands' parents and siblings. One can delineate, therefore, that so far as the maintenance of contact and communication is concerned, urban nuclear households are closer to wives' relatives than their rural counterparts.

In another respect also village households display greater solidarity towards the norms of the joint family. Compared to their urban counterparts, more rural nuclear households maintain contact with the husbands' third and fourth degree kin. In the town, 18 per cent of the respondents have reported 'no contact' with such kin. In all, 32 per cent of these respondents have reported that such contacts occur only rarely and they cannot remember when they last met such relatives. The corresponding figures for the rural respondents are 14 per cent and 20 per cent respectively.

At the same time, it is also to be noted that a section of the rural nuclear households has spoken very bitter relations with husband's parents and brothers. So much so, 8 per cent of them have reported 'no contact' with their husbands' parents, and 22 per cent with husband's brothers, though they live in close physical proximity. The corresponding figures for the urban sample are 2 per cent and 4 per cent respectively. Thus, it is observed that majority of the villagers maintain regular and frequent contacts with husband's kin though a substantial section of them also has a bitter relationship with that category of kin. Though the proverb "familiarity breeds contempt" is partly applicable here, the major bone of contention is the claim over the share of the ancestral property. In general, villagers' economic condition is poor and the amount of property is also meagre. So it becomes often difficult to satisfy the heirs with their due shares, and this becomes the major factor behind the disputes among the near primary kin, i.e., with whom co-parcenary rights exist. Sometimes it even so happens that the husband's relation with his paternal uncles and cousins with whom no co-parcenary interest exists, becomes more intimate than that with his father and brothers.

Two more facts emerge from the data. First, it is seen in both the village and the town that the respondents' ties and intimacy with married daughters are closer than that with their married sons who live separately with their wives and children. It shows the prevalence of the joint family values which do not look upon with favour separation of sons during the life time of parents. Both urbanites and ruralites regard such incidents, namely separation of their sons during their lifetime, as undesirable.

Next, as 'means of communication', villagers generally depend on visits. urbanites, however, apply other media such as postal correspondence and telephonic conversation than visits for this purpose. This is natural as villagers are generally illiterate and unable to correspond through writing. Telephone facilities are either not available in the village, or too costly for them to afford.

What seems interesting is that in spite of the easy availability of these modern and quick means of communication, urbanites are slow in maintaining contacts with husbands' kin compared to the villagers who have to depend on relatively expensive means for the purpose.

We have also collected data regarding the kind of relation which is maintained by the respondents with husband's first, second, third and fourth degree patri-kin who live in the same compound or housing complex or within a walking distance. Our purpose here is to assess the nature of the association between physical proximity and intimacy of relationship with husband's patri-kin. Patri-kin have been divided into two categories: husbands' parents and brothers (first and second degree kin), and husbands' father's brothers and their sons (third and fourth degree kin).

Data reveal that relation with kin living nearby is closer among the urbanites than among the ruralites. In the village, sometimes, the relation with husbands' parents and brothers does not remain cordial because of the disagreement or disputes over the share of the ancestral property. Another factor is that often these husbands separated after bitter quarrels, and hence a lot of bickerings occurred before the husbands parted with their families of origin. As such occasions of conflicts do not arise with the uncles and cousins (with whom separation of both hearth and property had already occurred), relation with such kin does not become that much bitter. Husbands even got help from such kin when they had separated from their parents.

In contrast, the urban fathers who have somehow adjusted themselves with the idea and practice that the sons may separate even during their lifetime, accept separation amicably and calmly. As a result, relation with the stem family generally does not worsen due to separation. As only a small number of the urban people have ancestral property, the chances of quarrels over its share are also less here. Anyway, our observation is that physical proximity does not necessarily lead to intimate relation with husbands' patri-kin. If it were so, then ruralites would have much surpassed the urbanites in maintaining the joint family solidarity. This is not our experience with the sample considered in this study.

Patri-local residence is the norm of northern India. It means that after marriage the wife should remain with the husband's family of origin. Even when the family becomes too large and breaks down on demographic ground, the norm is that the new household units should reside in the vicinity of or within the compound of the residence of the stem family as far as possible. However, though it may be possible to follow this norm in the village, it is impractical in the urban perspective where most people do not have any ancestral home. Besides, as social mobility is high in the town, men have to move to far-off places for pursuing their career. Anyway, the society has accepted that in the town non-compliance with the norm of patri-local residence, in itself, does not indicate the lack of joint family solidarity.

However, another development should not be lost sight of in this context. A tendency which has been found to have been developing slowly but gradually is that in place of patri-local residence, uxori-local residence is being practised by a section of the urban nuclear households, i.e., the trend is that after separation (or even before marriage) sons begin to hire/purchase apartments near to the residence of their wives' parents. Sometimes, however, they are following the neo-local residence where the couple resides in a place which maintains more or less equal distance from the parental residence of both the partners.

Considering the gravity of the issue, we have collected information whether and how far these new types of residence—uxori-local and neo-local—are being practised by the nuclear households. We have compared the distance between the respondents' place of residence and that of the parents of both the husband and the wife. In case, parents are dead, the place where other brothers of the husband reside has been counted. Our assumption is that the more respondents reside nearer to the paternal residence than to their husband's paternal residence, the weaker will be the joint family solidarity. Our observation has been presented in Table 6.3.

As expected, the norm of patri-local residence is generally honoured by the rural households. In all, 92 per cent of the rural nuclear households are situated in close spatial proximity of male householder's parents' residence. However, the residence of 24 per cent of the households is near to the paternal residence of the wife (respondent). The corresponding figures for the urban sample are 30 per cent and 37 per cent respectively. It shows that the practice of living near to the wife's parental residence is more common among the wives living in the urban nuclear households than among their rural counterparts. Yet, uxori-local residence in large scale is not yet the practice, rather the tendency is towards neo-local residence.

Many Indian family sociologists have assigned a special importance to the family developmental process for having a comprehensive understanding of the Indian family system. According to them, the nuclear family is an alien, atypical phenomenon in the Indian soil. It is evident if one looks at the

Table 6.3

Respondents' by Distance of their Residence from that of their Father and their Husbands' Father/Brothers in Rural and Urban Nuclear Households (in percentage)

Distance between respondent's residence and that of her parents	*Distance between respondent's residence and that of her husband's parents/brothers*						*Total*	
	Same compound	*Within walking distance*	*Takes ½ hour to 3 hours*	*Takes more than 3 hours*	*Outside West Bengal*	*No definite residence*	*%*	*f*
Same compound	- (4.0)	2.44 (2.0)	1.22 (-)	1.22 (2.0)	- (-)	- (-)	4.88 (8.0)	4 (4)
Within walking distance	2.44 (12.0)	6.10 (2.0)	9.76 (2.0)	7.31 (-)	1.22 (-)	4.88 (-)	31.71 (16.0)	26 (8)
Takes ½ hours to 3 hours	4.88 (60.0)	7.31 (12.0)	15.85 (-)	3.66 (-)	1.22 (-)	4.88 (4.0)	37.80 (76.0)	31 (38)
Takes more than 3 hours	2.44 (-)	3.66 (-)	1.22 (-)	7.31 (-)	1.22 (-)	1.22 (-)	17.07 (-)	14 (-)
Outside West Bengal	- (-)	1.22 (-)	4.88 (-)	- (-)	2.44 (-)	- (-)	8.54 (-)	7 (-)
Total	9.76 (76.0)	20.73 (16.0)	32.93 (2.0)	19.50 (2.0)	6.10 (-)	10.98 (4.0)	100.0 (100.0)	82 (50)

Figures within parentheses indicate rural sample.

family developmental process. Family system as a living entity is a continuous process passing through various phases mainly due to demographic factors (birth, death, marriage). Nuclear family structure is just one of these phases in the family developmental process, and the balance is always tilted towards the joint family structure, since neither the co-parcenary law nor the Indian tradition and value structure accepts separation of sons during the lifetime of the parents.

The above assumption can be logico-empirically tested if empirical data relating to the time of family break-up and different stages or phases of the family developmental process are collected. This very task has been attempted here. This inquiry, however, proposes that there are several, not one, family developmental processes. That is to say, all the households do not necessarily rotate between these preconceived phases: joint-nuclear-joint. Those nuclear households would never turn into joint households if the sons become separate just or soon after their marriage. Hence, data about the time of break-up of the respondents' husbands' families of orientation, i.e., at which time of their life cycle these people have actually separated from their parents, are absolutely necessary for comprehending the family developmental process. If it is found that these people remained in their families of origin after their marriage only for a short period, say upto five years at the most, the durability of the joint structure would be brief. It would be questionable in that case whether the fulcrum of our family system is oriented towards the joint structure.

We have, therefore, collected information on the break-up of the households in terms of time (phase in the life cycle of a man) and phase or stage. Information has been gathered also in relation to the quality of the impact of the break-up, i.e., which aspect of jointness—commensality, co-residence or co-parcenary—has been most affected by this break-up. In addition to collection of information about separation of the respondents' husbands, we also took care of the same in relation to the time of separation of the other brothers of the husbands, if any, That is to say, efforts have been made here to collect the complete information regarding the developmental process of the respondents' husbands' families of origin. Our supposition is: the more frequent are the cases (1) where sons separate from their stem family within five years of their marriage, (2) where sons separate within the lifetime of their parents and before their sisters' marriage, and (3) where separation of hearth is immediately followed by separation of residence and property as well, the weaker will be the spiritual and functional solidarity of the joint family.

Table 6.4 presents data regarding whether the respondents' husbands separated at all, and if separated, how many days before or after their marriage this separation matured. In Table 6.5 corresponding information relating to the other brothers of the husbands, if any, has been presented. Thus, Tables 6.4 and 6.5, if taken together, present data relating to the developmental process of the families or orientation of the respondents' husbands, that is, whether these families disintegrated at all, and in case they disintegrated what were the phases of their disintegration.

By 'separation' we mean parting of the respondents' husbands from their families of origin, i.e., families where the husbands' parents and/or other brothers, if any, live/lived jointly. The event when or where all the sons separate from the parents during their lifetime and the parents then live alone has been called a case of family disintegration, i.e., disintegration of the joint family. In contrast, the event when or where one or more sons separate from the parents' household but other sons remain with them till their death has been called the continuation of the joint family. As we assume that in place of one family developmental process, several such processes are there, our goal is to depict some of them.

It appears from Table 6.4 that in 31 per cent of the sample households husbands of the respondents have separated before or since their marriage. Some of them have deferred the separation, but as many as 72 per cent of them have separated within five years of their marriage. It seems that an early separation is a feature of a substantial section of the sample households. In case of only 5 per cent of the sample households the stem family never disjoined because the husband was the only son and he never separated from his parents, or the husband remained with his parents till the death though other brothers separated, or parents died long before the son's marriage and therefore the stem family never formed at all.

Table 6.4

Time of Break-up of the Respondents' Husbands from their Families of Origin, by Residence

Husbands separated from their stem families	*Rural*	*Urban*	*Total*
Before marriage	5(10%)	21(27%)	26(21%)
Since marriage	1(2%)	12(16%)	13(10%)
Within 1 year of marriage	12(25%)	6(8%)	18(14%)
Between 1 year and 3 yrs. of marriage	9(19%)	5(6%)	14(11%)
Between 3 and 5 yrs. of marriage	9(19%)	11(14%)	20(16%)
Between 5 and 10 yrs of marriage	8(17%)	11(14%)	19(15%)
Between 10 and 15 yrs. of marriage	2(4%)	4(5%)	6(5%)
Remained in the stem family for more than 15 yrs.	2(4%)	8(10%)	10(8%)
Total	48(100)	78(100)	126(100)
Never separated	2	4	6
N	50	82	132

Data presented in Table 6.5 provide more information in this regard. In case of 54 per cent of the sample households, the stem family disintegrated. Some of these households never took the joint shape as here sons separated since or just after their marriage. Sometimes it so happened that before the marriage of the respondents' husbands their elderly married brothers were already separate, and the husbands also followed suit. In some other cases, all the sons remained joint for some time and then parted with the stem family simultaneously. Parents then began to live separately. When this is the practice, the stem family loses its continuity and such a phenomenon may be treated as a case of family disintegration.

Table 6.5 further shows that 46 per cent of the sample households disintegrated only partly as in their case one or more sons disjoined while the rest remained with the parents. Thus, the stem family could survive from total disintegration.

What is noteworthy in this table is that in the sample 8 per cent households have been found where the respondents' husbands are the only son of their parents and as they parted with, parents had to live alone or had to stay with their married daughter or other relative(s). Such happenings have been identified as cases of family disintegration.

Striking differences have been noted between the behaviour of rural and urban households. Table 6.4 indicates that in the village the trend is not to separate just after marriage, but to stay for a few months with the stem family and then to separate.

Table 6.5 depicts that in the town most (55%) of the stem families have not totally disintegrated, i.e., one or more sons continue to remain with the parents when others separate. The corresponding figure for the village is only 33 per cent.

To summarise, it appears from Tables 6.4 and 6.5 that in the town a substantial section of men tend to live separately since the time before their marriage. However, the rest, namely, those who continue to remain in the stem family do no tend to split from it early. In the village, on the other hand, the rate of sons' getting separated after a few months from their marriage happens to be more frequent and the incidence of remaining with the parents and/or other brothers for more than 10 years after marriage is not at all significant.

Table 6.5

Separation of Respondents' Husbands vis-à-vis Separation of Husbands' Brothers from their Families of Origin, by Residence

When respondents' husbands separated from the stem family	*Rural*	*Urban*	*Total*
All brothers of the husband separated simultaneously/brothers separated before the marriage of the husband /just after their marriage/within 3 years of their marriage	31(63%)	27(35%)	58(46%)
Husband was only son; when he separated his parents live alone or with other relatives	2(4%)	8(10%)	10(8%)
Rest of the brothers of husband remained joint/remained with parents	15 (33%)	43 (55%)	58 (46%)
Total	48(100)	78(100)	126(100)
Never separated	2	4	6
N	50	82	132

On our inquiry we located some economic and demographic factors behind this phenomenon. In the village, those husbands who separated early were found to have lost their fathers at their childhood. Before their marriage they stayed with their brothers and widow mother, if alive. These elderly brothers who themselves were poorly educated because of the premature death of the father, could hardly arrange for the proper education and placement of the younger brothers. As a result, since childhood these men had to try for earning some money just to meet their own expenses, and sometimes even their widow mother's and unmarried sister's expenses. Obviously, their education and training cannot proceed far and most of them had to join the primary and secondary sectors as unskilled manual labourers or vendors. Quite naturally, their tendency would be to get married at their earliest opportunity and then separate from the brother's household. If their fathers had died before getting their sisters married, the elderly brothers or the widow mother had to do this by selling the remaining portion, though very meagre, of the ancestral property. These men in the rural nuclear households, thus, in the majority of the cases, are landless unskilled labourers. They separate from their brother's household mainly on economic grounds. The widow mother either stays with each of the sons by rotation, or herself manages for her own, if her health permits.

Thus, partition of the households in the village generally occurs between the brothers, fathers having met early and premature death, and not between the father and the sons. Hence, though the village displays higher incidence of early separation, these splittings mostly do not occur during the lifetime of the father. As the longevity of men is poor in our villages, the longevity of the LJ and LCJ type of households is also smaller in this region. One may note here what Conklin says in this regard (1968; 1969). He draws that though the norm in India is living in the joint family, the fairly high birth and death rates of India often makes the fulfilment of the norm difficult. For, "in order for a son to be able to live in a two couple lineal joint household, both father *and* mother must survive until the son's marriage, assuming that a son is born in that marriage" (1968, 29). Shah (1998, p.73) also corroborates this observation. What we like to point out is that one should not draw that since the rate of early separation is higher in the village, the attachment of sons to parents is comparatively weak in the village (in comparison with the urban scenario).

Moreover, the economic condition of the majority of the villagers is stringent and it is more precarious for those who live in nuclear households. These people neither have any regular and secure source of income nor any amount of arable land from the cultivation of which they could procure their livelihood. Under this condition it becomes difficult to remain in the joint household for a prolonged period.

Information on the family development process cannot be complete unless we present data on the phases of separation. Family sociologists pursuing the theory of family developmental cycle generally hold that demographic factors as birth, death and marriage are responsible for the changes in the cycle. It is argued that with the coming of brides through marriage, with the birth of children and with the death of the elderly members of the family the structural character of households changes. We have collected the relevant data in this regard which have been presented in Table 6.6.

The first point which draws our attention is that the majority of the respondents' husbands separated from their families of origin when those families were at the primary stage of their developmental process, i.e., when their parents were alive and marriage could not be arranged for all of their brothers and sisters. This stage is called 'primary' because the son, an adult and competent member of the family, is yet to have assumed all the major responsibilities. Duties to the aged parents through looking after their physical and mental health and providing emotional, and if necessary, financial aid should be performed by the sons of the family. In the Indian society, the elder brother is regarded second to the father, and one of his essential duty is to arrange marriage at least for sisters and help the brothers in getting established in jobs or professions. A substantial section of men in the sample households separated before completing these duties, and that is why we state that many of our sample households disjoined at the primary stage of their family developmental

Table 6.6

Phase of Separation of Respondents' Husbands from their Families of Origin in the Village and the Town

When respondents' husbands separated from the stem family their	*Rural*	*Urban*	*Total*
Parents were alive; all siblings were married	2(4%)	19(24%)	21(17%)
Parents were alive; only sisters were married	5(11%)	9(12%)	14(11%)
Parents were alive; all siblings were not married	5(10%)	20(26%)	25(20%)
Father was dead; all siblings were not married	7(15%)	6(8%)	13(10%)
Father was dead; only sisters were married	10(21%)	8(10%)	18(14%)
Parents were dead; only sisters were married	1(2%)	-	1(1%)
Father was dead; all siblings were married	16(33%)	8(10%)	24(19%)
Parents were dead; all siblings were married	2(4%)	8(10%)	10(8%)
Total	48(100)	78	126
NA (Never Separated)	2	4	6
N	50	82	132

process. A good many persons, on the other hand, has been found to separate when the family developmental process approaches near to its final stage, namely, when the parents/fathers are dead and all their siblings have got married. As a son of the family he has completed most of the duties by this time, and according to the present-day social norms and values, if men separate at this phase they are not to face much social criticisms and censure.

The table further shows that in 48 per cent cases sons parted during the lifetime of both the parents, in 43 per cent cases they separated leaving behind their widow mother, in 44 per cent cases they separated after the marriage of all the brothers and sisters, and in at least 70 per cent cases they separated after the marriage of their sisters.

It can be drawn from what has been depicted above that parents', particularly mother's, remaining alive or the fact of all the brothers and sisters not getting married, does not, to any appreciable degree, prevent men from being disjoined from their families of origin.

The tendency towards early and premature separation is found more in the town than in the village. Maybe, the higher longevity of urbanites is the reason. Separation during the lifetime of parents has been found to take place in 62 per cent of the urban sample, while only 25 per cent of the rural sample has reported the same. However, in both the village and the town men have been found to generally wait for their sisters' getting married before they decide to separate. The rate is 75 per cent for the rural and 62 per cent for the urban households.

In Table 5.11 of the preceding chapter we presented respondents' opinion about what they think to be the ideal time of separation. We now feel the relevance of comparing this opinion with respondents' (or their husbands') actual behaviour in this regard. On the whole, consistency has not been found in a large measure between respondents' opinion about the ideal time of separation and the time when they (or their husbands) actually separated. Many of them who opined that it is desirable to separate just after the marriage have, in fact, waited a long time before they finally separated. Before separation they performed many of their duties towards the husbands' parents and siblings from within the stem family. On the other hand, a great many cases have been found where the respondents expressed that one should not separate during the lifetime of their parents but actually their deed goes against their desire.

It should be pointed out here that the decision to disjoin is not always taken by the respondent. It may be her husband's, or it might be caused by some external factors like the transfer of the husband or lack of accommodation in the place where the stem family resides. Sometimes separation may be imposed on her by the other members of the stem family, say when her husband's father and/or brothers ask him to be separate or when brother(s) of the husband leave(s) the stem family. All these factors may cause the inconsistency between the respondents' opinion or words and actual behaviour or deeds.

In spite of all these, it has been found that a consistency between words and deeds have been observed in a higher number of cases from the rural sample. Maybe, urban people are more subject to extraneous factors. Another possibility is that when the respondents expressed their opinion they did it on the basis of their lifelong experiences. Thus, a respondent may discover at the fag end of her life (when she has been interviewed for this inquiry) that she has not been properly treated for all her sacrifices for her husband's stem family. Hence, now she feels that it would have been better if she separated at an early stage, as is being done by her sister-in-law or by her daughter-in-law. Instances displaying such late realisation are higher in the women from the urban sample perhaps because the urban sample is older by ten years on an average than the rural sample.

Sometimes the process of separation takes place step by step. That is, separation of the hearth may not be immediately followed by the partition of the house and the property as well. We, therefore, decided to collect data relating to the degree or depth of separation. That is, when the respondents' husbands separated from their stem families we inquired into whether the separation was in terms of hearth, residence or property or a total separation of all of them. Considering that the three major pillars of the joint family are commensality, co-residence and co-parcenary, we have assumed that if a man separates his hearth only and another both hearth and house, the depth of separation will be deeper in the latter case. If property is also divided, depth of separation will be still deeper. The functional solidarity of the family also will weaken correspondingly. Relevant data have been presented in Table 6.7. It is to be noted that this depth of separation was measured at the time when the sample households started the process of separation, and not their present status.

Table 6.7 reveals that the highest number of sample households (45%) were separated simultaneously in terms of both hearth and residence, i.e., they deviated from two joint family norms—commensality and co-residence. The depth of separation was less in case of 32 per cent households which separated their hearth only. The number of the households which simultaneously separated the hearth, house and property is comparatively low (17%). We have, however, kept outside from this account those 6 (5%) households which never separated. Anyway, it seems that co-parcenary is the last norm to be violated and there are many households which are in all intents and purposes separate units but still hold property in common.

Village and town display distinct difference in this matter. While the majority of the village households (54%) separated their hearth only when they parted with their stem family, the majority of the urban households (65%) were separated simultaneously in terms of both hearth and house. Next, while 23 per cent of the village households separated hearth, house and property simultaneously, only 14 per cent of the urban households did the same. It indicates that when the households split up, perhaps the process of nuclearisation becomes deeper for the urbanites than for the ruralites.

One thing becomes apparent from this table. Though co-parcenary is maintained in majority of the cases and separation occurs mostly in terms of hearth and house only, the respondents have not attached any special importance to this fact. They actually had categorised their households as 'separate' units though their property is shared with their husbands' agnatic kin. Hence, according to the indigeneous perception, splitting up of a family means separation of the hearth. Separation of residence provides an added depth to this process. And, whether or not property is held

Table 6.7

Depth of Separation of the Sample Households, by Residence

When separation took place	*Rural*	*Urban*	*Total*
Only hearth became separate; house and property remained joint	26(54%)	14(18%)	40(32%)
Hearth and house became separate; property remained joint	7(15%)	50(65%)	57(45%)
Hearth, house and property became separate	11(23%)	11(14%)	22(17%)
Hearth and property were separate; house remained joint	1(2%)	-	1(1%)
Husband was expelled from the home; no share of property was given to him	2(4%)	1(1%)	3(2%)
Separation of property and hearth took place before husband's marriage	1(2%)	-	1(1%)
Only house became separate; hearth and property remained joint	-	2(2%)	2(2%)
Total	48(100)	78(100)	126(100)
Na (Never Separated)	2	4	6
N	50	82	132

in common does not affect their behaviour in significant ways. This is the reason why in Bengali the joint family is called *ekannabarti parivar*, i.e., the familial unit whose members share a common hearth. Hence, whatever may be the legal and religious definition, the indigeneous interpretation emphasises that when households separate their hearth, they should be counted as separate familial units.

For measuring the attachment of the members of the nuclear households towards the husband's (householder's) family of orientation a relevant information would be the reasons behind their disjoining, more specifically, to ascertain whether the members liked the separation or whether they had to accept it under some external pressures and unavoidable situations or because of their helpless condition.

Relationship among the members of a joint family may be affected significantly when the household units separate due to mutual bickerings and jealousy, or due to spatial mobility of the sons. The after-separation interaction patterns among the members will be substantively different under these two conditions. And, for one who is committed to measure the functional jointness of our family system, such differences are highly relevant. Hence we collected information relating to the factors or reasons behind separation.

One common reason for which household units disjoin is clash of personality between the members. When members are assertive of their status and rights, are concerned with their own interest and benefits only, are self-righteous, are not ready to consider other's views and problems, it becomes difficult for them to remain peacefully in the same household. Personal bickerings, abuse, quarrels, jealousy, non-co-operation, impatience then become the part of daily life. And, when this is the case, members would like, if situations permit, to part with.

Another factor bringing separation may originate from the helplessness of the members. Helplessness may be of various kinds. It includes those factors over which people have no control. Lack of adequate space in the home is one such factor. Another factor is the job/career requirements of the malefolk of the household, who may be required to move to different places on transfer or for availing themselves of better career opportunities.

In the rural context where men are generally the landless poor or unskilled industrial labourers who lack any secure and regular source of income this helplessness of members has another dimension. Conflict over the share of economic responsibilities of the household is here a regular event. They have no savings and their one day's illness and absence from the place of work may lead to starvation or borrowing. To these people maintenance of a joint family is a 'luxury' which people of poor means can ill afford. Hence, when these people separate purely on economic reasons, i.e., due to incapability to afford a big family, it indicates the helpless condition of the members rather than their unwillingness to sacrifice for one another or lack of mutual affection and understanding or lack of commitment to the joint family solidarity and values.

There may still be a third factor responsible for the disjoining of the family. It occurs when the members feel or realise that for many reasons it is no longer convenient or viable to continue their present living arrangement and agree that it is better to amicably part with each other. These people do not dishonour the joint family values, nor are they helpless, but they simply want to disjoin when the family becomes too large to be maintained properly. They apprehend that if they do not take timely measures, many problems and complexities would emerge. Separation in such a situation comes through mutual discussions and settlements. This is possible only when the members of the family have a feeling of affection towards one another and commitment to the joint family values. This is the situation where the households 'divide to unite'.

It has been found that the separation came through amicable settlement in only 6 per cent cases and these are mainly urban households. In the majority of cases (59%) separation occurred since the majority of the members desired to separate. They found joint living both undesirable and inconvenient for many reasons. Such examples are equally prevalent in the town and in the village. In all 35 per cent of the households separated under the pressure of circumstances and members' helpless surrender to the adverse economic condition. We have, therefore, categorised the households on the basis of the 'primary' reason(s) behind the separation as reported by the respondents. In reality, however, the matter is not that simple, and as occurs in case of other spheres of human behaviour, here also in most cases separation is an outcome of the interplay of several factors.

Almost one-third of the respondents from village households have pleaded that they had to separate solely under economic stringency, being unable to maintain a large household. Only one case has been found among the urban respondents having similar ground for separation.

For obvious reasons, separation due to lack of space in the home and career advancement of the malefolk of the household are features of the urban households and in the village such situations are almost non-existent.

Though the reasons behind split up of the family differ to a great extent for the rural and urban households, almost no difference has been found among the rural and urban respondents when they plead that they had to separate because of lack of solidarity, unity and mutual understanding among the members of the household. The mode and language of expression of these two types of respondents, however, differ. There was difference in taste, culture, familial background, socialisation pattern and mentality with others in the husband's family. The hobbies which were nurtured in the paternal home as singing or dancing could not be practised here in the face of the other member's opposition and banter. The atmosphere of the parental home was lenient and permissive. Acts like singing, dancing, attending functions were natural events in the parental home, but in the husband's home the atmosphere was too uncongenial to pursue these hobbies. In fact, here people were unfamiliar with the event that the wife of the family would make public appearance in the stage or attend public functions.

The educational standard of the women members of the husband's family was poor and much inferior to that of the respondent, according to some respondents. These people did not like wives' being gainfully employed outside the home. Sometimes they were jealous on seeing the respondents' freedom of movement and economic self-sufficiency.

Some respondents stated that their husbands' parents were conservative, and therefore, they did not accept their inter-caste marriage. Differences over the amount of dowry paid by the respondents' fathers, or respondents' being not very good-looking or fair-complexioned also have sometimes been pointed out.

A few of the respondents, on the other hand, have reported that the environment of the husbands' household could not be adjusted with since it was too indulgent and loose. Brother-in-law often used to drink, sister-in-law returned home with boyfriend and late at night but parents-in-law did not seriously object to these things. These incidents set unhealthy examples before the children. Besides, streams of guests used to come and everytime there was a hue and cry, noise created by the TV., tape-recorder, etc., for which children felt disturbed and difficulty in concentrating on lessons.

According to some other respondents, the husbands' household being too large in size and due to frequent coming of relatives of the mother-in-law and her married daughters much pressure was laid on the respondents' health. Often meal time became very late. Still, according to some other respondents, as husbands' brothers' wives were too lazy much pressure of the household chores was to be borne by them. Often there were quarrels over the division of labour in the household. Some village respondents said, among the brothers there were often bickerings over the division of labour in the activities related to farming and cultivation—those who were employed outside, took this opportunity to avoid toiling in the farm.

Some of the respondents have reported that the diet, food habit and cooking in their husbands' households were too different to be adjusted with. They used too much chilly or sugar in cooking. Though none of the respondents has pleaded that this was the primary reason behind their separation, many of them have referred to this factor in conjunction with other reasons. Thus, this factor can be regarded as a contributory cause influencing separation of households.

Still to many respondents, they were unable to perform their duties toward their parents while staying with the husband's kin. Those who had no brother particularly felt this problem. Neither they could look after their old parents/widow mother while staying in the joint household, nor their parents could be requested to stay with them together with the husbands' kin in the same household. Some others alleged that they were not allowed to offer gifts to their parents or younger brothers and sisters as husbands' parents did not like it. Parents-in-law did not like frequent coming of their natal relatives to the home, some respondents complained. The mother-in-law was very miserly and did not like to expend on food, dress, exchange of gifts with relatives, entertainment of guests, some respondents experienced.

Some of the respondents confined that the mother-in-law was of the interfering and bossing type. She objected to chatting with the husband, going with him for shopping or on excursion. She always had a tendency to guard the husband, and husband too, being the only son, was too fond of his mother and always tried to satisfy her. This was very irritating to the respondent. Even if the husband brought any small gift for her, mother-in-law insisted that the same should be brought for her daughter too, a few respondents complained. Some of them have pointed out differences of opinion with the mother-in-law over imposing discipline over the children.

Some of the respondents said that the excessive attachment of their husbands towards their parents, brothers and sisters irritated them. Husbands had to assume much economic burden of the whole family, which stood in the way of arranging healthy diet, better coaching for his own children. Sometimes it so appeared that these kin exploited the respondents' husbands' gentleness and dutifulness.

Some respondents have mentioned selfishness, lack of the sense of responsibility and sympathetic understanding on the part of the husband's kin. Sometimes brothers of the husband were jealous of him. The respondents argue that if these things are present in the household, peaceful living is bound to be disturbed, and this will come to surface over petty matters. To avoid such almost daily disturbances, it is better to part with. According to several respondents, cordial relationships can be maintained with relatives if they live at a distance, for "familiarity breeds contempt".

Many urban respondents have admitted that a major factor behind their decision to separate was their independent, self-righteous mental make-up. They wanted to live according to their own liking and they disliked others' bossing and domination. Hence, they disliked living in large households.

A few respondents emphasised the need for an efficient and neutral head of the household who should not be biased to any member or discriminate against some members. For example, each son should be equally urged to bear the responsibility of the family, each daughter-in-law should be asked to do her duty, and whenever a member deviates from his/her assigned duty, steps should be taken rather than overlooking or bypassing the matter or making it light or insignificant.

In a few cases disputes over the share of the property have been the reason for splitting. Such cases have specially been noted among the villagers who possess a very meagre amount of land. These people are so poor that they quarrel over even a small plot of land.

It appears, then, that the reasons behind the splitting up of the family are many and diverse. However, as has been observed, the lack of the spirit of being selfless and making adjustment is the single biggest factor behind the breaking up of the household units, and this is equally applicable to both the village and the town.

Another fact worth mentioning is that in the village it is mostly the malefolk of the household who take the decision to separate. Disputes occur mostly between the father and the sons or among the brothers, and these disputes mainly centre around the economic reason: who will bear how much economic responsibility of the household or who will work how much in the farm. In the town, on the other hand, the wife's opinion is honoured and she is a party to this decision in most cases. The common factors leading to the outburst of disputes among the members of the urban households are excessive pressure of household chores, imbalanced or unjust division of household work among the family members, attachment to the wife's relatives, difficulty over the adjustment with diet and cooking of the husband's home. These factors, however, do not matter significantly to their rural counterparts. It shows that in the matter of separation, the urban husbands show much concern for the wife's convenience, liking, opinion and wishes. In the village, economic factor seems to be most vital. As this is the domain of the men who have to bear the responsibility of providing for the family, men are here the main decision-makers.

For measuring the joint family solidarity information on the wherewithal of the parents when sons separate during their lifetime is relevant. For, the care of the aged parents is a primary concern for the Hindu sons. We, therefore, inquired when the respondents' husbands separated who looked after their parents, under whose care they lived, who provided for them, what the husband's role was in these matters. By 'looking after' we mean being in regular touch, regular visits, if required extension of physical help like accompanying them to the hospital or the doctor's chamber, etc., extension of financial help if and when required, to provide emotional support and security, and so on. In other words, our goal was to inquire whether and how far the husbands of our respondents perform(ed) their duties and responsibilities to their parents.

The issue is mainly qualitative in nature and, therefore, we tried to appraise its functional or subjective aspect, e.g., whether any change occurred in the status of the parents, in the authority structure of the households, owing to the sons' separation. At the same time such concrete information as whether sons extended financial, physical and emotional support and security towards their parents after being separated also were counted. While preparing the category-set for analysing the relevant data all these aspects were appreciated. What to be pointed out is that here we have categorised the families of origin of the respondents' husbands—the households they have left behind when they established their own families of procreation.

Categories 1 and 2 comprise those cases where the stem families of the respondents' husbands do not disintegrate and no substantive change occurs in the status of the parents due to one or more sons' separation. Though one or more sons have separated the rest continue to remain in the stem family, and the father continues to enjoy the status of the head of the household as before. Even when one of the parents dies no structural and positional change occurs in the status of the widower father/widow mother in these households. Structurally, these households may be of any variety of the joint type—LJ, LCJ or supplemented CJ (when one of the parents dies). In such households, the parents are not regarded as dependent or burden even though the respondents' husbands (and some of their brothers) left home; sometimes, however, sons extended financial, physical and emotional support to their parents after separation (Cat. 1), and sometimes with structural separation they become to a certain extent functionally also detached (Cat. 2).

Households put in categories 3 and 4 differ both structurally and functionally from categories 1 and 2. These are the supplemented nuclear households where the son becomes the head of the household and the widow mother is his dependent. In category 5 those cases have been put where the living parent(s) become the dependants of sons and all the sons share the responsibility of the parents. The parents by rotation stay as guests in the household of each of their sons for a specific period. For instance, if a widow lady has three sons, under this system she would stay by rotation with each of them four months in a year. Married sons of the households put in category 6 generally have avoided the responsibility of their parents. Just after or within a few months after their marriage they have separated and their parents have begun to live with the unmarried sons and daughters. Sons of the households put in categories 7,8,9,10 and 11 have shirked the responsibility of their parents either fully or partly. Either the daughters or other relatives look after them. Sometimes they have none to depend on (Cat. 11). Sons may or may not extend financial, physical and emotional support and assistance to them.

It appears that the problem of looking after parents when sons separate has not been found by a substantial section of the sample households. In majority of the cases, however, parents were not that fortunate to keep their families of procreation intact till their death or to enjoy the status of the head of the household. In case of not more than 10 per cent of the sample households sons did not separate till parents' death. In some of these cases parents faced early and premature death (Cat.12).

Parents in 45 per cent of the sample households (Cats. 1 and 2) remained in the stem family with one or more married sons when other sons left. These are the instances where the joint nature of the households did not totally disappear at least during the lifetime of the parents. In these households parents somehow managed to enjoy the status of the head of the household. They were not treated as dependants or guests. This trend is much more prominent in the town (56%) than in the village households (29%).

In categories 3 and 4 those cases have been put when the widow mother is not financially dependent (maybe, she owns some property or enjoys a pension). This trend is more marked in the village (22%) than in the town (8%). In the village, a custom generally followed when the joint family property is divided among the heirs after the father's death is that a portion of the property is vested with the widow mother and the son who looks after her, should enjoy the property. After her death, that property is shared among all the sons. Here the mother enjoys an option regarding with whom she will stay. It seems, in the village when the parents have some property or a source of income they need not be anxious of their future.

This problem is rather faced when parents are economically helpless (Cat.5). Here sons, sometimes grudgingly, share among themselves the charge of the parents. Parents remain with each son by rotation. This occurs more often in the village (17%) than in the town (3%) since in the village men mostly are not financially capable of bearing the sole responsibility of their parents singly. In the town since generally people are not financially dependent (as is the nature of our sample) on their sons they do not like this system. In the village often the widows themselves are not willing to stay with one of their sons permanently. They feel that it will make them appear as burden or obligation in the son's family. They will have to labour much to please the daughter-in-law to make their presence viable. On the other hand, if they stay with each son they will enjoy the status of guest, will be treated by the members of the son's household with more care and respect, enjoy more freedom of action and movement, and if physically fit, can even earn some money as their hand allowance which is not available from sons. If they live with their sons as guests, they can spend their income according to their own liking. Sons cannot claim any share of it since in that case other sons will interfere and come to rescue the mother.

Another trend noted (Category 6) is that when men separate after their marriage their parent(s) lives/live with the unmarried son(s) and daughter(s). This occurs more frequently in the village (22%) than in the town (8%). In the village this is the practice among those people who live below the subsistence level and have no regular source of income. It seems that men in this category of households have avoided the responsibility of their parents after their separation.

In case of 20 per cent of the sample households (Categories 7, 8, 9, 10 and 11) also sons seem to deviate from discharging their duty towards their parents in one way or another. Parent(s) here live with the married daughter or any relative (12%) or alone (8%). Sons sometimes (12%) financially and/or physically look after them (Categories 7, 9, and 10). In 8 per cent cases (Categories 8 and 11) sons do not maintain any contact whatsoever with them. The prevalence of these phenomena is more common in the town (25%) than in the village (10%).

It seems, then, that the rate of the parents' remaining alone occurs more often in the town than in the village. In the village when sons separate and they are not much economically solvent, they do not generally avoid the responsibility of their parents. Hence, excepting the very poor households in the village, the problem of looking after of the parents in the old age is not still serious. Parents, however, remain in their sons' households as dependant and generally they are deprived of the status of the head of the household.

Urban people, on the other hand, who are employed in the secondary and tertiary sectors are economically self-sufficient compared to the villagers, and they generally need not financially depend on the sons. Instead, they are capable of helping their sons. Sons, therefore, often do not like to separate from these parents unless serious differences of opinion or clash of interest among the members arise. Parents, on their part, think it more dignified, if they are financially solvent and physically fit, either to remain as the head of the household in their families of procreation, or to live alone rather than staying in their sons' families of procreation as their dependent or guests. The prejudice against residing with the married daughter is also less in the town than in the village.

These findings are consistent with the information presented in Table 6.5 which shows that in the town in case of 10 per cent sample households men (householders) live separately even when they are 'only sons' of their parents. Thus, in the town, it is no longer considered as exceptional or rare phenomenon where the couple lives alone even when it has son(s). This trend is no longer visible in the village where such behaviour on the part of the sons is still regarded as disgraceful and deviant. In the village, those couples who have male child are not required to be anxious of who would take their responsibility when they would be old, ill or infirm. And, this is a major reason why still the villagers strongly hanker after having a male child and hesitate to limit their family until a son is born. In the town, this longing for male child is less strong as here parents are less hopeful that they would be taken care of by their sons in their old age.

In this chapter we have tried to depict the elements of functional jointness and spiritual solidarity observed in the opinions expressed by and the familial behaviour reported by the respondents living in nuclear households in rural and urban areas. It appears that looking after the parents when sons live separately is not yet an immediate and serious problem faced by our society on a large scale since generally sons make some provisions for their parents in such cases though that arrangement may not appear to be adequate and satisfactory to the parents. Though not worried about their sheer wherewithal, parents in both urban and rural areas have grounds to be anxious about the survival of their families of procreation as a substantial section of these households has disjoined in the early stage of the family developmental process. In the village, majority of the stem families have disintegrated when parents, particularly fathers are dead. It is to be noted, however, that the longevity of the rural men below the subsistence level is still poor, and most of the villagers belong to this category. When they face an early death, their families of procreation most often tend to break up. Besides, disagreement over the share of economic liabilities of the household is a vital factor behind the split up of the stem family for a substantial section of the village population.

In the city, though the poor life span of the fathers and economic factors are not the problem, spatial and social mobility of the sons, lack of adequate accommodation in the ancestral house when the family expands are relevant factors behind separation. However, the factors like selfishness and lack of mutual understanding among the members and their unwillingness to sacrifice for each other and tolerate each other's opinions and causes are equally prevalent in the village and the city. This is singularly the most serious factor behind separation for the majority of the households. It seems that the remnants of the function and the spirit of the joint family have been mostly reduced to the acceptance of the responsibility of the parents, making some arrangements for them when men separate. Another element of jointness can be noted in the opinion expressed by a substantial section (42%) of the villagers that men should not separate during the lifetime of their parents, particularly fathers. Their behaviour mostly follows their opinion.

The traditional concept of the joint family, of course, includes a much larger circle of kin than simply the parents. Thus, by remaining dutiful to one's parents only is not enough for having one's compliance with the joint family values and norms. As our data reveal, however, this is being the fact. Urban men who are generally spatially dispersed from their patri-kin, have been found to maintain regular contact with their parents and siblings only, and their contacts with the uncles and cousins (third and fourth degree kin) are mostly irregular, infrequent and poor. Many of them meet one another during some social ceremony (for instance, a marriage ceremony) only and some cannot even remember the present address of these kin. This problem has not emerged in this scale in the village where patri-kin live in close physical proximity. But here also the issue has taken another form: relationships with the husbands' parents and brothers are so bitter for a good many respondents that they do not have even speaking terms with these kin. Their behaviour evinces the proverb: "familiarity breeds contempt".

In another respect, i.e., joint performance of rituals with the husband's kin also, the respondents evince a poor degree of solidarity towards the joint family norm. Most of them perform the rites and rituals separately in their own house and according to their own convenience (Table 6.2).

At the initial stage of separation villagers generally separate the hearth, and gradually separate the residence and property. The urban men, on the other hand, become separate simultaneously in terms of both hearth and residence, and many of them do not show any interest in the share of their ancestral property because their share (in most of the cases a small portion of the ancestral home) is too meagre or because by foregoing the share they also forego the responsibility of their parents and parents' burdens and liabilities (Table 6.1).

The fact that emerges from our data is that to the respondents the fact of separating the hearth is the indigeneous definition of the breaking up of the joint family, whether or not residence and/or property are held in common. The moment they cease to share the common hearth, they count themselves as persons belonging to separate households. Subsequently their attitude and behaviour to the stem family also begin to change and solidarity weakens from that time on.

One more trend which emerges from our findings is that respondents from the nuclear households are more attached to their parents and sibs than to their husbands' kin. Urban respondents maintain more regular and frequent contacts with their kin. However, we have not got evidence in favour of uxori-local residence pattern, and the modern townsmen show the tendency towards neo-local residence pattern (Table 6.3).

7

Functional Solidarity in Joint Households

In this chapter, we shall compare the degree of intra-household solidarity or compactness of joint households in the village and the town. This is required since our assumption is, as has already been stated, that structural jointness does not necessarily and invariably ensures functional jointness as well. To measure the degree of functional jointness of a joint household, one should analyse such things as the authority structure and division of labour of the household, consumption pattern of the members with a view to measuring whether the household functions as a solid and compact economic unit, whether members share one another's joys and sorrows, experiences and aspirations, and so on. Hence, in this section we have tried to show how far the households which are structurally joint, are functionally, i.e., in letter and spirit, joint as well.

Of all the indices of functional solidarity of a joint household, economic solidarity, i.e., how far the household acts as a solid economic unit, how far members share one another's liabilities and cooperate in this regard, is important since economic factor has been reported to be a major reason behind the dissolution of the joint household. What is to be noted in this context is whether the household functions as a solid, unified economic unit, for instance, whether a single person controls the accounts and budget of the household, whether all the earnings of the members (both individual and joint) are reserved in a common purse wherefrom the needs and requirements of the members are met. It is assumed that to the extent members of a joint household pool their earnings (when they have individual and separate sources of income) in a common fund which is controlled by the head of the household who also decides the budget of the household, the household appears as a solid economic unit and is therefore joint in both letter and spirit. It indicates not only the spiritual unity of the members, but also ensures that the consumption pattern of the members, irrespective of differences in their earnings, is more or less homogeneous and patterned. Alternatively, to the extent the members deposit only a fraction of their income to the common fund wherefrom the minimum expenses only, for example, expenses on meals, electricity, salary of the maid servant, etc., are met, and then separately bear their other expenses—those on dress, health and medicine, education of children and the like—according to their individual capacity, standard and taste, the consumption pattern of the members will be divergent and unequal. It will ultimately lead to poor co-operation and sharing among the members. Ultimately, the economic base and the jointness of the household will weaken. As co-operation among the members of a household in the economic field is an indicator of co-operation in other fields as well, we propose to present information in this regard as collected from the respondents, at the first instance.

The present inquiry for this purpose has collected information regarding

1. whether all the members of the joint households deposit their earnings, both individual and joint, under the care of the head of the household or pool together in a common purse from which all the expenses of the members of the household are met; and
2. under whose supervision and authority the budget of the household is decided and whether the head of the household has any active and effective role in the matter.

It is our assumption that from the sociological perspective such information would be far more useful and relevant to jointness than that regarding the mere presence and absence of co-parcenary.

We have observed that when the economic solidarity of the household is poor, the mere sharing of a common hearth and residence indicates members' urge for serving their narrow immediate interest, e.g., to save the expenses on fuel, salary for the maid servant, expenses on social liabilities and obligations, etc. One can legitimately express doubt about how far the spirit of the traditional joint living is maintained hereby. Such living arrangement is more akin to living in some kind of boarding house or inn where boarders pay a specific charge in lieu of which they receive some specific services.

The relevant information has been presented in Tables 7.1 and 7.2. Table 7.1 shows whether the respondents (and their husbands) deposit their earnings under the care of the head of the household to meet all their expenses.

The table shows, first, that there is a striking difference between the consumption patterns of the rural and urban respondents in several respects. Secondly, the economic solidarity of the urban joint households is relatively higher than that of the rural households. The number of those households which share the hearth only keeping most of the other expenses under the individual control, is higher in the village than in the town. This sort of behaviour indicates that in spite of living in a joint household the husband-wife-children units or entities are eager to maintain their separate or distinct existence. It seems that the ruralites are more sincere to their spouses and children and are more careful to meet their requirements themselves rather than depending on the consideration of the head of the household. This is consistent with our findings depicted in Table 5.13. Poverty is the main reason behind this sort of behaviour. When one's income is too inadequate to meet one's own basic needs one cannot afford to be generous or great. Thus, the economic stringency mostly compels ruralites to be less considerate and benevolent to the others.

It has already been pointed out that in the village, as there is more economic and social pressure to remain with the stem family, sons often cannot separate from it, particularly during the lifetime of their father. They cannot seek division and claim their share in the ancestral property so long as the father is alive. Moreover, their individual income being inadequate and insecure they cannot afford to take the risk of being separated and foregoing their share

Table 7.1

Pattern of Expenditure in Rural and Urban Joint Households (in percentage)

Residence	Type of household	Expenses are met from a common Fund	Expenses are individually made in										Some brothers only pool	Share the hearth only	Total
			Cat.1	Cat.2	Cat.3	Cat.4	Cat.5	Cat.6	Cat.7	Cat.8	Cat.9	Cat.10			
Rural	LJ	27	11	18	16	-	4	-	16	4	-	-	-	4	100(n=26)
	CJ	6	6	6	-	12	-	-	26	25	-	-	6	13	100(n=16)
	LCJ	-	-	-	13	-	12	-	12	38	-	-	25	-	100(n=8)
Total		8	4	6	5	2	2	-	9	8	-	-	3	3	50
		(16%)	(8%)	(12%)	(10%)	(4%)	(4%)		(18%)	(16%)			(6%)	(6%)	(100)
Urban	SuNu	68	-	14	-	-	-	18	-	-	-	-	-	-	100(n=22)
	LJ	24	5	2	-	-	24	16	-	-	19	5	-	5	100(n=42)
	CJ	42	-	8	-	-	-	16	-	-	34	-	-	-	100(n=12)
	LCJ	19	6	-	-	-	-	37	-	-	19	-	-	19	100(n=16)
Total		33	3	5	-	-	10	19	-	-	15	2	-	5	92
		(36%)	(3%)	(6%)	-	-	(11%)	(21%)	-	-	(16%)	(2%)	-	(5%)	100

Note: Cat. 1 = only dress; Cat. 2 = only guest/ gift; Cat. 3 = dress+ medicine+ Guest/milk; Cat. 4= dress+ guest+gift/milk; Cat. 5= dress+medicine+gift+education; Cat. 6 = dress + medicine + edn. + milk; Cat. 7 = dress + guest + gifts + edn/ milk; Cat. 8 = dress + medicine + guest + edn + milk; Cat. 9 = dress + medicine + gift + edn + guest + milk: Cat. 10 = dress + medicine + edn + gift + guest + milk + tiffin.

Table 7.2

Who Decides the Budget of the Household? (in percentage)

Residence	*Type of household*	*Fa-ther-in-law*	*Mother-in-law*	*Husband*	*Self*	*Brother-in-law*	*Son*	*Jointly*	*Total*
Rural	LJ	11	11	59	4	4	-	11	100(n=26)
	CJ	19	12	25	-	25	-	19	100(n=16)
	LCJ	26	12	25	-	-	12	25	100(n=8)
Total		8	6	21	1	5	1	8	50
		(16%)	(12%)	(42%)	(2%)	(10%)	(2%)	(16%)	100
Urban	SuNu	-	9	50	18	-	5	18	100(n=22)
	LJ	42	10	26	10	-	2	10	100(n=42)
	CJ	-	17	33	-	42	-	8	100(n=12)
	LCJ	38	6	19	6	-	-	31	100(n=16)
Total		24	9	29	9	5	2	14	92
		(26%)	(10%)	(32%)	(10%)	(5%)	(2%)	(15%)	100

of the property. When this is the case they have the tendency to keep the cooking arrangement only joint. This is also convenient for those who have a small plot of land from which the demand for vegetables, serials can be met at least partially. But since the amount of land is not adequate, they are required to have some other source of cash income as well which is kept under the control of the individual earners from which many of their needs, for instance, those for dress, medicine, children's education, milk (when people can afford), entertainment of friends and their wives' relatives, offering gifts, etc., are realised. In the village, it has also been seen in a few CJ type of households that some of the brothers (those who are engaged in the cultivation of the ancestral land or in any business) deposit all their earnings in a common fund and spend from it jointly, while the rest of the brothers (those who have individual source in income) share the hearth only in lieu of a specific amount of monthly contribution. These latter brothers meet their other expenses individually. Thus, within the same household different economic units work simultaneously. No such instance has been found in the town.

In the village, those households which do not own any piece of land and depend totally on the members' cash income, have displayed a special type of arrangement. Everyone of the brothers is assigned with the charge of supplying one or more items whose cash value is more or less equal. For instance, one brother may have the responsibility of bearing the expenses of rice, another brother of fuel and grocery, another with supplying the potato and green vegetables, and so on. Here, there is no head of the household determining the budget. Sharing of expenses is kept at a minimum level under such arrangement.

Let us come to the expenditure pattern on some common items. It seems that in both the village and the town members tend to expend individually on dress materials. It means that people generally choose and buy their clothes according to their own taste and purchasing power. This is so because there are so many varieties in design and price in this respet that people like to spend on this item according to their need, taste, standard and purchasing power. In the village, this has also been found that sometimes while dress for daily use of all the members is bought from the common fund, costly and fashionable dress is bought by the individuals themselves on their own.

In both the village and the town, it has been seen that while offering of gifts to the respondents' husbands' agnatic kin is regarded as an item in the common budget, that to their own natal kin generally becomes their (and their husbands') responsibility. Division in this respect is highest in the CJ households and lowest in the LCJ households. The father being generally the head of the LCJ households, has the obligation to maintain the relationships of give-and-take with the relatives. That is, invitations are issued in his name and he has the obligation to honour the same. Either he himself should do it or in case he is unable, others in the household should assist him in doing so. In CJ households, however, there being no such head in this sense, invitations are extended to the brothers separately who have the obligation to meet them on their own.

A pattern noted among the urban joint households is that expenditure on health and medicine and on children's education is generally borne by the respective brother/son. Like dress, here also persons spend according to their own capacity and level of aspiration. In the village, this tendency is not very notable since villagers who are generally poor and are themselves poorly educated, mostly are less serious about their health and their children's education. Their capacity and consciousness to regularly spend on these items are less than the urbanites. However, those villagers who are a bit enlightened and better-off, do not depend on the household budget for these, and individually spend on these items. In the village, it has also been seen that though in case of petty illness people take care of themselves, when they become seriously ill, they are assisted by their relatives—from both inside and outside the household. However, these are outside the regular budget allotments.

Division in respect of expenditure on buying milk is greater in the village than in the town. Here also poverty of the villagers is a major reason. In most of the village households milk is not included as a regular food item even in case of children. Hence, those who like to consume milk regularly, have to buy it out of their own fund. Sometimes even when some members of the respondents' households (mother-in-law or the daughter-in-law) have milchy cow, it is regarded as their own property and individual source of income. They themselves are in their charge, look after the animals and enjoy earnings from them. If other members like to consume milk, they have to buy it in cash as ordinary buyers.

It means that whatever financial arrangements are to be made, are done among the malefolk who are in charge of providing for the household, and the earnings of the wives are their own and not to be deposited to the common fund of the household. Urban ladies also enjoy such facilities when they earn something through private tuition, handicrafts, etc.

A major difference observed among the respondents from the urban and rural households is in the mode of entertaining the guests. In the village, in the majority of the sample households (60%) individual members, and not the head of the household, are the hosts. Hence the expenditure on entertaining guests are to be borne by the persons concerned. That is, when the daughter-in-law's brother comes to the house, she (or her husband) should arrange for his tea and snacks. The joint kitchen would provide his meal only. Here also the reason is poverty. Villagers generally eat *muri* (parched rice) as their tiffin and there is no arrangement in most of the village households of regularly preparing tea and snacks in the kitchen. When need arises, as when a guest comes to the house, some sweetmeats are purchased from the market. Now when the question of immediate cash expenditure arises, this is to be done by the persons whose guest has come. In the town, on the other hand, as the kitchens have readymade arrangements for preparing tea and some fast food, entertainment of guests can be made from the kitchen. If only the guest is to be specially entertained, individuals become the host.

A feature noted in both the village and the town is that at both the places the economic solidarity among the CJ households is higher than that in the LCJ households. People mostly live in the CJ household out of their own choice and convenience and not for any social compulsion. And, when the household works as a solid, compact unit, it becomes more convenient to live in it. Hence, it is expected that the brothers in a CJ household who enjoy almost the equal status and share the responsibilities evenly among themselves, consciously will try to make their household a solid economic unit and minimise the uneconomic, useless expenditures. In the LCJ households, on the other hand, often people, particularly in the village, have to stay against their wishes for various reasons (already discussed). So they have a tendency to make the 'sharings' as little as possible and protect their autonomy and freedom as far as possible. This attitude becomes reflected in their pattern of expenditure as well. Often the respondents from these households have informed that they dislike cooking or the recipe, the lifestyle or the consumption pattern of their households, but are helpless, and so they are forced to make separate arrangements on their own whenever they face any difficulty. Thus, though the norm of commensality is not violated, sharing in other respects is indeed poor in these households.

However, the number of households where sharing has reached the minimum possible level, i.e., excepting the meals everything is separately arranged, is a few in both the town and the village. It shows that our joint households are yet to reach the status of the boarding houses or inns.

Table 7.1 presents the patterns of expenditure on some major items. Obviously, there are many more items on which a household is to spend. It is not possible to include all of them in this report, though data have been collected in this regard. We have tried to highlight the trend only, not to present the total picture of consumption patterns of the households.

The information regarding who distributes the economic responsibilities of the household among different members, under whose care members deposit their income (or portion of it), who keeps the account of the household and takes decision on the heads of expenditure is relevant for measuring the economic solidarity of a joint household. Also to be seen is whether it is the eldest male member of the household who is assigned with this responsibility and honour, or it is he who earns and contributes the highest amount to the family purse, enjoys this status. This information we assume to be relevant since the person who is entrusted with this charge is generally regarded as the 'effective' head of the household. We shall show whether there is any difference between rural and urban households and among different categories of the joint households in this regard. The relevant data have been presented in Table 7.2.

A difference has been noted among the rural and urban households in respect of the role and status of the fathers of the respondents' husbands. Urban fathers, it seems, enjoy a more vital role in this regard than their rural counterparts. This is so because urban elderly men are economically self-sufficient (having pension, income from rent, from family business interests, from savings and investments, etc.) compared to the rural men most of whom were marginal farmers, share-croppers, agricultural labourers, unskilled industrial labourers or self-employed in petty business like vending, small shop-keeping or the like. Obviously, they lack any savings and in their old age they are dependent on their sons. However, those fortunate few who own a substantial amount of land or enjoy a pension in the capacity of being ex-servicemen, can have a say in controlling the family purse.

Another difference noted is that the urban respondents' role in this regard is more prominent than their rural counterparts.

Still another fact should not be overlooked. In the village, in some (10%) cases brothers of the husband have been entrusted with this responsibility while in the city the corresponding figure is only 5 per cent.

On the whole, however, the picture that emerges is more or less similar in the village and the town. In both the areas, the most effective role is of the respondent's husband and then comes the role of his father and mother.

Another pattern observed equally among the rural and urban joint households is the tendency of taking decisions jointly. These households, mostly of the LCJ type, are 'democratic' in the sense that here the father takes decision in consultation with his sons. This occurs when the father has no regular income and it is the sons who are in charge of providing for the household.

What is to be noted is that malefolk of the household are generally entrusted with the task of handling the economic matters. Women, particularly in the village, are not generally regarded fit for this purpose. This is not at all a hopeful symbol for those who aspire for expanding the domain of women's decision-making, which is a step towards the emancipation and the enlightenment of our womenfolk. At the same time it indicates that so long the decision-making in the economic matters remains the privilege of the men, the future of the joint households also will be in their hand, contingent on their choice and interest.

What appears from Tables 7.1 and 7.2 is that most of the joint households in the sample do not work as solid and compact economic units in the sense that in majority of the households members do not deposit their earnings in a common purse from which their needs are satisfied. Nor does the eldest member of the household always control the budget.

On further analysis of data it has been found that in case of a substantial number of households the accounts and budget are under the control of a single person, not necessarily the oldest male member of the household, ensuring that all the members should follow, at least in respect of the major items of expenditure, a consistent and uniform pattern and standard. The number of such households in the village is 21 (42%) and in the town it is 41 (45%). Let us make a depth analysis of the internal arrangements of these households.

It appears that in both the village and the town the LJ households betraying economic solidarity are mostly run from the earnings of one person. In the sample, the number of such households is 12 in the village and 8 in the town. In the town, these households are mainly run by the father. In contrast, in the village it is the son who provides for these households. Here the father (or other members) either has no separate income or it is too meagre.

In some other LJ households, the pattern is that both the father and the son are engaged in the cultivation of the ancestral land or running the ancestral business, and none has any other individual source of income. Expenses are met from their joint income. Still, in a few other cases, both the father and the son have their separate sources of income a portion of which they contribute to a common fund from which expenses are realised.

It means, then, the economic solidarity of the LJ households depends on the extent that one person earns enough to bear the sole responsibility of the household. In the well-off households, the father mostly bears the liability of the household. He is/was generally a professional or a businessman or employed in a high rank in any office, and therefore, is financially solvent. If he can afford, he does not like to depend on the son or create any pressure on him to make any regular contribution. In these households, father remains the head of the household. This pattern has been noted mostly in the town. An opposite picture emerges in the poor households, mostly rural, where the father has no income and it is the son who is in charge of earning the bread. Obviously, here also all expenses are met from a single fund, that of the son who becomes the head of the household. In a smaller number of cases, mostly from the town, however, the economic responsibility is jointly borne by the father and the son.

A different picture is observed in case of the CJ households where married brothers share the same hearth and residence with or without dependants (e.g., widow mother, widower father, unmarried brother(s) and/or sister(s). Here all the brothers are earners and have to bear the responsibility of their wives and children and also of the dependants, if any. Generally, the trend observed in such households is that each of the brothers has separate source of income, none of them is dependent on the other, they contribute a specific amount of money to the common purse from which all the expenses are met. It is not necessarily the eldest brother or the brother who earns highest, who controls this common purse. When there is a good mutual understanding among the members, such households emerge as the most solid economic units. The number of such households is higher in the town than in the village since urbanites are better-off than villagers and to maintain such an arrangement a minimum degree of economic self-sufficiency and security (that nobody should be dependent on the others) are a necessity, which villagers often lack.

It appears that the LCJ households where parents live with more than one married son, bestow the least degree of economic solidarity. For maintaining this solidarity in such households the primary prerequisite is that the household should possess a property from which the expenses of the members can be served, or that all the earning members of the household (father and sons) be engaged in a common venture, that means, the source of income should be common, or that the head of the household (generally, the father) should be so much solvent that he can bear the sole or major responsibility of the household and need not create pressure on sons. But when members have independent source of income and are forced to remain joint, their co-operation and sharing will be minimal. They tend to share the hearth only. Structurally though these households are still undivided, functionally there are several (nuclear) units within each of them. Hence, in our sample we have found only a few LCJ type of households which display economic solidarity, and these few ones are provided from the undivided household property or the earnings of one person, the father.

It can be drawn, then, that unless there is economic solvency and security (existence of some property), the economic base of the LCJ households becomes weak, while the LJ households can still remain solid even when the household is economically insecure. For their survival, CJ households require that the brothers should have a regular income which should be more or less adequate, and also they (and their wives) should have mutual understanding and willingness to stay together. Anyway, the survival of the joint households is facilitated when members have economic security and the household owns some property.

In Table 7.3 the pattern of taking meal by the members of the joint households has been shown. The information is relevant in the present context since mealtime chat or discussions have a special implication indicating family solidarity. The family meal, specially, the main meal of the day, is a distinct aspect of the family's life. It holds the members of the household together over an extended period of time. The length of its duration and details of the occasion naturally vary from one household to another; but, in general, a meal should be an extended session of the household personnel with a relatively high rate of attendance. Mealtime is the family council time, particularly today when under the stress of the differing preoccupations of its members, the household is not likely to get together at any other time. In many households the dining table is the focal point for most of the family interactions (cf. Bossard and Boll, 1966, p. 136).

It is at the dining table that the household is most apt to be its true self. This may mean that it is at ease, relaxed, friendly,

Table 7.3

Pattern of Taking Meal in the Joint Households (in percentage)

Residence	*Type of household*	*Women and men eat in two batches*	*All members eat jointly most of the times*	*Members take meal according to their own convenience*	*Members take meal with their respective spouse and children*	*Total*
Rural	LJ	54	23	23	-	100(n=26)
	CJ	44	31	25	-	100(n=16)
	LCJ	64	-	25	12	100(n=8)
Total		26	11	12	1	50
		(52%)	(22%)	(24%)	(2%)	100
Urban	SuNu	14	18	68	-	100(n=22)
	LJ	19	10	64	7	100(n=42)
	CJ	42	8	50	-	100(n=12)
	LCJ	31	-	63	6	100(n=16)
Total		21	9	58	4	92
		(23%)	(10%)	(63%)	(4%)	100

enjoying itself. It may also be the household in haste, operating with direct bluntness, tense or at war. The family meal, in short, represents the household in action, focussed upon a common interest.

It is significant in any attempt to appraise the social significance of the family meal, to recall that its role is one of continuing repetition. Many households meet around the table three times a day; most households should do so at least once a day.

Finally, it is obvious that the social significance of the family meal and the role of the table talk would vary depending on the relationships among the household members, particularly in the context of a joint household where this mealtime offers unique scope for discussing various issues and events among the members. This is the occasion when the members present can exchange their views and experiences, can collect information on the well-being of the others, can be aware of various problems faced by the others, and also anybody can lodge complaint against the others and seek some adjudication. In short, provided there are close and cordial ties and understanding among the members, they should enjoy and earnestly feel the usefulness of this mealtime get-together. Each of them should try to be present there in time and if anybody is late, others should motivate him not to miss this mealtime assemblage (cf. Kapadia, 1959, p.88).

Our traditional joint families followed a specific norm of taking meal. Generally, the norm was that the children of the household should be fed first. The turn of the malefolk should come next.

Lastly, the womenfolk of the household used to take their meal. In a large family where there are several adult women, they choose to dine together where they could openly and freely discuss anything and everything excluding perhaps politics and national budget. Now they are in a relaxed mood since their husbands and children have already been served and have gone to rest.

These mealtime behaviours bear the norm of the traditional joint family. But in the present days where nearly all members are pre-occupied and busy, it is not always feasible to abide by the above pattern. At every stage we are modifying and adjusting ourselves under the changing circumstance and the mealtime behaviour is not exception. So it is not possible for all the members of a joint household to remain present during the mealtime session. Moreover, as egalitarianism and democratic values are now in vogue, it is an old fashion that different categories of members—children, men and women—should not dine together. Hence, to be realistic we have not rigidly followed the traditional norm of taking food as an indicator for measuring family solidarity. Still, considering the vital role of the mealtime behaviour, we have included this indicator in a somewhat modified form with a view to noting whether our respondents (and other members of their households) still enjoy this mealtime and whether there is any correlation between family solidarity and this enjoyment. Our supposition is: if members of the household have cordial ties and understanding with one another, they should try to find some time when they can sit together and freely talk to each other, and the mealtime offers the best opportunity for this. If it is not possible to arrange it during the lunch time, they can utilise the dinner time or the lunch time on holidays for this purpose.

On the other hand, when members of a joint household do not feel for attending the mealtime discussions even either at night or in holidays, and instead of taking the meal with the others, they are eager to take the meal according to their convenience only, or they show interest in sharing the meal privately with their spouses and children only, the weakening of the joint family bonds is indicated thereby. Thus, if the respondents report that they take meals in hours convenient to them, it symbolises that they are so much preccupied with their own business and motto and give primacy to their own interest and well-being that they do not bother to undermine the satisfaction obtained from the others' company, that they are not ready to share, or at least be sympathetic listeners of the others' problems and experiences. The above behaviour signifies that to these persons the appeal and charm of living in a joint household is weak or absent.

Further, compliance with the norm of commensality exists only in paper when sharing the hearth means that the cooking will be done in a common place while members will take food separately and privately with their own spouse and children. The spirit of the mealtime family gathering is totally absent here. Sometimes, these people have separate cooking arrangements too of their own where they prepare some additional dishes or delicious items for the tiffin or the meal. The pleasure of belonging to a joint household is absent in this case, and members see it only a botheration which they have to tolerate for some material gain, (e.g., to reduce the cost of living, labour, or to avoid the hazards of separate establishments, or to assert their rights on the ancestral property). These households are already in the process of nuclearisation.

Let us come to our findings. First, Table 7.3 shows a distinct difference between the rural and urban joint households in this respect. While an overwhelming majority of the urban respondents do not have the experience of mealtime assemblage, the majority of the rural respondents faithfully comply with the traditional joint family norm in this respect.

The pattern of taking food separately or according to the members' convenience has been observed more frequently in the urban households. Urban CJ households are an exception. This indicates that the solidarity of the CJ households is greater than other types of urban joint households at least in this respect.

One of the basic things which the family gives to its members is the satisfaction of "the desire for intimate response". Every normal human being aspires to be wanted, to be understood, to be appreciated, to be loved. It is these affectional bonds and satisfactions which bind a person to his/her family emotionally. These bonds between the members of the family are of vital interest under any circumstances of family life and become specially important under the growing complexity and impersonality of the social life. It is to be seen, then, with which member(s) in the household a person maintains these bonds.

It is a general supposition that with the strengthening of the romantic love between the husband and the wife, i.e., as more husbands will regard wives as their friends with whom they can share and discuss their problems, experiences, plans, programmes and aspirations, and depend on them for their emotional satisfaction, their attachment with their consanguineal kin will lessen to extent. In the same vein, it can be further assumed that with the expansion and intensification of the egalitarian values and norms of behaviour, the hierarchical role relationships on the basis of age and gender—a feature of the joint family authority structure—will be feeble and ultimately fade away. For, by definition, joint family is bound to nurture hierarchical role relationships and cannot survive when egalitarian and democratic values become strong and popular.

The present inquiry has collected following data to test the above assumptions:

(1) to whom the husband is more attached—his consanguineal kin or wife (Table 5.13);
(2) whether the wife desires his husband in the role of her guardian or friend (Table 6.1);
(3) whether the husband obliges his wife in this regard (Table 6.1);
(4) pattern of taking meal (Table 7.3);
(5) who accompanies the wife when she goes to the market for shopping;
(6) whether the husband accompanies the wife when she goes to any place of amusement or recreation; and
(7) whether the wife celebrates the *Bhatridwitiya* ritual in her husband's home or goes to her brother's place.

Tables 5.13, 6.1 and 7.3 have already been presented. In the following pages some more information will be presented.

It has been inquired with whom the respondents generally go for shopping—their husbands, husband's kin living within and outside the household, their own relatives, or with friends and colleagues. Data indicate some differences between the rural and urban respondents in this matter. Compared to rural wives, urban wives prefer a bit more to accompany their husbands.

Our data also indicate that urban women enjoy more freedom in this matter, and at least 12 per cent of them have reported that they go for shopping alone. This freedom is totally absent for the rural wives.

In both the places, however, the tendency for going to shopping with wives' own relatives, (e.g. their mother, sister) or with friends and colleagues is negligible.

It has also been seen from the data that in the village the tendency of going to shopping with husbands is highest among women belonging to the CJ households and lowest among those living in the LCJ households. Also, it is the wives in the former category who personally participate most in shopping while those living in the LCJ households mostly avoid going to the market.

It can be drawn from above that village women show more interest in personally going for shopping when their husbands accompany them, and the CJ households offer this scope most while the LJ and LCJ households where wives have to live with their parents-in-law, curtail this freedom to some extent. In CJ households, women are more free and independent as there are no parents-in-law who watch their movements and activities and from whom sometimes permission is to be taken for going out of the home. Often these elderly people do not like their daughters-in-law going to any public place or market place.

In the town, however, the freedom of women already being won to a great extent, the above feature is absent. Here the tendency of accompanying the husband while going out for shopping is more or less comparable in different types of joint households.

On the whole, then, as our data show, rural women are more traditional and conservative than their urban counterparts in the above matter.

We have data regarding with whom respondents generally go to the places of recreation and amusement like cinema, fair, exhibition and the like. It has been observed that urban wives, when they go at all to these places, go with their husbands. A substantial section of urban respondents, however, do not feel the urge for going to these places as in these days of electronic media when in each house (in our urban sample) there are TV sets or cable connection and sometimes VCR, VCPs also are used, they can enjoy at home and need not go outside for recreation.

Rural women, on the other hand, go to these places on a larger number. They go with their husbands, and contrary to the urban wives, they also go to these places with the other members of their husbands' households (26%).

Respondents from the rural CJ households mostly accompany their husbands when they go to these places, and this tendency is least observed among those from the rural LCJ households. Urban households do not show any such consistent pattern. Indeed, respondents from the urban LCJ households show quite an opposite trend. These women either do not go, but when they go, it is only with their husbands. Anyway, our data show that rural women living in the CJ households where there are no parents-in-law, enjoy freedom of movement more than the women living in the other varieties of rural joint households. As urban women are already enjoying more freedom, it does not matter much which category of households they live in.

Bhatridwitiya is a very popular and holy ritual celebrated by all the Bengali women wishing their brothers' prosperity, well-being and good health. Every girl or woman having a brother , even cousin, would celebrate this ritual irrespective of her age and pecuniary condition. Sisters invite their brothers at their residence, arrange a grand feast in their honour, and offer some gift according to their ability. Brothers also reciprocate and honour the invitation. The ritual cannot be celebrated only when brothers are abroad or there is a serious breach with them. Otherwise, generally both the parties—sisters and brothers—do not fail to falicitate this occasion and to rejoice.

In deference to the orthodoxy, married sisters should invite their brothers, and brothers should go to the sisters' place (when the latter are married). It is against the correct norm and an unpreferred practice that sisters should come to the brother's place to jubilate the occasion. That is, married women are required to rejoice this occasion with other female members (mother-in-law, sisters-in-law) in their husbands' household, and not in the company of their paternal home. One universal function of the performance of rites and rituals by the members of a group is that they reinforce, revitalise and rejuvenate the social solidarity among the members, and hence these events are to be performed along with the others. Thus, though the manifest function behind the celebration of this ritual is to elevate and refresh the ties between the sisters and the brothers, one of its latent function is to strengthen the ties and solidarity among the women in the household who should arrange and perform it jointly. Also, the brothers of each of the wives in a household would come to know one another thereby, and thus this festival creates an opportunity where representatives from several families can be familiar with each other.

Hence, we have included the mode of celebrating the *Bhatridwitiya* ritual as an indicator of the functional solidarity of the joint households. Its performance in the husband's residence has been supposed to indicate the collaboration and mutual understanding between the mother-in-law and the daughters-in-law or among the sisters-in-law. On the other hand, if wives show the tendency to perform the occasion in the company of their own relatives in their paternal house, the less is the understanding and co-operation among the members of the joint household.

Moreover, joint celebration of the ritual in the husband's place provides evidence in favour of the solidarity of the joint family from another angle too. It evinces the authority of the mother-in-law. More and more the rites and rituals are performed jointly and members are to participate therein, the authority of the head of the household also is betrayed and reinforced thereby. This is so because joint family solidarity is generally accompanied by hierarchical authority structure.

Our findings reveal distinct differences between the respondents from the village and the town so far as the mode of performance of this ritual is concerned. While 25 per cent of the urban respondents comply with the traditional norm, only 4 per cent of the rural respondents pay attention to the same. In the village, the general tendency is that either all the married women of the household go to the residence of their respective brothers for celebrating the ritual (42%) according to their own standard and choice, or some of them celebrate it at the husbands' place while others leave for their brothers' place (48%). It means that in the village the traditional norm of celebrating the ritual is only rarely honoured. Though the urban picture is not as such encouraging, it is relatively better than that in the village.

Another point of difference that emerges is that while there is a trend among the respondents from the urban LCJ households

(44%) to celebrate the ritual with their mother-in-law and/or sister(s)-in-law, rural respondents in the corresponding situation tend to go to their brothers' place (88%). In an urban LCJ household when the brother of the mother-in-law comes to the house, the daughters-in-law are often obliged to stay there. This shows that the urban mothers-in-law still enjoy some effective power over their daughters-in-law while their rural counterparts show weakness in this respect. This is consistent with the earlier findings.

In urban areas, not only the LCJ households, but the CJ households also appear to be more strongly organised when measured on this criterion. Not a single case has been found in the rural sample where all the sisters-in-law celebrate the ritual jointly, while 33 per cent of the urban CJ households do it. This occurs partly because of the income disparities among the brothers of the respondents' husbands and partly because of the weak bonds among the sisters-in-law.

Another feature which emerges from the data is that this ritual has ceased to be performed in many (about 28%) urban households. Women in these households either have no brother (a function of the implementation of the family planning measures) or brothers live abroad.

Anyway, the overall picture that emerges from above is that women generally tend to celebrate this ritual in their brothers' home in the company of their natal relatives (generally their sisters who also come to this place to join them) than with their mothers-in -law or sisters-in-law. Compliance with the traditional norm is the weakest among the rural joint households. Some of the urban LCJ and CJ households, however, still stick to this norm.

One more behaviour of the respondents has been noted as an evidence of their cordial ties and mutual understanding with the other members in their husbands' households, namely, the division or distribution or certain daily activities among themselves. It is our assumption that when members help each other in performing these tasks, they act as a compact work-unit; on the other hand, to the extent the members do these jobs by and for themselves (or for their spouse and children) only, the feeble family ties are evinced thereby.

Actually, in any household there are many such tasks where there is a scope for sharing or co-operation among one another. One household is one unit, and therefore, all the tasks performed within it—cooking, serving meals to the members, purchase of vegetables and other household items which are used for daily and frequent consumption, cleaning utensils, washing clothes, feeding children, looking after and coaching children, shopping, maintenance of ties with relatives, and so on—should be done from one centre. Member(s) who are in charge of performing a particular task, should do it for the whole of the household, rather than doing a part of it for himself/herself, his/her spouse and children only.

Though we have collected data on the mode of performing of many such household chores, we do not see it useful to present all these (whether these tasks are performed jointly) because these tasks being a part of our daily life, a minimum degree of sharing is to be followed in case of at least some of them. For example, commensality being the first and foremost condition of joint living, it is obvious that tasks related to cooking should be performed jointly. This may not be so, however, in relation to certain other activities, such as, serving meal, washing of clothes, looking after children, or shopping where there is a scope for following both the patterns—joint performance and separate performance. Hence, we have selected a few spheres of activities belonging to the latter category with a view to measuring whether there is mutual co-operation among the members in performing these tasks, or alternatively, whether the members do these tasks independently and separately.

To make the presentation manageable, we have limited our discussion to five spheres of activities only, namely, purchase of dress, washing of clothes, looking after babies, coaching or supervising children's education, escorting them to the school, and maintaining communication with the relatives who are directly related to all the members of the households such as respondents' husbands' parents' brothers and sisters or husbands' married sisters. Communications with the respondents' natal relatives have been kept outside this discussion since contacts with this category of relatives are usually done by the respondents themselves. The criteria for our choice are, first, these activities offer the scope for both joint and separate performance; and secondly, these are common and frequent tasks to be performed in any typical household.

It appears that there is least sharing in case of purchase of dress. Sometimes elderly respondents and/or their husbands also assume the responsibility for buying the dress material for all the members. In the village, the division in this sphere is more prominent than in the town. Here either members themselves or the head of the household (respondent's husband) do this job. In the town, in a few cases at least, other members also participate or help.

In the town, washing of clothes mostly is done by the persons concerned or by the maid servants. Only in a few cases other members share this job. In the village, however, co-members' help is obtained in the performance of this job in a greater number of cases. That is, division is less sharp in the village than in the town in this respect.

At both the places, the responsibility of looking after babies generally lies with the persons concerned. As expected, young respondents participate more in this task than the elderly ones.

Coaching or supervising children's education or escorting them to the school also is generally done by the persons concerned. Consequently, young respondents' participation in performing this task seems to be higher. In the town, in a few cases the help of the respondents' parents-in-law is obtained in this regard.

Some differences have been noticed between the respondents from the village and the town in respect of maintaining contacts or communications with the relatives, particularly those relatives who are regarded as 'common' to all the household members, e.g., parents' relatives, married sisters and their relations, etc. In the village, generally this is the responsibility of the malefolk (father and sons) or the elderly womenfolk (mother), while in the town the participation of the women members in this respect is a bit higher. The participation of the elderly people in general is higher than that of the younger members, and this has been noted in both the areas.

It seems, then, the task of maintaining contacts with relatives is assumed to be a task of the aged persons, while the young members, perhaps, show more interest in friends. If this is so, ties with the relatives are bound to be less frequent and irregular in the coming days. For the survival of the joint family feelings it is required that all members, particularly the young ones, should interact with the relatives, rather than leaving this function to the domain of the parents or the grandparents.

Solidarity of a joint household depends to a great extent on the members' willingness and efforts to protect its joint structure. On the other hand, solidarity weakens to the extent to which members are unhappy with the present form and wish to get relieved of it.

In the present inquiry we, therefore, have seen whether the respondents and members in their households are eager to keep up the present nature of their households, or alternatively, desire to part with them. Sometimes a member himself/herself may not desire separation, but others may not be willing to continue with him/her, and when this is the case the solidarity of the household is questioned. The question we put to the respondents for this purpose is: "Do you have any member in your household who likes to live separately, or who, you think, should separate?"

It has been observed, first, that respondents (or other members in their households) in general do not think that there is any such serious problem of adjustment or clash of interests among the members of their households that the household may disintegrate in the near future. Neither they themselves are planning to leave the household nor do they think that the presence of any member is seriously injurious to the peace and unity of the household. This feeling is more prevalent among the ruralites (72%) than among the urbanites (67%).

Still, some of the respondents have reported that their households may disjoin. Among this category of people, it is the respondents themselves who are thinking in terms of separation (10%). In the town, however, another 10 per cent of the respondents think that their husbands' brothers and/or their wives also are thinking in terms of being separated. Some of the respondents have expressed their desire to be separated from their daughters-in-law. In the town, their number is 9 per cent while in the village it is 6 per cent.

Next, it has been noted that those who have expressed their desire to be separated mostly belong to the urban CJ households. This may seem a bit baffling since this category of the households have appeared to be relatively compact when measured in terms of some other indices which suggest that some sort of understanding prevails among the members of these households. Actually, these respondents who are thinking in terms of separation have never expressed their satisfaction with the existing arrangement. They only try to make their living somewhat peaceful. Also, even when one brother fails to adjust and wants to separate but the rest are desirous of maintaining the solidarity, a CJ household is not in danger.

Respondents from the LCJ households also have admitted the existence of some problems in their households. Respondents from 62 per cent of the rural and 50 per cent of the urban LCJ households have expressed that it would have been better if they or some other members were separate.

The above finding is consistent with our earlier observations that compared to other categories of the joint households in general the degree of solidarity is relatively low in the LCJ category, and that it is still lower in the village.

It can be drawn, then, that the possibility of disintegration remains relatively strong in case of the LCJ and CJ households compared to the LJ and SuNu ones. It confirms our notion that generally women do not face the problems of adjustment with their parents-in-law as with the other kin of their husbands, e.g., husbands' brothers and their wives.

A fact is to be noted here. A deeper analysis of our data shows that the LJ households in the sample which generally face the problem of adjustment are mostly supplemented by some other members as well. That is, excepting the parents, their son and daughter-in-law (i.e., the respondent), there remain other persons as well, e.g., unmarried son(s), daughter(s), any relative of the parent(s), etc., and in some cases the respondents have expressed their unwillingness to continue with such kin. That is, adjustment is not generally difficult between the parents and their son and the daughter-in-law when there is no other adult person in the household.

Still another fact needs to be pointed out. In a substantial number (26%) of urban SuNu and LJ households the respondents' husbands are the 'only son' of their parents. In at least 6 of these cases, a possibility has been noted where the household faces the problem of disintegration. It has already been pointed out that in 15 per cent of the urban nuclear households husbands are the 'only son' whose parents are still alive and live separately. It shows that the problem of adjustment may occur in the small households as well. However, maladjustment and clash of interests and personalities occur more often and in greater intensity when there is a larger number of persons in the household. Since with each addition of members the number of interrelationships and interactions will correspondingly multiply and the problems of adjustment also augment to that extent, greater care needs to be taken in such circumstances to maintain peace and solidarity in the household. Anyway, our data unmistakenly suggest that even when the sons are the only son of their parents and there is no other person to take care of the parents or share their responsibility, the daughters-in-law (and also the sons) are being separate or are thinking in terms of separation. Having only one son is, therefore, no deterrent to family disintegration.

We have presented how many of our respondents are thinking for parting with their husbands' stem families. At the same time, one should discuss, to make the story complete and vivid, the contexts and reasons behind this thinking. Hence, we decide to quote our respondents in their own words which, we think, will be self-explanatory and reveal the story beneath the surface.

Let us first look into the statements of the rural respondents living in the CJ households:

"My husband's second brother does not properly bear his share of the economic liabilities of the household. Also I myself and other brothers-in-law desire to separate. But it is because of the mother-in-law that her sons do not dare to split."

"The wife of my husband's youngest brother wants to separate because it is her strong belief that she has to toil hard. Also, the preparation of food is not according to her taste. Her husband, however, does not like to separate since the third brother of the husband (at present the head of the household) has declared that so long the mother is alive whoever will separate, will have to leave the house simultaneously and also will not get any share of the ancestral land.

"I myself intend to separate, but I am helpless since the occupation my husband is engaged in is joint with his elder brother. He is a simpleton, is extremely gullible and hence is unable to run the business independently. Also, my brother-in-law is the head of the joint household and keeps all the earnings with himself (or his wife). So we are fully dependent on them."

"The wife of my husband's third brother wishes to separate, but her husband does not like it. She is not in the good book of my mother-in-law since her marriage with my brother-in-law was self-arranged and my mother-in-law did not like it."

Let us turn to the situation prevailing in the rural LCJ households:

"It would have been better if the wife of my husband's eldest brother were separate. Her husband earns highest and bears the major responsibility of the household, which is not liked by her. For this she always boasts, often becomes insolent, obstinate, has vanity and does not like to mix and talk freely with the others. She often neglects her assigned role in the performance of the household chores. In short, she displays her dissatisfaction and non-co-operation in every possible way. But since her husband respects and fears his mother, she fails to convince him of separation."

A respondent from another supplemented LCJ household likewise reports that she herself and the second brother of his husband like to separate. The household is large; her husband has four brothers, and he is the third of the five brothers. Three of the brothers (including her husband) are married. The household possesses a substantial amount of arable land, and the second and the youngest brothers are in its charge. The father of the respondent's husband who is still the head of the household, keeps the account of the produce of the land. The problem of the second brother is that though he is given a weekly allowance of Rs. 50 by the father (in addition he is spared of all other expenses), he is not satisfied and does not feel secure with this arrangement. He feels that he has no security for the future since he has no savings and no other source of income. Though he devotes all his labour and time to the cultivation of the ancestral land, the earnings go to the father on whom he is totally dependent. In his absence when the land is equally divided among all the five brothers, his share will be inadequate to meet all his expenses. So he feels that it is high time for him to get separated, for in that case he can find out any alternative or supplementary source of income, as has been done by his other brothers. The father, however, is not willing to release him since in that case the land, he is afraid, will not be properly cultivated. This second brother of the respondent's husband twice earlier tried to part with and both the times his father persuaded him to rejoin him. But his grudging continues. The respondent herself also wishes to separate but on different ground. She feels that she is not being a gainer in any respect by remaining in the joint family. Since her husband is in service and has cash income, he does not get any share from the income from the land. In lieu of a specific contribution, he only shares the common hearth, and all other expenses are to be borne by her husband himself. Thus, though all the five brothers live under one roof, the styles of living is unsatisfactory. But nothing can be done at this moment since her husband cannot disobey his father and cannot say or do anything in defiance of the paternal authority.

Another respondent from the rural LCJ household who herself is a mother-in-law and lives with her three married sons reports, "The wife of my second son desires to separate. The workplace of the son is in Kolkata and he comes back home only in the weekend. He bears the cost of the rice consumed by the whole of the household. But he does not take food at home throughout the week; only his wife and sons take meals on all the seven days of a week. So his wife thinks that her husband's share of the economic liability is disproportionate to what she consumes. My son, however, is not willing to oblige his wife."

Respondents from the rural LJ households have referred to some other grounds as reasons for seeking separation. One such respondent who belongs to a supplemented LJ household reports that she herself wants to separate since she utterly resents the behaviour of her husband's mother and brother. Her mother-in-law is of excessively dominating type and does not permit her to go outside the home. Her brother-in-law is a drunkard and creates disturbances. However, her desire for being separate cannot be materialised since her husband's earnings are not adequate to maintain a separate establishment. Also, if they get separated, they will have to leave the house.

Another respondent from a similar type of household explains, "I myself intend to separate because the atmosphere of this home is not congenial to my child's education. Because of frequent sickness of my mother-in-law, I have to assume the major responsibility of the household chores, and this load is so excessive that I cannot find time to supervise my daughter's studies and coach her. But I am helpless since my husband is only a petty hawker. His income is irregular and inadequate for maintaining a separate establishment."

Another respondent belonging to a supplemented LJ household also holds the excessive load of the household chores responsible for her desire to be separate. This is a big farmer's household where the women have to help in farming activities as well in addition to their routine household chores. However, her problem is that her mother-in-law is extremely lazy and does not like to do any work. But her father-in-law is unwilling to get his other sons married. If husband's brothers were married, their wives might share with the respondent the burden of the household chores. He apprehends that the incoming brides might split up the household. Consequently, the heavy workload seriously falls upon her health. She feels very weak and cannot supervise her children's education. Another difficulty faced by her is that her father-in-law does not like that any of her relatives comes to his house. He suspects that she passes clandestinely large quantities of rice and vegetables to her parent's home through them. She is not even permitted to give any gift to her relatives, though she can afford. However, since her husband's (who works as a compositor in a press) income is not adequate, he cannot take the risk of getting separated. Besides, if separated, they will have to forego the share of the ancestral property and the house as well.

What appears from above is that in the village the economic factor is the prime cause which both encourages and discourages family disintegration. It acts as a deterrent when the parties are unable to afford the cost of separate establishments, or when they apprehend that they will be deprived of their share in the ancestral property in case they separate. On the other hand, members feel the urge for separation when their economic status is better than that of the others in the household and they think that the joint living is becoming a liability for them as they have to assume the liabilities of the others depriving themselves. Of course, there are other factors as well which motivate separation such as excessive workload, lack of individual freedom, differences of taste from the other members in the household, but these factors are less frequently reported than the economic factor. Only a few respondents have reported their dislike of their parents-in-law. Maladjustment with their husbands' brothers' wives has often been reported in the CJ and the LCJ households. Another noteworthy fact is that though the wives insist on separation, their husbands are not often ready to oblige them because of their poor economic condition or lack of confidence that they would be able to provide for their wives and children. Sometimes because of their attachment towards their family of origin they are unwilling to separate.

Let us compare the rural situation with the urban situation where the socio-economic condition is much different from that in the former.

A widow respondent from an urban supplemented nuclear household who lives with her son, incidentally the son is her only issue, informs that her daughter-in-law occasionally insists on her son's being separated. Her son, however, does not attach any importance to what his wife says. Being the only son, he is conscious of his duty towards the mother when the father has passed away.

Though the above experience is typical in most of the households of this category, certain other kinds of events also sometimes occur. In the words of one such respondent whose allegation is against her widower father-in-law: "I wish my father-in-law should live separately because it is difficult to adjust with him for his cantankerous nature." In another case, the charge is raised against the unmarried brother-in-law: "My brother-in-law drinks and does not behave properly. Nor does he regularly contribute to the family purse. He should be separated, I wish."

It appears, then, members of SuNu households want to separate only when there are serious differences of taste or clashes of personality. Otherwise, compared to the other categories of joint households, this type is more or less tied and safe.

Let us turn to the urban LJ type of households which may or may not be supplemented by the respondents' husbands' other relatives like his (unmarried/widow/widower) uncle or aunt, brother or sister.

A respondent from an LJ household who herself is a mother-in-law, states: "My daughter-in-law desires to separate, but retreats since it will be costly at the same time." In this household the father (the respondent's husband) shoulders the major share of expenses for the household. The son bears only the costs of dress and medicine of his own, his wife and children. Here the economic factor works as a deterrent to the son's seeking separation.

Another mother-in-law who lives with her 'only son', expresses, "It would have been better if my son and his wife were separate, but they themselves are not willing. It is from the earnings of my husband that the household is mostly provided". What to be noted is that though the son is the only son, the mother is seeking partition with him. The interesting fact is that the economic factor here both encourages (mother's behaviour) and discourages (son's behaviour) partition.

Both the above cases are typical and several such cases have been found in the present sample.

Another respondent who lives with her son and the son is the 'only son', opines, "My daughter-in-law intends to separate since she suffers from an inferiority complex, but my son is not at all eager." This lady is highly educated and was posted in a high rank of the Indian railway service. The daughter-in-law is only moderately educated, nor is she economically active. In another case where the daughter-in-law is the respondent, has stated, "I feel the need for separation from my mother-in-law since she always tries to guard my husband (who is her only child). It is disgusting to me." The bone of contention in the last two cases is the clash of personalities between the mother-in-law and the daughter-in-law, which also is a very common factor in the joint households, particularly of the LJ type.

Another type of problem is faced when the household is supplemented by other relatives. One such respondent whose husband is the only child informs, "My mother-in-law is very insistent on keeping her widow sister in the household. But that lady is a maniac and neurotic. I do not at all like to a live with that lady."

In the above case, the conflict is not directly between the parents and the son and/or the daughter-in-law but between the respondents and the dependants of their parents-in-law, particularly the dependants of the mother-in-law. It means that though women anyhow accept and adjust with their husbands' parents, they are against taking the liability of parents' relatives and more so when these relatives are economically dependent. This is also a typical event and similar other cases have been found in the sample.

Let us turn to the urban CJ households: A respondent from the CJ household supplemented by the widow mother-in-law comments, "The wife of my husband's second brother intends to separate but retreats since she lacks ability and courage to shoulder the responsibilities for leading a separate or nuclear family of her own." Another respondent in a similar context reports, "I myself want to separate since my sister-in-law does not equally share the household chores. Accordingly, my workload becomes unbearable."

It appears that a common bone of contention in the CJ households relates to the division of household chores among the sisters-in-law. If somebody fails to do her assigned tasks, problems crop in.

Problems may crop up on other grounds as well. As one of the respondents informs, "It would have been better if my husband's elder brother were separate with his wife and children. Since his income is low, my husband is to bear his liabilities. As a result, my children are being deprived; I cannot arrange for them the best possible diet, education, schooling, etc., according to my capacity, standard and aspiration."

In a similar context another respondent states, "The wife of my husband's second brother intends to disjoin. She has only one son and I have three daughters. She thinks that she has to spend more than what she along with her husband and son consumes."

It shows that in the CJ households where the economic statuses of the brothers are unequal, the brother who earns the highest, will have a tendency to be separate. Clash of personalities, interfering or bossing in-laws are not the most serious problems here. Rather, the presence of the widow mother or widower father works as a deterrent to family disintegration since, if other conditions are not too uncongenial, sons prefer to remain joint till the parents, even either of them, are alive.

A somewhat different picture emerges if we analyse the internal arrangements of the urban LCJ households. A respondent from a large LCJ household which has a depth of four generations (i.e., husband's cousins also live jointly) and has 18 members, conveys, "The wife of one of my husband's cousins finds it difficult to adjust with our giant household. She is employed while we, the other sisters-in-law, are housewives. She wants to separate but her problem is that her husband is posted outside West Bengal. Hence if she parts, either she will have to live alone or leave her job for joining her husband in the latter's place of work."

Though the above case is not typical, it is mentioned because of its special dimension. It shows that the integrity of a large LCJ household is possible if only members are sincere to protect the same. Also, it is not a fact that people always dislike large households.

Let us come to the problems which injure the integrity of the LCJ households. One respondent living in such a household opines, "I wish my husband's youngest brother should separate along with his wife and children. He contributes less than others to the family fund. Moreover, my father-in-law is biased in his favour since he does not ask him to share the economic burden of the household equally with other sons."

This is a typical case and several other LCJ households have been found in the sample which face problems due to conflict among the brothers over the disproportionate sharing of the economic liability by some of them, and/or alleged partiality of the head of the household (usually, the parents) for his allegedly deliberate failure in being just to all the sons and daughter-in-law. Still, there are other grounds of conflict as well.

A respondent narrates her problem in a somewhat different way: "I like to separate because of my bitter relationship with my mother-in-law. Moreover, neither our living in the joint household is helpful from the economic aspect since we have to share fully all responsibilities, nor does it save my time and labour. Workload is here backbreaking and that is why I hardly find time to coach my daughter.

A similar opinion has been expressed by another respondent who works as a clerk in a nationalised bank: "I find no reason in living together since it means nothing else than sharing one hearth and living under one roof. I have no sentimental ties or feeling for the members of my husband's household. We live here simply as paying guests. Nothing is done or held jointly. I have an *ayah* for looking after my son, and if she is absent, either I have to absent myself from my office or keep my son under the care of my mother. So I get neither any physical help from the others nor any financial support. Excepting that for the meals, I have to bear separately all the other expenses. So much so that even when my son wants to eat an omelette, I have to buy it from outside or prepare it myself.

From the extracts presented above some hints about the problems faced by the urban LCJ households may be obtained. First, the head of the household, generally the father, is required to play an impartial and authoritative role in relation to all the other members. He will not be excessively affectionate to any of the sons, and will be fair and just in distributing the economic liabilities among the sons and household chores among the womenfolk of the household. The LCJ households are the largest in size. As both the parents are alive the frequency of visits by the relatives is likely to be high in such households. For the same reason the married daughters will more frequently come to such households and stay for a couple of days here. Thus, the members of the LCJ households are to be specially skilled and careful in adjusting with various types of people. The workload of the women members also is heavy here because of frequent visits of guests and relatives. Often it is not possible to follow a regular routine of work. Hence, the working wives have to face real difficulties in such households particularly when all or most of the daughters-in-law are not employed. The working wives cannot devote as much time to the household as is given by their non-working counterparts. And, for this inability often they are criticised and accused. They are called to be selfish or at the least self-centred. They, it is alleged, exploit others in the household to serve their own interest. Whatever they earn is used by them for their own purpose. Those who share their household work do not get any share of their income. So why should the others share their part of the burden of the household chores?

Besides, like the wives, sons/brothers are not often happy with their respective duties and liabilities. When the household is run mainly from the earnings of the sons, they often do not find such households as convenient and suitable.

Let us try to summarise and see whether any pattern of behaviour emerges.

It is our observation that unless the household possesses a substantial amount of property (land, business) from the earnings of which most of the expenses of its members can be provided, or unless one person assumes the responsibility of meeting the major expenses of other members in the household so that they are relieved from making any regular and substantial contribution to the family purse, the joint households, particularly the LCJ type, generally do not act as a solid, unified unit. What has been found is that in joint households generally cooking is done in one hearth while expenditures on many other items, for instance, dress and milk, health and medicine, children's education, entertaining friends and relatives, providing gifts to relatives, are in various degrees borne individually by the members according to their respective capacity, taste and standard. Often it is noted that within one joint household several economic units are functioning, and instead of one family purse where the earnings of all members should be deposited, accounts are maintained and decisions on expenditures are taken by several centres comprising the husband-wife-children groups. This is the pattern when members have independent sources of income and they mainly depend on their individual income for making their living.

Compared to the LCJ and LJ type of households, the economic management of the SuNu and CJ types of households seems to be relatively compact, but on different grounds. In the SuNu households it is generally the son who is in charge of providing for the household and hence there is little division of expenses. The CJ households, on the other hand, survive when brothers consider and calculate that this type of living arrangement will be convenient and economic. Hence members in CJ households consciously try to increase the economic viability and compactness of the household. However, when there are any social or other types of pressures, such as the presence of the widow mother or widower father against whose disapproval sons cannot quit the stem family, the economic solidarity of such households may weaken.

Overall, the economic solidarity of the joint households is weaker in the village than in the town.

The solidarity of the households is poor in respect of following a harmonious division of labour or distribution of household chores as well. Excepting the tasks related to cooking, in other spheres members' mutual co-operation or joint participation is on the whole minimum. Rather than performing the jobs for the whole of the household members either do them for themselves (and their spouses and children), or depend on the hired help.

Members' lack of commitment to the traditional joint family values is evident in their behaviour in certain other respects also. Urban people now pay little regard to the mealtime discussions and talks. Instead of taking meal with other members of the joint household, they generally take either according to their own convenience or with their own spouse and children. This is not so, however, in the village where the respondents mostly take meal either with other women members (men take meal with other male members), or all the members have lunch/dinner together. In another respect, i.e., while going to the market for shopping or to the places of amusement or recreation centres also rural respondents are more often accompanied by the members of the husbands' household. Urban respondents, on the other hand, overwhelmingly prefer their husbands' company on such occasions.

Urban respondents, however, show a bit more respect to the traditional norm of celebrating the holy *Bhatridwitiya* ritual than their rural counterparts. While the rural respondents almost en masse celebrate this ritual in their brothers' place, which practice is against the scriptural norm or prescription, the behaviour of a little more urban women is conformist in this respect, i.e., a relatively higher number of urban women celebrate this occasion with other women in their husbands' household.

When the respondents were asked whether they sought separation from any member(s) of their existing households, they, however, have mostly answered in the negative, and this opinion has been expressed by a higher number of rural than urban respondents. Further, this opinion is shared more by residents of the SuNu and LJ households than those from CJ or LCJ households. It shows that people who at present live in the joint households on the whole do not intend to bring alteration in their household structure. Though they have sometimes expressed their dissatisfaction and inconvenience on several grounds and also have modified the traditional norms in many ways to suit their present requirements, most of them think the present arrangement workable.

Respondents from the LCJ households, however, do not belong to this category. Unless there is economic support and benefit, members do not like to live in such households. The CJ households as such are not a desired type, but members' grievances and dissatisfactions in the CJ households are less than that in the LCJ households since the survival of the former rests on mutual convenience and understanding. Whenever members feel this arrangement unpaying, they are free to disjoin without any serious repercussions in the circle of the relatives and neighbours. This is not so for the LCJ households for various reasons (discussed in detail). And, that is why members' dissatisfactions with and dislike for the LCJ households is highest. Moreover, in the absence of the parents-in-law, wives in the CJ households enjoy more freedom of action and movement. These households are more democratic and the LCJ households are mostly authoritarian. The LJ households in general are not disliked provided there is a good understanding between the mother-in-law and the daughter-in-law. The former should not be too bossing or domineering or jealous of the daughter-in-law or try to guard her son from the daughter-in-law. The latter, on the other hand, should not be selfish or self-centred and have a strong longing for living in a small household of her own.

It appears that quarrels, strives and dissentions due to economic factor are common to all types of joint households in both the village and the town. Its gravity is more felt in the village households because of their poverty. For the same reason the workload of the women members of the large joint households in the village becomes still heavier because villagers cannot take the help of the labour-saving devices or can hire help from outside. However, the allegation that parents-in-law are not impartial or just has been heard from both the rural and urban LCJ households.

The LJ households particularly face the clash of personalities between, or mutual dislike of, the mother-in-law and the daughter-in-law, and this is more evident in the urban than in the rural LJ households. It is not that the village women do not face this problem. But because of their financial infirmity, they have to tolerate all these things.

Our typical observation is that when the father bears the major economic responsibility of the household, members do not like to separate. Also, when the economic status of all the brothers is more or less comparable and they can make an equi-distribution of all the liabilities among themselves, they do not intend to disjoin provided there is no serious problem among the sisters-in-law over the division of household chores.

One more fact to be noted is that in general wives are more eager to separate than their husbands. Hence, it has often been conveyed by the respondents that though they desire to part with, their husbands hesitate or are unwilling. It follows from above that the joint family is an important component and pillar of the patriarchal social system. More and more women will be conscious and assertive of their rights and succeed in persuading their husbands to accept or even cognise their viewpoints, the bonds of the joint family will be inactive and stagnate to that extent.

8

Mobility and Joint Family Solidarity

I

Since Parsons argued (1949, pp. 191-92) that the relatively isolated nuclear family is the most functional type for the democratic industrial society, a popular point at issue among the family sociologists is whether the extended family would survive in a geographically and occupationally mobile society. The issue seems to be further complicated since it is hypothesised that both these types of mobility are interrelated, and they are closely associated with industrialisation. Later on, other researchers (e.g., Goode, 1963) elaborated the above hypothesis of Parsons taking evidence from the empirical world. Goode has concluded that under the impact of industrialisation and urbanisation conjugal family is being more favourite and that the kindred and lineage are losing most of their functions. Still, it seems impossible to cut down the size of the family to its nuclear core only either in the West or in any other society without some type of political or coercive force. Thus, there remain additional kin who are included because of a direct emotional tie with some members of the nuclear core, a tie supported by the institutional structure. And, it is impossible to eliminate these additional kin ties without disrupting the nuclear family itself (1963, pp. 370-71).

Family sociologists of the 1950s and 1960s working in the cities of America, Canada, Great Britain and Western Europe, however, sharply reacted to the above hypothesis. They have presented many counter-evidences to show that the extended family instead of being disintegrated is becoming more significant to the individual because of the difficulty in developing satisfactory primary relationship outside the family in an urban environment. Furthermore, visits, get-together, exchange of gifts and goods and services among kin outrank similar interaction patterns among friends, neighbours and co-workers. Litwak (1960a, 1960b, 1965) has shown that the 'modified extended family' is being the prevalent family pattern, since it does not require geographical propinquity and since occupational and social mobility does not weaken this type of family.

The conclusions of Litwak can be reduced to five major propositions:

1. that the extended family exists in the modern urban society, at least among the urban middle class;
2. that extended family relations are possible in an urban industrial society;
3. that geographical propinquity is not a necessary condition of these relationships;
4. that occupational mobility is unhindered by these activities; such activities as advice, financial assistance, etc., can be interchanged among mobile persons; and
5. that the classical extended family of the rural society or its ethnic counterpart is unsuitable to modern society, and on this point Litwak agrees with Parsons. Neither is the isolated nuclear family the most functional type. The most functional is what he calls the 'modified extended family'. He is, however, against dichotomising all families as either nuclear or extended, and, instead, tries to popularise his concept of modified extended family.

Inquiries into the patterns and kinds of exchanges of aid among kin were a favourite research topic among the family sociologists of the West during the 1950s and the 1960s. Axelrod, for example, concludes: "The extended family may have lost its function as an economic producing unit in the city, but relatives continue to be an important source of companionship and mutual support" (1956, p.17).

Bell and Boat also hold that compared to neighbourhood and co-workers, kin are generally more important in each neighbourhood by all the measure of informal participation used (1957, p.391).

Bell has made a detailed empirical inquiry into the kinds of interactions among the British socially and geographically mobile middle class families. He emphasises, "It is central to my argument that middle class extended family aid is not dependent upon crisis and ceremonial; and that it is not only on these occasions that the middle class extended family is a functioning social entity but that it works continually..." (1968, p.88). Aid may be exchanged directly, for example, in pursuing or advancing careers, purchase of a house or looking after children, or it may be given in indirect form as through children, i.e., from grandparents to grandchildren. Extended family aid often is used to provide important status and helps in the purchase of status signs (precious furniture, household gadget and equipment). Another mechanism frequently utilised by the families, as has been noted by Bell, is the giving of aid on socially approved occasions, such as wedding. This is acceptable and can be received without any loss of independence.

Sussman has made empirical inquiries into the aid patterns of the American middle class families (1953; 1970). His conclusions are similar to those of Bell. In an investigation he observes that the majority of the nuclear family units in his sample are in a propinquitous and functionally integrated kin network which cuts across caste, race, occupation and education, suggesting the existence of a pervasive social system with the *gesellschaft* characteristics of modern urban society (1970, p. 485).

On an intensive analysis of his data, he further notes that the relations of nuclear families to kin in his sample approximate Parsons' onion ring structure. The greatest number of kin are in the inner ring composed of parents' sibs and children's family units. As one moves from the intermediate ring of grandparents' and sibs' children's and grandchildren's family units to the outer ring of cousin's and other relatives' family units, the number of contacted kin declines (1970, pp.485-86).

Blood has discussed in detail the nature and type of exchange of aid among kin (1970). He has also inquired into (1) the relationship between exchange of aid and geographical and social mobility of the incumbents, or, the economic progress of the society through large-scale industrialisation; and (2) the future trends of interactions within the kin network. He finds that large-scale industrialisation by virtue of corporate size overshadows that potential significance of kin groups (p.195). He sees a close analogy between the impact of spatial mobility and social change. Ordinarily kin ties thrive under conditions of social stability. By contrast, we normally assume that social change undermines kin ties. At the same time he notes that the relationship between kinship and social change is not wholly linear. When the broader social environment collapses, people are thrown back on more immediate resources which means on their kin ties (p.197).

Blood has developed certain trends in the kinship interaction. He draws: "Today the trend is away from the kindred as a social organisation to kin as a category of people" (p.199). Hence, a boundary line, though arbitrary, develops between the 'nominal' kin and 'effective' kin.

Next, a tendency from unilineal to bilineal kinship interaction is noted. With the breakdown of monolithic kin group systems, nuclear families are forced to interact with the kin of either spouse. The usual result is that networks of effective kin become bilateral. Under some modern circumstances, they even acquire a matrilateral bias. The latter rarely goes as far to exclude contact with the husband's kin. Rather insofar as females become the chief performers of modern kin functions, the personal ties of the wife with her family of orientation give interaction a matrilateral emphasis.

Another important trend noted by Blood is what he calls is "from hierarchical kin structure to diffuse equality". The trend of change is away from hierarchical organisation. In today's kin networks, very little power is exercised (on the basis of age-grading, for example). Where power occurs, it is seldom based on the power-wielder's status in the kinship but flows from his personal attributes or his status in external systems.

Another important trend is from 'hard' functions to 'soft' functions. Political and economic functions (specially productive economic activities) are dwindling kinship functions as the world urbanises and industrialises.

Lastly, a trend has been noted from 'obligation' to 'choice', a lessening role of ascriptive obligations in determining kin behaviour. Whereas hierarchical structure, for example, obligates high status members to assume responsibilities of low status members to conform loyally, members of modern kin networks are free to choose whether they will interact at all and if so how and with whom. By definition, the choice is not unlimited. Most of the world falls outside the category of kin. But within that broad category, there is freedom to choose which relatives will become effective kin.

Literature on family sociology in India lacks such detailed and intensive analysis of interactions and exchanges within the kinship network. Most of the Indian family sociologists have just mentioned about the existence of functional solidarity among the kinship group (namely, the joint family). Thus, any critical and intensive analysis of the evidences of functional solidarity such as patterns and degrees of exchange of aid among the kindred is lacking in our literature on family sociology. A few notable exceptions, of course, are there. Desai (1955), for instance, has examined in some detail the types of exchanges of aid among the kin (*kutumba* or *kula*) which are generally fulfilled during the ceremonies. In the writings of some other writers, for instance, Ishwaran (1974), Sarma (1964, p. 196), Shah (1998, p.94) also we get some references about this event. Chekki (1974) has analysed in detail the functional ties and patterns of interactions among kin in the urban context. He assumes that the nature and extent of social interaction between kin can be measured through an examination of the exchange of services among them (p.51). In this context, he has analysed, first, which category of kin is regarded as the 'intimate' or effective kin, and secondly, which type of interactions or contacts are maintained with which type of kin. He has also tried to analyse whether these contacts and interactions decrease when some of the kinsmen are spatially and socially mobile.

II

It appears, then, that the exchange of help and services is the life-blood of the kin system. However, the relationship between the exchange of aid and the class position of the givers and recipients of aid is yet to be adequately explored. Also, it is to be inquired whether such interchanges increase or decrease with the spatial dispersion or proximity of the kinsmen.

In Chapters 5, 6 and 7, we have shown the degree of functional solidarity as is currently displayed in the opinion and behaviour of the women members (respondents) of our families. In the present chapter, we shall try to analyse whether this degree of functional solidarity is linked to (1) respondents' economic status and (2) respondents' physical proximity with their husband's kin. In other words, we shall see here whether interactions with kin are related to incumbents' income and their physical proximity. Rather than treating interactions with kin as a static concept we have classified it and have shown the trends of exchanging aid with different types of kin on different occasions.

While measuring exchange of aid among relatives only those occasions of exchange have been considered which are regular, frequent, recurring and the amount of exchange is substantial.

Obviously, it is rather difficult to recall, report and record exactly which category of aid has been exchanged with which category of kin how many times. However, it is possible to work out a rough rank order of different categories of kin with whom aid of any kind has been exchanged. At the same time, it must be pointed out, our categorisation of different kinds of aid as financial, physical, psychological, etc., is not always accurate, and we have simply followed a broad, general pattern.

We have studied patterns of exchange of aid in many forms including the exchange of goods, services, gifts, advice and financial assistance. Such help patterns are widespread among all classes. Exchange of aid may be direct and indirect or subtle. Sometimes aid may be exchanged in cash and sometimes in kind. The predominant form of economic aid exchanged among the poor households, particularly in the village, is not in cash but in kind. Farming activities demand the help of relatives. First, a marginal farmer living in a nuclear household cannot afford all the hired labour and the agricultural implements he requires, and secondly, he cannot entirely depend on his meagre resources for livelihood. Under such circumstances, he is compelled to seek the co-operation and assistance of his relatives in farm-work. Thus, mutual help and co-operation among relatives during sowing, weeding and harvesting seasons may be observed in the form of exchange of labour and agricultural implements.

Exchange of goods and services among those kin who live in close physical proximity might be a usual practice. It includes the giving and receiving of loan of articles needed for domestic use and consumption such as a cup of sugar, food grains, rice, flour, edible oil, and so on. Poor households often do not possess adequate utensils and furniture to entertain respectable guests, and if they are in need of such items, the members of the related households in the vicinity are the people to be approached first. If the loan is not paid back it may be excused because the people involved are kinsfolk. Womenfolk often help each other in such tasks as baby sitting, preparation of food, shopping, etc., especially on occasions of family ceremonies and festivals.

Though there are government maternity hospitals, women during their child-birth still usually receive support from kin, particularly mother or mother-in-law. During their first pregnancy, women generally go to their parents' home where they get all types of care and aid. But during their subsequent pregnancies they have to depend both on their kin and their households' kin (mother-in-law, sister-in-law), since this time they may not always go to the parental home and stay there for a prolonged period. Now they have more children, the previously born ones, besides the new-born baby, who must also be taken care of. Also, women in nuclear households have to make arrangement for their husbands as well. So it is not possible for them to remain absent from their home for some length of time. Often the mother or any of her elderly female relative comes to help her and take the charge of her household. In their absence, women have to depend on their husbands' mother or any other relative. Anyway, during the pregnancy and child-birth our women are still dependent on relatives.

Moreover, the public health agencies have not in any way displaced the role of relatives. During illness the relatives have the moral obligation to help the victim in every possible way including financial aid.

Care of the parents, when they are aged and ill, providing a resort for a primary relative such as uncles or aunts, widow sister or brother's widowed wives and their children are still regarded as a duty on the part of our people.

Occasional aid would include services performed at weddings or other festive events or during periods of crisis, illness, death, accident, disaster and personal trouble of family members. A sense of moral obligation and commitment to give service appropriate to the occasion is found among the kindred. The habit of turning to kin when in trouble, before approaching friends or other agencies established for such purposes, is expected rather than the exception.

Mutual aid, cooperation and active participation of kin can be observed on various occasions such as that of first pregnancy rites, child-births, naming ceremonies, ancestor worship, mate selection, betrothal ceremonies, weddings, religious rites and festivals. As marriages are arranged by parents and other intimate kin, they take active interest and responsibility in choosing a matrimonial match for the sons and daughters. Kin are often entrusted with the task of finding a 'best' bride/groom and are requested to collect the relevant information about the bride or the groom. Sometimes, intimate kinsfolk are invited to decide suitability of the new matrimonial match. This is one of the occasions when the team spirit of the kindred is overtly displayed. Even now the intimate kin group functions as a marriage guidance bureau.

The preparations for a wedding ceremony begins weeks or even months in advance in which relatives play a major role in purchasing ornaments, clothes, utensils, furniture and many other goods. Going to relatives' house for informing and inviting them is a major task in which intimate kin often help the parents of the bride/groom. Some of the pivotal kin assemble much before the actual day of the ceremony. They identify themselves with the whole affair and try their best to make it a success in all probability.

In performing a wedding ceremony aid and assistance are exchanged among relatives in various forms. Besides the physical participation and emotional involvement, intimate relatives often share the financial burden also through precious gifts in cash or in kind. It is not obligatory to return such gifts to the respective givers when similar occasions arise in their households. These actually mark and suggest kinship solidarity and tend to augment kinship bonds. The intimacy of relationship can be measured from the conduct of relatives during such occasions.

Attendance on funerals is equally obligatory for intimate kin. An event of grief such as death among the kindred needs sympathy, consolation and help from relatives and is to be shared with them.

Observance of ancestor worship is another occasion to be celebrated by the kin group. It fortifies kinship bonds and the authority of the head of the lineage. Other members are required to perform their duties assigned by him. On such occasions, function of the kin group is more of psychological than physical or financial in nature.

More such psychological functions are performed by the kin group when one unit extends support to another in each one's effort to achieve and maintain community status, family growth, occupational and career achievement and mobility, and established economic status. The status of one's family in the community is related to kin connections. Sponsorship and achievement of educational and occupational goals and economic security are enhanced by the activities of the kin network.

Exchange of financial aid among relatives occur on various occasions, and it may be provided in cash or in kind. Actually, the scope and occasion of exchange of such aid are many. Some such common occasions are: building or purchase of a place of dwelling, marriage of the daughter, serious illness, providing capital in business or in farming, and so on. Sometimes, particularly in the poor households of the village, exchange of financial aid is a recurring event and no special occasion is marked for the same.

Before we go into a more detailed discussion of some of the field materials relating to the exchange of aid among relatives, we must admit that all the data we have gathered are likely to be underestimations. These topics are considered as private and a common and usual part of our life. Respondents often fail to remember many such occasions, or cannot simply think them as mentionable or reportable as 'exchange of aid'. Hence, we have collected data in this regard in unstructured, conversational style. Accordingly, we have simply reported the pattern or dimension of the exchange. Here our objective is to highlight which type of aid is exchanged with which type of kin under what circumstances or occasions, viz., whether exchanges occur mostly with the husband's kin or with the wife's kin, with brothers or cousins, etc. We have tried to exhibit the nature of kinship bonds and functional ties among the kindred, and not to count the frequencies of the respondents who have exchanged aid with their relatives highest or lowest times.

Economic status of the respondents may be a vital factor influencing the pattern or dimension of help. By 'economic status' we mean the per capita monthly income of the respondents' households. We have presented the findings indicating whether there is any association between the economic status of the respondents and the types of aid exchanged by them. Respondents have been dichotomised into two categories using the median income as the cutting point, namely, those whose income is above average and those whose income is below average.

Our data reveal, first, that of all the types of aid exchanged, the physical help is exchanged highest times and this is done among the residents of the nuclear households whose economic status is below average. These people live mostly in the rural areas. In fact, as our sample shows, the economic status of the ruralites is much inferior to that of the urbanites, and among the ruralites, the low-income people mostly live in the nuclear households. It is quite reasonable that this category of people will most often physically help one another since lacking in financial and other resources, they generally assist their relatives through their toil. Also, since people belonging to nuclear households lack sufficient manpower resource, they have to rely on their kin whenever any such exigency arises. People of joint households may obtain such help from within their own households. Hence, the reciprocal exchange of physical assistance is higher among people living in nuclear households than in joint households, and this is still higher among those who are unable to come to others' help through other means.

Moreover, exchange of physical help requires geographical proximity among the givers and the receivers, which is more often found in the village than in the town. This is another reason why rural people, compared to the urbanites, more often physically help one another.

Next, while urban people are more prone to exchange information, advice, suggestion with their relatives, the exchange of financial aid is more frequent among the villagers. This is quite natural since because of their inadequate, insecure income, villagers often have to accept financial aid from others, and these 'others' are their relatives. Because of their low social, educational and occupational status and little exposure to the world outside, they cannot effectively help their relatives by providing them with timely and sensible advice, helpful information, effective suggestion or competent professional help, which urbanites can and often do. Thus urbanites depend on relatives' assistance in such matters as getting their children admitted to a famous educational institution or enhancing the career prospect and securing a respectable job for the children or finding a suitable matrimonial match for the children or looking after relatives in their old age or arranging medical treatment in one's illness, and so on. Villagers also come to one another's help under such circumstances, but their capacity and competence are limited. Hence, they try to reciprocate one another by rendering physical aid.

Another striking difference noted among the ruralites and the urbanites is that while the poor villagers tend to depend on the affinal kin (wife's parents and sibs) during their financial stringency, urban people, if any exigency arises at all, approach to the agnatic kin (householder's parents and brothers). Thus, financial transactions with affinal kin mostly occur among the poor villagers who generally live in the nuclear households. It must be pointed out at the same time that poverty observed in the rural nuclear household sample (where the average monthly per capita income is only Rs. 300) is much more acute than that observed in the urban sample (average income being Rs. 2,900). It shows that in our sample the urban households below median are no match for the rural households below median. Thus, what might have been the behaviour of the urban poor in similar circumstances of economic hardships (i.e., whether they would approach their affinal or agnatic kin for financial aid) cannot be ascertained from this sample. What we can draw is that people below the subsistence level, who mostly live in the rural nuclear households, are financially more dependent on their affinal kin than on their agnatic kin. Though agnatic kin's financial helplessness is one reason behind such behaviour, the fact that still our people (however poor they might be) do not shirk their duties towards their married daughters/sisters is proved by this. Among the poor people, stem families generally disintegrate due to economic reasons, and when this occurs husbands' parents and sibs often do not feel obliged to economically support the household units which disjoin. Under such circumstances, the wife's kin extend their co-operation and support to these people. In respect of mutual aid and co-operation in other matters, e.g., physical and psychological, however, men interact more with their agnatic kin than with affinal kin.

It appears, then, that in general the exchange of aid with the respondents' husbands' kin is more frequent than that with their (respondents') natal kin, and there is no difference in this respect between the nuclear and the joint households, rural and urban households, and households having different economic status.

In another respect, however, a difference has been noted in the behaviour of the rural and urban joint households. While the former interact less often with relatives (both affinal and agnatic), their urban counterpart's behaviour in this respect follows a different trend, i.e., residents of the urban joint households have been found to interact more frequently with their relatives. Moreover, in the village, better the economic status, less is the frequency of exchange with the kin. The reason is that when a household itself is more or less self-sufficient in money and manpower, its dependence on the others outside the household lessens. Exchange of aid with the respondents' husbands' married sisters, however, does not follow this pattern and it is, in fact, higher in joint households than in nuclear households. Economic status of the household is not related to this type of exchange.

Unlike their rural counterparts, urban households, even when do not require financial assistance, often lack sufficient manpower.

This is so because of two factors: (1) As urban middle and upper-middle class people limit their households to one or two children only, the number of malefolk in these households is reducing. (2) As social and spatial mobility is a feature of the urban males, brothers/sons are often geographically dispersed. It seems then that while the rural joint households tend to restrict their interactions with relatives outside the immediate family circle, urban households, due to their shortage of manpower, cannot afford to do so.

It has been observed that while villagers regard their married daughters/sisters as *kutumba* and do not like to involve them in day-to-day matters (thus most often here exchanges are of the financial type), the urbanites do not mind to exchange all sorts of services with this category of relative. Further, the mother-in-law in urban joint households often enjoys effective power compared to their rural counterparts. Quite naturally, she likes to involve her brothers and sisters with her household matters.

Thus, the trends which emerge from our findings indicate that though the behaviour of the urban and rural people and those living in nuclear and joint households is more or less in the same direction, several differences also are observed. Exchange of economic aid is higher in the village and among the residents of nuclear households in the village who mostly are below the subsistence level. They exchange such aid mostly with the wife's kin. On the whole, exchange of aid with the husband's kin is higher than that with the wife's kin, and this is still higher among the residents of the joint households. Excepting the help which women still enjoy from their mothers (in the absence of the mother other female relatives like aunt, sister) during their pregnancy and child-birth, interactions with the wife's kin are not regular and frequent. Compared to the ruralites, urbanites more often exchange physical and informative help with their paternal uncles, aunts and cousins. In the village, functional interactions with kin are highest among the residents of nuclear households which are economically weak. Rural joint households which have adequate manpower and money exchange least with the kin outside their immediate circle. In the town where economic divergence among the kin and status differentiation among the brothers are comparatively more prominent than those in the village, people often feel uncomfortable to approach their kin for financial aid.

Opinions of the family sociologists vary in respect of the possible impact of class differentiation among the kin and the exchange of aid. For example, in their classical study Young and Willmott (1957) have emphasised that there is a considerable relationship of dependence and mutual aid between the wife of a family and her own mother particularly when they are from the working class (1962, p.238). Bell observes that the pattern of help exchanged among kin vary with the social class: "...the middle class extended family performs functions that the working class extended family cannot, through financial inability rather than differences in sentiment" (1968, p.91).

Blood (1970) has seen the issue from a different perspective. He notes that within the kin network the flow of goods and services is from points of high resource concentration to low resource points, following the old maxim "From each according to his ability, to each according to his need". However, the sheer existence of need (which low status families have in abundance) is not enough. If everyone in the system is needy, there is nothing to flow.

The high status families, on the other hand, as Blood observes, have a discretionary margin of resources to be flowed not necessarily within the immediate circle. It also enables them to devote more resources to non-kin. High status people participate more actively and more responsibly in such external systems as the economy and polity and the community (1970, p.191).

The observations of the Indian family sociologists in this regard is not clear and conclusive. Chekki has drawn: "Usually class is no barrier to kin contacts... Blood bond is stronger than class differences" (1974, p.106). At the same time he notes, the other side of the picture is that the kinship system is subject to the influence of class structure. In his sample, he has seen that 45.22 per cent of the respondents indicated that class acted as a barrier in kin contacts, whereas 54.78 per cent said that it did not. Wealth and poverty create differential nature of kin contacts (ibid.).

Our observation in this regard is as follows: Most of the times wealth creates a barrier in maintaining cordial ties between the members of the kindred when their status differs widely. People experience a significant change in kin relationships when a member of a kin group rises to a class position above that of most of the group members or when another sinks to a lower class due to economic loss or otherwise. In such cases, loyalty to one's kin, which is a *sine qua non* of the kinship system, is strained. People then become selective to a certain extent in maintaining intimate relations with members of the kindred, following which several interaction groups based on class differentiations emerge. At the same time, it must be pointed out, economic differentiation is not alone responsible for bringing about divisions among the kindred. It is not that those who are economically better placed always tend to avoid their poor kin. The degree of kinship relations, the extent of intimacy and personality factors sometimes undermine the economic ones. In normal and in difficult times people forget class differences among kin and help one another.

This inquiry, therefore, does not point to any linear relationship between the kinship interaction pattern and differentiation in the economic status of the members of the kindred. About 88 per cent of our rural respondents and 42 per cent of our urban respondents who live in nuclear households and whose husbands are not 'only son' of their parents, have reported that they do not maintain equal degree of intimacy or reciprocity with each of the brothers of their husbands.

It seems that the impact of class differentiation on the kinship bonds is of dubious nature and the truth is that more research is needed on this issue. Status differentiation, perhaps, affects one's relationships with one's uncles and cousins than those with one's brothers.

III

So far we have only shown which type of aid (financial, physical, etc.) is exchanged more frequently (or rarely) with which type of relatives. To make the picture complete information on the occasions when aid is exchanged is also relevant, and this has been presented in this section.

Here also our goal is not to present data about the total frequency of exchanges incurred by our respondents. Rather, the trend or dimension of the exchange has been explored here. Next, though data collected from the nuclear and joint households and from the village and the town have been compared with one another, respondents have not been categorised on the basis of their per capita income. While analysing data it has been seen that income is not an important factor here in general. However, when income has been found to influence incumbents' behaviour significantly, it has been mentioned.

It appears that interaction and co-operation among relatives occur highest times on the occasion of solemnising and smoothly performing a marriage ceremony in the family. Though aid is exchanged with the close kin like parents and siblings of the couple on many other occasions, the interchange of aid with distant kin is mostly limited to this occasion only. All sorts of aid—financial, physical and emotional or informative—are exchanged on this occasion. The kind of aid exchanged, however, varies with the closeness of the kinship bond. While the close kin help one another in every possible way, the distant kin generally extend only informative help like providing information about the possible bride/groom, supervising the arrangement on the day of the ceremony, entertaining guests, etc. Exchange of aid on this occasion is more common in joint than in nuclear households and in the town than in the village households. Rural joint households, however, are more prone to extend aid to relatives rather than themselves being recipients of aid. They are more or less self-sufficient in money and manpower and so do not require help and assistance from relatives. Urban joint households even when do not require financial aid often have to depend on relatives for physical help owing to their shortage of manpower.

Kinsfolk come to one another's help in large measure during such other occasions as death, illness and old age. Dependence on kin in such matters is higher among people in the town than in the village, in nuclear than in the joint households. When a person becomes a doctor and is somehow attached to the medical profession or any institution of health, it becomes almost an obligation on his part to offer professional aid to relatives. Moreover, village low-income group people, particularly in the nuclear households, cannot hire help from outside during their illness and so whatever aid they can expect, is from their relatives. Besides, if their illness is serious, they get financial aid from their relatives.

The function of offering shelter to kin is performed more frequently by urban joint households. Often these households are supplemented by widow/widower/childless relatives or relatives whose son/daughter lives far away. Number of such relatives is day-by-day increasing under the circumstances when the number of child-births is controlled, children live far away due to social and occupational mobility, and taking refuge in the old age home is not considered as prestigious or comfortable, nor are such homes sufficiently available to the common people. Thus, urbanites living in both nuclear and joint households play a significant role in this respect. Women who have no brother, have to regularly visit and look after their parents. During their illness they themselves get help from their mother when they live in nuclear households. Thus, exchange of physical aid among the kin when people are old, ill, infirm or single occur frequently in the town.

When men part with their stem family and leave their ancestral home they need a new residence. If they cannot buy a new one by themselves, they have to take help from kin in this regard. Quite reasonably, wife's kin extend help in this regard more often since a man's father and brothers generally would not like the whole matter. However, lack of space in the ancestral home may force members to settle in different places. Under such circumstances separation takes place through mutual understanding when a man's patri-kin, if they can afford, help him in finding a new place of dwelling. Not only financial aid, but physical and informative aid (supervision of the construction, providing useful advice or information about a land or negotiation with the contractors, etc.) also are exchanged in this regard. Respondents of the rural nuclear households require this aid most often.

In the Indian society still this is the norm that parents, so long they can afford, should assist their children in pursuing and advancing their career. If alive and able, all normal persons do this and hence this job has not been separately mentioned by our respondents as an 'aid' received from the parents. But when other relatives do this job (generally in the absence of parents or when parents are not capable) this has been reported as an 'aid' received from the kin. Aid obtained by the respondents or their husbands and children has been included under this category.

It has been observed that aid in this regard has been exchanged more by the urbanites than by the villagers. This is reasonable since villagers, because of their poor education, lack capacity to help in this regard. Also, the urgency to extend and accept such aid is less felt by the villagers. In the town, however, people often take help even from distant relatives for advancing the career of their children, and under the present circumstances this aid is regarded as a substantial one.

Besides, when there is somebody within the circle of kin who is well-established in such professions as medicine, engineering, law, architecture, etc., others expect him to help in advancing career in these fields. Similarly, when a person holds a high rank in any office and is capable of getting his relatives admitted to such organisations, it is considered as right and proper to do so. Though this behaviour may be labelled as indulging in favouritism or nepotism, Indian values are still strongly in favour of such behaviour. It is considered as quite natural and proper for one in an office to be personally involved with one's kindred so that they can manage some advantage from an office. Such comments are not rare as: "If my cousin cannot help me in selecting a job in his office, what is the use of this relationship?" Though Beteille noted the prevalence of such 'ambidextrous class' in the countryside (1974, p.106). In our inquiry we have found it to exist in both the village and the town and among people from all income and occupational groups. As joint households contain a higher number of members, the number of givers and recipients of such aid is also higher in such households than that in nuclear ones.

In both the village and the town and in nuclear and joint households, the trend is that respondents' exchange of aid with their mothers is highest. Most of this aid is provided by their mothers during their pregnancy and child-birth. Sometimes, particularly in nuclear households, during respondents' illness and when they are gainfully employed outside the home, their mothers help them by taking care of their home and children. Respondents, particularly living in urban nuclear households, too look after their mothers (also fathers) when they are ill and old.

What to be noted here is that the urban respondents mostly depend on their husbands' kin for looking after their children when they go outside for their job or profession. Even when they live in nuclear households, they equally depend on their mother and mother-in-law for this. In the village, however, women living in nuclear households have to depend on their mother for this purpose since women's going outside home for job is not here still viewed favourably, and also because working women are still a tiny minority in the village. Hence, if they are economically active, the other women members in the respondents' husbands' households are jealous of their freedom and economic solvency.

Next in order come respondents' husbands' brothers, their wives and children. All sorts of aid are exchanged with these kin who come to each other's help in a variety of ways. In fact, whenever a man faces any difficulty he first turns to his brother (next to his parents) for help who also oblige. Parents will be old and die some time, and hence it is the brothers who will be looked to for help and assistance.

IV

It is commonly believed that social and geographical mobility has an important impact on the functional ties and exchange of aid among people who were earlier members of one stem family. Western family sociologists have inquired into this issue in detail. For example, Bott related spatial mobility to the type of network of which family is the centre. She draws: "A family's network will become more loose-knit if either the family or the other members of the network move away physically or socially so that contact is decreased and new relationships are established" (1971, p.106). She continues that in general the network of socially mobile families tends to become less connected not only because they move physically but also because they are likely to drop old social ties and form new ones. At the same time, she emphasises, however mobile the family, husband and wife feel an obligation to maintain contact with their parents (p.107).

Parsons strongly pleaded that the mobility of the occupational system requires a great deal of shifting in the place of residence. Since it is the individual, as such, who is in demand for new jobs in such a way as to necessitate his changing of residence, it is essential that his family be able to change with him, and this would not be possible if it were not an isolated conjugal family (1949, p.192).

Since the present inquiry is not primarily concerned with the relationship between industrialisation and urbanisation and the conjugal family system, we need not elaborately discuss the arguments and counter-arguments of or against Parsons' hypothesis. We are simply concerned with the joint family solidarity and spatial and social mobility. Further, since our sample does not include enough cases who are spatially and socially (educationally and occupationally) mobile it does not permit us to test the hypotheses of Parsons and his critics. We, therefore, see no point in discussing them in detail. For the present purpose we shall concentrate on those portions of these arguments and counter-arguments which are directly related to our inquiry.

The arguments put forward by those who believe that mobility hampers kinship bonds are: (1) Persons who are closely tied to their stem families will be reluctant to move physically even if better career prospects are available elsewhere. (2) It is less likely that ties and identification with the stem family will remain intact where only a fraction of it (say, one son with his wife and children) moves while the rest of the family is immobile. And (3) it is impractical for an individual to move with a large family and locate suitable jobs for all his sons/brothers simultaneously. The critics of Parsons generally do not counter the argument that occupational mobility may be accompanied by spatial mobility. But the issue is whether these mobilities are accompanied by weakening of ties and functional bonds with the kindred which is left behind. The issue is further buttressed by the more general analysis of Homans who draws that contact is one of the four major prerequisites for primary group cohesion (1951, p.36).

Against Parsons Litwak counterargues that extended family relation can be maintained over great geographical distances because modern advances in communication techniques have minimised the socially disruptive effects of geographic distance

(1960b, p.386). Moreover, he pleads that extended family identification can be retained despite breaks in face-to-face contact since distance does not prevent or seriously hinder such aids to family members as help in times of illness, emergency loans or gifts, purchase of a house, and the like (p.387). Thus, there are many spheres of life where aid can be exchanged among the relatives where physical proximity is not required. We are to look into the behaviour of people in such circumstances, i.e., whether and how far geographical dispersion hampers (or strengthens) kinship ties.

Bell who has made a thorough inquiry into this issue has observed that geographical mobility has obviously affected the amount of contact between members of the extended family, i.e., the locals saw more of their kin than the non-locals. However, in terms of the functioning of the extended family it was social (occupational) mobility, and not geographical mobility, that was the important variable (1968, p. 160). Bell defines social mobility as "movement from a manual occupation to a non-manual occupation intergenerationally" (p.44).

Blood accepts the positive role of modern means of transport and communication in neutralising the disruptive effects of geographical dispersion of kin. Thus, these facilities make distance an increasingly penetrable barrier, an increasingly illusory obstacle to kin interaction (1970, p.194). At the same time, he admits that technology has not totally destroyed the effects of geographical factors: "Geography has become *less* important, not unimportant" (ibid).

In India little empirical work has been done to test the above hypothesis. In fact, the joint family is *believed* to be an unchanging institution, spatial and social mobility has nothing to do with it. Desai, however, feels the urgency of inquiring into the impact of occupational and social mobility and migration on the "sentiment of jointness of the joint family". For the future family sociologists his suggestion is to test, among other hypotheses, how much did residential separation lead to the effective separation from the joint family. How much individualisation of the individual has taken place (1955, pp.112-13).

Madan finds a sort of association between geographical proximity of kin and their interrelations (1989, p.168).

Chekki has observed that geographical distance to some extent influences kinship interactions. Distance is given as the reason when they could not maintain contacts with a certain set of kin. On the whole, however, distance is no barrier to close contacts among intimate kin (1974, p.60). He notes that the frequency of visits to the ancestral home in the village and the degree of attachment to their kin and place of origin are largely determined by the presence of kin, existence of property at the native place and the spatial distance (p.108).

In our inquiry we cared to collect data in this respect and tried to measure whether geographical dispersion affects the interactions and contacts among the kin.

"Geographical dispersion of a household" has been measured here in terms of the physical distance between the present residence of the respondents and that of their husbands' patri-kin. Respondents' households have been divided into five categories on the basis of the geographical dispersion of their husbands' male patri-kin. Category 1 comprises those households where majority of the sample households are located in kin-based 'compounds' or adjacent houses. Category 2 contains those households where the kin live within the walking distance, or, it takes not more than half an hour to reach one another's place; in case of the village sample, those respondents whose husbands reside with their patri-kin in the same village but not in adjacent houses, have been put in this category. Category 3 is constituted of the households where the respondents' husbands live with their patri-kin in the same town/city and it takes from half an hour to three hours to reach one another's place. Category 4 includes those cases where the kin live at a certain distance, but within West Bengal. Category 5 comprises the cases where the kin live outside West Bengal (or outside India). Another category 6 has been framed to include the cases where no regular or fixed pattern in the living arrangement of the kin has been noted, e.g., some of them are in transferable service having no definite address, or each of them lives at different place and thus the kin are widely scattered.

Table 8.1 presents data relating to exchange of aid among the respondents' husbands' patri-kin when the latter have different

Table 8.1

Geographical Dispersion of Respondents' Husbands from their Patrikin and Exchange of Aid, by Residence and Type of Household (in percentage)

Residence	*Type of household*	*Share same compound/ plot of land*		*Live within walking distance*		*Takes 1 to 3 hours*		*Live within W.B.*		*Live outside W.B.*		*No pattern*		*Total*	
		*1**	*2**	*1*	*2*	*1*	*2*	*1*	*2*	*1*	*2*	*1*	*2*	*1*	*2*
Rural	Nu	33.7	37.1	7.9	6.8	2.2	2.2	-	1.1	-	-	2.2	6.8	46.0	54.0
															100.0
	Joi	65.5	21.9	-	-	3.5	5.8	-	1.1	-	-	1.1	1.1	70.1	29.9
															100.0
Urban	Nu	9.1	1.5	7.6	5.3	17.4	17.4	13.7	10.6	6.1	5.3	3.0	3.0	56.9	43.1
															100.0
	Joi	40.1	4.1	7.5	0.7	10.2	10.9	4.7	6.8	6.8	6.1	1.4	0.7	70.7	29.3
															100.0

Note: *1 indicates cases where aid is regularly exchanged among kin.
*2 indicates cases where there is little exchange of aid among kin.

degree of physical proximity. Among the patri-kin, husbands' brothers and their relatives, and husbands' fathers' brothers and their relatives have been included.

It has been found that exchange of aid among the kin is lower among the rural nuclear households than among the urban nuclear households. Among the joint households, on the other hand, in both rural and urban areas, the number of interactions are almost equal and are higher than that in nuclear ones.

Geographical dispersion among the patri-kin in this sample is higher in urban than in rural areas (this is actually the feature of rural society in general), and among nuclear than among joint households. Thus, it is highest in the urban nuclear and lowest in rural joint households.

It appears that rural joint households are least geographically dispersed of all the household categories (87% of the sample fall in Cats. 1 and 2), and exchange of aid among kin is also comparatively high in these households, i.e., it occurs in case of 70 per cent of the sample households. Urban nuclear households are geographically most mobile (only 24% fall in Cats. 1 and 2), and the exchange of aid is also less in these households, that is, only 57 per cent of the respondents from these households have reported of such exchange. At the same time, however, it is found that though the rural nuclear households are literally almost surrounded by the patri-kin (86% fall, in Cats. 1 and 2), exchange of aid with patri-kin is least (only 46% of these people have reported of it). The incidence of the exchange of aid is almost equal in rural and urban joint households, though the latter are geographically much dispersed (only 52% fall in Cats. 1 and 2) than the former.

What to be noted is that in the rural nuclear households we find evidences which are partly against the common perceptions. Majority of the people in these households (54%), whether or not they live in close physical proximity, rather tend to avoid interchanges with the respondents' husbands' patri-kin. In rural joint households also a sizeable number of the respondents (30%), though fewer than those in rural nuclear households, have bestowed a similar tendency. Thus, in the village, physical proximity with the kin does not necessarily create a favourable condition for exchange of aid.

The urban picture is a bit different. Some amount of association, though feeble, has been observed here between higher spatial mobility and less interactions among kin. And, this tendency is equally visible in both types of households. Thus, among the urban people we find a tendency to exchange aid or maintain functional ties with those kin who are less spatially mobile. That is, closer is the physical propinquity, higher are the frequencies of exchanges with the respondents' husbands' kin.

It can be drawn, therefore, that some sort of association between geographical dispersion and exchange of aid among the patri-kin prevails. As geographical dispersion is specially the feature of the urban society, this association has been noted in the urban society only. Spatial mobility not being a variable for the villagers, its association with other variables, say exchange of aid with relatives, cannot be tested in the village perspective.

On further analysis of data it has been noticed that both physical proximity and exchange of aid of the respondents are low with the brothers of their father-in-law and persons related with them. Among the rural nuclear households, such interactions have been reported to be almost insignificant since as many as 79 per cent of the respondents have reported that they have little exchange of aid with such kin. What to be noticed is that physical separation is no bar here in interactions with kin as bulk of these respondents (83%) live in kin-based 'compounds' of adjacent houses. Situation is a bit hopeful for the rural joint households where persons reporting 'little exchange' is 52 per cent. Urban households, however, interact relatively more frequently with these third and fourth degree kin than their rural counterparts and here the frequencies of 'little exchange of aid' are 53 per cent for the urban nuclear and 44 per cent for the urban joint households.

Next, whatever exchanges take place with these kin mainly relate to the exchange of informative aid. Though there are some incidents of exchange of physical aid as well among the urbanites, the exchange of financial aid with such kin occurs rarely. These kin are regarded as distant or nominal kin whose presence and participation are generally expected on the occasion of any ritual or ceremony in the family. Moreover, whatever aid is exchanged, is exchanged mostly among kin having physical proximity. It seems, then, that exchange of aid with the third and fourth degree patri-kin is as such low and it is still lower when there is no physical proximity with those kin. It can be drawn, then, that physical distance weakens ties with the third and fourth degree kin and makes them functionally ineffective.

If we turn to spatial dispersion and exchange of aid with the respondents' husbands' brothers and their relations, it is seen that the rate of interactions is a bit higher in rural than in urban areas, and in joint than in nuclear households.

In terms of geographical proximity also the respondents' husbands' brothers are closer than husbands' fathers' brothers'. Respondents from 87 per cent of the rural nuclear, 89 per cent of the rural joint, 29 per cent of the urban nuclear and 70 per cent of the urban joint households live either in the same plot of land or within the walking distance of the places of their husbands' brothers. Thus, some association between exchange of aid and physical proximity with the kin is discernible within the close circle of kin. Most of the rural joint households are physically close to their first and second degree patri-kin, and the exchange of aid of any kind is also highest (91%) in them. In order then come urban joint (88%), rural nuclear (70%) and urban nuclear (67%) households.

Hence, as our observations point out, both physical propinquity and the type of household structure incumbents live in are strong intervening variables influencing kin group interactions. Under the same degree of physical propinquity, members belonging to joint households interchange aid more frequently than those living in nuclear ones, and this is the trend in both the rural and urban households.

Our data, however, do not permit us to argue that though exchange of aid with the respondents' husbands' kin is somewhat positively associated with physical proximity, the opposite is true. Neither can it be pleaded that physical separation does not matter in interactions with kin, that the familial bonds remain unaffected or intact even when brothers are physically disintegrated. On the whole, we see that the interchange of aid occurs more often among those kin who have physical proximity. One can then assume from these data that physical proximity is a contributory condition for continuing interactions among the kin, even among the close circle of kin like brothers. But at the same time one must not overlook the fact that in spite of close physical proximity, brothers in 8 out of 31 rural nuclear households rarely interchange aid with one another.

It is comprehensible that physical help cannot be feasibly exchanged among those kin who live scattered. There is no bar, however, in exchanging financial and informative aid. And, if spiritual bond of oneness or identity of belonging to the same joint family were there, brothers should have been found to exchange these latter types of aid even when they are dispersed. But most often this does not occur. Our findings are thus in tune with those of Blood who draws, "At a micro-ecological level, it makes a great deal of difference whether nuclear families establish separate households according to a neo-local residential system or whether they are literally surrounded by kin in extended family households or in kin-based 'compounds' of adjacent houses. The greater the geographical proximity of kin, the greater their influence on one another" (1970, p. 193). And, "the greater the distance between households, the less the interaction among them (i.e., the stronger the nuclear unit becomes at the expense of kinship ties" (ibid).

We can summarise the discussion with the following observations:

First, a thin but positive association between geographical propinquity and mutual exchange of help and assistance among the respondents' husbands' patri-kin has been noted: higher the spatial propinquity, higher the exchange. Second, the association seems to be prominent

1. in the behaviour of members of the joint households;
2. in urban than in rural areas; and
3. in case of exchange of physical help than that of informative and financial aid.

Third, though geographical distance somehow limits exchange of aid, its prevalence does not ensure the same. That is, it cannot be drawn that if kin live adjacent to one another, they will enter into regular and frequent interchanges of aid and assistance among themselves.

V

Our sample does not include enough cases where the respondents' husbands are occupationally and educationally mobile either intergenerationally (father-son) or collaterally (brother-brother). Definitely there are occupational changes and variations among the brothers of the respondents' husbands, but they cannot be labelled as occupational mobility causing any substantial change in the social and economic status of the incumbents. With more or less the same status being retained, such changes only lead to horizontal social mobility. Hence, any attempt to inquire into the relationship between social mobility (vertical mobility in respect of occupational and educational achievements) and kinship interactions or exchange of aid has been dropped.

But since differentiations are there in the fields of education and occupation in the sample households (in this case, among the male members of the respondents' husbands' families), we have made an effort to see whether men like to separate their residence from their patri-kin when their levels of educational standards differ in some way. Since interactions with one's brothers is more critical than that with one's father when the occupational and educational status of men varies, we have noted whether respondents (and their husbands) live in close physical proximity with their husbands' brothers. In the absence of marked vertical mobility, the level of education and occupation has been simply dichotomised into two categories: cases where the levels of education and occupation of the respondents' husbands and their brothers are more or less comparable or similar and cases where there are marked differences in this regard.

The present sample is more heterogeneous in terms of occupation than education. In 42 per cent of the sample households brothers are occupied in diverse types of jobs and professions, whereas in respect of educational standard this diversity exists in case of 35 per cent of the sample households. Occupational diversity is more prominent in the rural (47%) than in the urban (39%) households. However, as has already been reported, this diversification mostly indicates horizontal mobility. So we have referred to this feature as 'occupational diversification' rather than occupational mobility.

In both the village and the town, the educational and occupational standards are more divergent for men who live in nuclear households than those who live in joint households. It means that joint households comprise men whose occupational and educational status is more or less comparable to one another.

Our data do not provide any strong evidence in favour of the hypothesis that when there is occupational and educational differentiation among the brothers they would prefer to separate their residence and be spatially dispersed, or that when there is similarity in these respects they would reside in close vicinity. A feeble tendency has, however, been noticed, particularly in the village nuclear households to move to a separate dwelling place when there are such differentiations. In contrast, in joint households, both rural and urban, the educational and occupational similarity of brothers is evident. So it can be drawn that if situation permits, men in general prefer to maintain close physical proximity with those brothers with whom their social status resembles.

9

Will Joint Family Survive?

Already we have discussed the factors behind the break-up of joint families. We have seen that a joint family would survive as long as the adult, earning members, find the arrangement convenient, economic, comfortable and enjoyable. But when social and occupational divergences crop up in the household, some of the members may deliberately try to disturb the peaceful atmosphere and create tension and bickering. If all the earning members are engaged in a joint venture, income differentiation would not emerge. But when the brothers are engaged in different jobs and vocations according to their capability and qualifications, individual income is likely to vary. The brother who earns the highest, would find the joint living uneconomic and inconvenient. He would find some context of excuse for being separated from the stem family. This excuse often leads to conflicts, more so amongst the women that finally leads to disintegration.

Sometimes a stem family may split up without disturbing the peace or injuring family bonds. In such a situation, amicable separation through mutual understanding generally occurs after the death of the parents, particularly after the death of the father in cases where the ancestral property is not substantial, or there is no ancestral home (father lived in the office quarters or rented house), or the living space in the home is insufficient to accommodate all the members, or it is for the career advancement of the son that required migration to a far-off place, that the married brothers find no separate advantage in continuing a large household, that they may decide to separate peacefully through mutual agreement. But frictions arise when the property to be divided is sizeable and the share of which is denied to a son who unilaterally decides to separate against the desire of the father. For the poor, however, any amount is regarded as substantial and often they view their share as unjust.

In some cases stem family may disintegrate during the lifetime of the parents due to quarrels and tensions and economic considerations may become secondary. In such a situation the couple decides that the peace acquired by setting up a new home would be more important than the economic loss incurred in leaving the security and comforts prevailing in the stem family. Thus, economic considerations and peace are compared and the final decision is the result of their delicate balance. Besides these two, there may be a host of other factors that may become insignificant or secondary while the final decision is taken.

It is only in a minority of cases that the whole stem family simultaneously collapses, i.e., all the brothers separate at a time. Generally, the disintegration process is gradual. The older sons separate and the parents might live with any of their married sons (including their dependants like widow mother or unmarried children). In some cases, particularly among the rural poor, the older sons separate just after or within a few years of their marriage and the parents live with the unmarried son(s). When all the sons get married, parents either live with one of them, generally the youngest one, or stay with each of them by rotation, that is, they (generally it is the widow mother who survives her husband) perambulate between their sons.

The above story is based on the respondents' description about what they have practised. Now we shall present the beliefs, opinions and perceptions of the respondents regarding the condition for the survival of the joint household or the future of the joint household. Our mode of presentation will be mainly descriptive since the interest of the research lies in the exploration of a social process. Hence detailed and verbatim report or the citations from the respondents' experiences are needed to elicit their unique views, philosophy or goals.

Another point deserves mention and clarification. Some of the statements of the respondents may appear to be apparently inconsistent and even contradictory. For instance, often it would appear from the respondents' answers that they still cherish the ideal of joint family living. In practice, however, they have sought partition from the husbands' stem family. It may be viewed as a disparity in their work and word. Sometimes, the same respondents may apparently make contradictory statements as "blood is thicker than water", and "you can't keep going on to see your sibs"; or "in an emergency one ought to turn to one's kin first"; and "one has to stand on one's own"; or, "all the family should stick together", and "you have to make your own way". Often it has been found that the same respondent who lives in a joint household, opines that it is more convenient to live in a joint household than in a nuclear one. He apprehends that the future of the institution of the joint household is bleak and that most probably it would not survive in future. Though, as it appears from the data, people receive the highest amount of aid from their kin, they maintain an appearance of independence and self-reliance. These apparent contradictions are, in fact, statements of alternatives faced by the respondents. These statements must not be seen as mutually exclusive but as a realisation of the room for manoeuvre within the system. On further re-analysis of these statements one would get some important clues to the familial behaviour and attitude to familial issues of our people.

II

We shall first present the opinion of the respondents to the queries such as the "reasons why joint households are better than nuclear ones", "reasons why nuclear households are better than joint households", "reasons for break-up of the joint households", "the conditions for the survival of the joint households", and "the anticipated familial structure of the future".

In response to such queries the respondents communicated their experiences, expectations and apprehensions in their own words and terms. It is not possible, nor is it desirable to forcefully eliminate the variations in answers with an attempt to present the same within a limited number of answer categories or under specific codes. As a result, we have not tried to present the information in mutually exclusive categories. Many of the statements may seem to be overlapping.

Also, our emphasis being on the multifarious dimensions of the issue, we encouraged the respondents to provide as much information as they could. Thus, while some of them expressed their experiences and views in one or two sentences, some others used a couple of sentences to make their answers comprehensive and exhaustive. Hence, in Tables 9.1, 9.2 and 9.3, the total frequency represents the total number of statements comprising explanations and opinions of the respondents, and hence it does not match with the total sample size (N).

In Table 9.1 we have presented what has been thought by the respondents as the advantages of the joint households compared to the nuclear ones. The respondents more or less agree that joint households provide relief and rest to the women members, are economic, provide security and emotional support, and help to remove boredom and loneliness. For clarifying their position it is better to directly refer to how the respondents conveyed their opinions and experiences.

Table 9.1

Advantages of the Joint Household

Advantages of the Joint Household	*Frequency*
Lessens the pressure of household chores and provides relief to wives	93
An economically rational form of organisation	82
Provides strength, support, defence, protection and security in crisis	64
Permits one to go outside home without having any anxiety for the home, husband and children	42
Convenient for the upbringing of young children	39
To maintain a joint family is a 'good thing'	37
One does not feel lonely, bored here	36
Convenient to the working wives	23
If ill and physically unfit, women need not be anxious of husband and children	20
Teaches children the art of adjustment	18
Co-residence with husband's kin looks good and enhances prestige	15
Safe and secure for the aged	11
Strengthens bonds between the husband and the wife	10
In a big household one can get companion of the same age group	5

Joint household is an economically rational organisation. It is less costly to cook on one hearth. As there are more earning members in the household, standard of living can be raised. Such costly and luxurious consumer goods and articles as VCR, washing machine, car can be afforded. As economic pressure is less, one can buy fashionable ornaments. Some expenses as on maid servant, cook, meeting social obligations and offering gifts to relatives on various socio-religious occasions can be commonly borne. If the husband dies, or becomes unemployed (due to lock out or closure in the workshop or following any accident) or his income is inadequate and irregular, one need not be anxious at least for the basic cost of living.

To maintain a joint household is itself a good thing. The large joint family may supply every member with contemporaries in age and gender in whom one finds companionship satisfaction and sympathiser and with whom one can share one's interests and problems. There are funs, pleasure in living in a big household. For enjoying life and being happy we need others' company as well. It is good to be dependent on and benevolent to one another. Living in the nuclear households makes one narrow, self-centred and selfish.

Joint household reduces members' loneliness and boredom. There is plenty of love, affection in it. Here one can share one another's sorrows and satisfactions. In a nuclear household one feels bored and life becomes routinised and monotonous particularly when children are grown-up. There is none within the household with whom one can pass the time of day. This makes people mentally sick and physically tired. In a joint household, on the other hand, as the parents co-reside, other kin also frequently come to visit them, which lessens monotony and reminds and reinforces the feeling that "I am not alone". Living in a joint household permits one to make trips outside home like travelling or going to the residence of any relative without having any anxiety for the home, husband and children. While going to the parental home, the housewife need not think about who will cook and serve the meal to her husband or send her child (if left behind) to the school and take care of them.

Joint household provides strength (unity is strength), support, defence, protection and security in the event of any crisis situation. If any problem arises, others can share it and help to come to a wise decision through mutual discussions and deliberations.

Joint household is convenient to the working women. As one need not be tensed with the home and children while at work, one can be sincere and committed to one's job and career. Also, if the maid servant or *ayah* is absent, one need not take leave of absence from the workplace. This viewpoint is, however, not accepted by all. In fact, it will be seen in the following pages that several of our employed respondents find joint households as uncongenial. Accordingly, the observations of family sociologists vary on this point. For example, though Kapadia (1959, 1966) agrees with this point, empirical observations of Chakrabortty (1978) go against it.

Living in joint households is convenient to the upbringing of young children. They get plenty of love, affection, care and attention, particularly from their grandparents, and do not feel lonely. Also, as the burden of child-rearing is shared by others, the mother can find time for herself. She can give more time to children's health and education.

Joint household lessens the pressure of work and provides rest, relief and leisure to women members as here the household chores are divided among several hands. So, for the housewife, life in a joint household is physically less tiresome and arduous.

If ill and physically unfit, women in the joint household need not be anxious. Also they can get relief, rest and respite under such circumstances.

When the couple lives in a joint household, their relationship becomes closer and pleasure-giving. Romanticism between the husband and the wife gets chance to be constantly renewed here as their children are taken charge of by their grandparents. Further, as there are many people in the household they can mediate between the husband and the wife in case any marital maladjustment pops out. Also, unlike nuclear households, here the couple can talk over a variety of issues and problems besides concerning themselves and children, which brings variety and colour to the marital bond. Moreover, here the husband can enjoy the company of his parents and can look after them closely. It makes him relieved and joyful.

In a joint household the socialisation of children becomes perfect as they learn to sacrifice for the others, share things with the others, do not become self-centred and selfish, become mentally healthy and normal, and get accustomed to communicate and adjust with the others.

Joint households are safe and secure for the aged. When people become old and infirm, they suffer from a feeling of insecurity and anxiety in nuclear households.

When a lady resides with her mother-in-law/daughter-in-law or sister-in-law, it looks good and earns admiration and prestige in the eyes of the others. It is thought to be a part of our hoary Sanskritic tradition. Quite irrespective of the material advantages, co-residence and adjustment with the husband's kin in itself provides prestige to a wife, and more so, to her parents as well.

Like all other things in the world, joint households have disadvantages as well which are no less important. In Table 9.2 we have presented the experiences and opinions of the respondents in this regard. The respondents', arguments are:

In a nuclear household one need not shoulder others' liabilities and hazards. Standard of living can be upgraded according to one's earnings and taste.

Nuclear households reduce tension, frustrations and grievances as one need not every time compromise with the others or obey a rigid, assertive, unsympathetic head. This is a real problem for the young wives particularly when they are reared in a different cultural and socio-economic atmosphere. Some of their habits such as late rising, putting on modern or western dress are not favoured by the people in their husbands' household, and it is uncomfortable and irksome to change these habits at this matured age. In the nuclear household, on the other hand, one can take decisions and act independently; freedom need not be curtailed or sacrificed.

Respondents in this respect have further added that life is short and everybody should, therefore, try to live according to his/her own way. And this is possible in nuclear households only. Moreover, nowadays people are more enlightened and have exposure to the world outside. So, generally they have their own opinion and taste which they like to assert. When this is so it is difficult to arrive at any decision in a big joint household. Thus, as

Table 9.2
Advantages of the Nuclear Household and Disadvantages of the Joint Household

Advantages and Disadvantages	*Frequency*
In a nuclear household	
One need not share or bear others' liabilities and hazards	63
Tensions, frustrations and grievances are reduced, as one need not compromise with others or obey a rigid and asservive head	55
Peaceful living is possible; there are no jealousy and quarrels over small issues; no clashes of personalities or temperaments	47
Husband-wife relationship becomes more cordial	21
Husband's married sisters cannot dominate or intervene or disturb	10
One can rear children according to one's aspirations; others cannot intervene	14
Women can be dutiful to their parents	12
Freedom of women is better protected	20
Nuclear household is convenient for employed and career-minded women	10
Nuclear household is economically viable particularly when brothers' earnings vary	26
Nuclear household makes people responsible while joint households foster idleness and discourage individual initiative	15
Nuclear household lessens the pressure of household chores for the wife	14
When kin live apart relationship improves as they are free from every-day tensions and accusations	26
In a joint household	
One is required to make many sacrifices which are not always acknowledged by the others	8
The atmosphere often becomes unhealthy for children	4
Frequent visits of guests hampers children's education	5
Women cannot supervise their children's education due to heavy workload	7

the number of heads increases, decision-making becomes a real problem. Also, temperamental differences and clash of personalities become almost regular phenomena in joint households. In nuclear households, on the other hand, peaceful living is possible. There are no jealousy, bickerings and quarrels over trivial matters. When kindred live apart relationship between them improves, or at least does not become too unsympathetic as they are free from everyday tensions. So it is wise "to divide to unite". At the same time, if they like, they can exchange aid with one another without sacrificing their individual freedom. That is, people are at liberty to decide with whom or when they would interact with their relatives. Next, there is no reason to suppress one's opinions and desires or mould one's lifestyle just to avoid others' criticisms and aspersions, particularly when this suppression makes one utterly unhappy, frustrated and aggrieved. Conformity is good but too much of conformity may be uncongenial to the development of one's personality.

In a nuclear household, privacy between the husband and the wife can be maintained. Physically and mentally they can come closer to one another as there is none to intervene or disturb. Also, this type of household fosters egalitarian relationships.

In a nuclear household, the wife can impress and influence her husband rather than herself being restrained by the others. The husband gets habituated to depend on his wife, solicit her advice and suggestion, takes decision in consultation with the wife. Also, the husband can be persuaded to help the wife in household chores without being criticised by the others as a henpecked, spineless man. In a joint household, on the other hand, the relationship between the husband and the wife deteriorates as the others are there between them who may incriminate the wife or irritate the husband against the wife.

In joint households as parents are there, husbands' married sisters frequently come and stay for a longer period. They often poke their nose in the family matters against the interest of the wife.

Nuclear households are convenient for employed and career-minded women. If all or most of the women in a joint household are not employed, it is inconvenient for the working wives, since here their problems are not to be sympathetically felt by the others. Also, they are not spared for any lapse in performing their assigned household chores. So either they are to work hard or they are taunted by the others who are jealous of their economic well-being and freedom of movement. In nuclear households, on the other hand, working wives can set their household routine according to their own convenience so that their dual roles and responsibilities can be synchronised.

Nuclear households are economically viable when there are economic differentiations among the brothers. In a joint household as purchases are made from a common purse, members sometimes show a tendency to be prodigal. Also, those who are relatively economically weak, are required to adapt themselves to and imitate those other members who are economically better off. Thus, against their will, capacity and need, these economically weak members are often forced to be extravagant. In a nuclear household, on the other hand, one can cut one's coat according to one's cloth.

Those who earn less cannot make savings in a joint household. Moreover, joint household fosters idleness, creates parasites and discourages individual initiative. Those who want to shirk responsibility can do this in this type of household. This may lead to a disproportionate sharing of burden among the different members. Thus, those who are conscientious, dutiful and peace- loving are exploited by their work-shy, indolent and parasitical fellows.

Due to frequent visits of guests, wives in a joint household do not get any leisure or rest. Most of the times they remain busy as a bee.

In a joint household, one is often required to make many sacrifices which are not even acknowledged by the others.

In a nuclear household one can rear children according to one's standard and aspirations. There are no parents-in-law who may intervene or pamper or spoil the children.

A joint household offers an unhealthy atmosphere for the children when there are bickerings and jealousy among the elderly people.

In a joint household, frequent visits of guests, everytime hue and cry, noise of the TV and the transistor hamper children's concentration on their lessons. If anybody has any bad habit like drug-taking, excessive drinking, insobriety, having a bad company, children are adversely influenced.

As there is heavy burden of household chores in a joint household, mothers often cannot devote adequate time and attention to their children.

If is often alleged that the atmosphere of the joint household is not congenial to the proper upbringing of children for various reasons. Often others intervene when the parents take disciplinary action against their children for any of their misdeed. Also, if the mother is preoccupied with household chores all the time her children are neglected, particularly their education hampers. Women can perform duty towards their aged and infirm parents in a nuclear household, which cannot be done when they live with their husbands' kin. They can keep their parents with them when they live separately. Nor in a joint household can they frequently visit their parents' home and look after them, as this is not often liked by their husbands' kin.

Freedom of women is more secure in a nuclear household. They, particularly the young wives, prefer nuclear households as they do not like to be supervised by the seniors.

As appears from above, respondents have pointed out the advantages and disadvantages of both forms of household. The issue has been viewed from many angles and perspectives. There are several advantages of a joint household which are accepted by all people, even by those who live in the nuclear household and are its staunch supporters. The same is true for the nuclear household system as well. At the same time, several contradictory opinions also have been found where the respondents are doubtful about which one of the household structures would be better. Several such spheres are: whether the joint household would be convenient to the working wives; whether the husband-wife relation becomes closer in the joint household; whether the joint household helps in the socialisation and proper personality development of the children. Though there are dissenting views, majority of the respondents think that a joint household is an economically rational organisation, and that housewives get some rest, relief and respite here. As advantages of a joint household, the respondents more or less agree that it is the shelter of the aged, the ill, the infirm, that it provides physical and emotional support and security, and that it reduces members' loneliness and boredom. Similarly, respondents generally do not hesitate to speak that in the nuclear household individual freedom can be more freely and fully enjoyed, that this type of household is popular among the young wives since they can live independently and need not obey the others; that here people are not to shoulder others' liabilities and hazards and therefore can upgrade their standard of living and fulfil their level of aspiration for themselves and for their children.

It is quite pertinent to know whether the popularity of a joint household (and also nuclear household) is higher among those who themselves belong to this particular household structure. Similarly, whether the rural/urban background of the respondents influences their opinions is also important to know.

In Table 9.3 we have tried to seek answers to these questions.

Table 9.3

Why are Nuclear Households Better than Joint, or Joint Households Better than Nuclear Ones?, by Residence and Type of Household of Respondents (in percentage)

Residence	*Type of household*	*Joint households are best*	*Joint households are better*	*Both types have merits and demerits*	*Nuclear households are better*	*Nuclear households are best*	*Total*
Rural	Nu	16.0	4.0	22.0	40.0	18.0	100(n=50)
	Joi	62.0	10.0	22.0	4.0	2.0	100(n=50)
	Total	39.0	7.0	22.0	22.0	10.0	100(n=100)
Urban	Nu	19.6	14.6	14.6	17.0	34.2	100(n=82)
	Joi	42.4	28.3	14.1	5.4	9.8	100(n=92)
	Total	31.6	21.8	14.4	11.0	21.2	100(n=174)

Table 9.3 shows that respondents in higher number admit that the merits of the joint households are more conspicuous than those of the nuclear households. The trend is similar in both the town and the village though there are some differences in degree. It appears that the proportion of these respondents who categorically believe that the joint household is the best form of household is higher in the village (39%) than in the town (32%). It is also to be noted that more respondents from the town (21%) than from the

village (10%) have opined that the nuclear household structure is the best form.

The table further reveals that in the town those who themselves live in nuclear households experience that nuclear households are the best form (34%) compared to their rural counterparts (18%). It means that living in the nuclear households seems to be less hazardous and more convenient to the urban wives than it is to the rural wives. On the contrary, proportionately more rural women who themselves are the residents of the joint households, experience that joint households are the best (62%) than their urban counterparts (42%).

There are valid reasons why village women are cautious and sceptical about the merits of the nuclear households. It is because the advantages of the joint household are better accessible to the villagers than to the urbanites. Villagers are generally short of cash and most of them do not have a regular source of income. Hence, they have to depend on their kin for economic aid more often. As the economic status of the kin is more or less comparable to them, generally all of them are in need of such aid, making the exchange of aid among the kindred a usual practice. Actually, in the village, relatives are the only source of help, and the role of the state or voluntary agencies is very meagre here. Hence co-residence with the kin is advantageous to them.

Moreover, villagers cannot afford to hire physical help from the outside in times of exigencies like illness, child-birth and pregnancy, old age, farming activities, and the like. Thus, physically also they are regularly dependent on their kin. Now, if they can manage to live in a joint household they will usually avail themselves of aid smoothly (as they are now members of the same household).

Further, compared to their urban counterparts village women are less educated, enlightened, conscious, assertive and vocal of their rights and freedom. Also, they exercise less control over their husbands. They are also less ambitious and aspirant for their own career or their children's education. So they have less complaint that children's education suffers in a joint household. Clash of personalities between the mother-in-law and the daughter-in-law is here less evident. Further, rural women feel less urge to look after their parents in old age (as most of them have brothers). Accordingly, the 'sacrifice' of the rural women is less when they live in the joint household compared to what they gain from it.

The situation is much different for the urban women many of whom feel a special attraction for the nuclear household. They are economically much better off than the villagers and so are not in need of economic aid from the kin. Moreover, they can afford to hire a cook, maid servant, *ayah* for helping them in housework and child-rearing, instead of depending on the mother-in-law or the sister-in-law. If required, they can take help of the creche, or can buy cooked food from outside. Thus, in their daily life they have to depend on their kin less than their rural counterparts.

Urban women are enlightened, educated, have more exposure to the world outside, and are often economically active. Hence, often they face clash of personalities with the other women members in the household and complain against its suffocating atmosphere. Being only child of their parents or having no brother living nearby, often they have the onus of looking after their parents in their old age, for which living in the joint household is not convenient.

It does not mean that the urban women are not aware of the disadvantages of the nuclear household. Actually, a substantial section of the residents of the urban nuclear households (34%) have opined that the advantages of the joint household is more felt than its disadvantages (joint households are best or better than nuclear ones). It shows that the popularity of the joint household is still there in the town.

As expected, generally residents of the nuclear households emphasise its advantages, and those of the joint households stress the advantages of the joint households. This is so because generally people get habituated and adjusted with their present arrangement and like to highlight its merits.

In conclusion we may then draw that the joint household is still capable of meeting many of the needs of its members. One finds that because of this (that it is still functional to the societal needs) many people are not prepared psychologically to break away from it. Their grievances and dissatisfactions are not so much against the system itself as against the atmosphere created by certain members of their immediate, specific households. This is one reason why there are several contradictory opinions about the advantages of the joint household (mentioned above). Many of its disadvantages originate due to the personality and mentality of its members. Still we do not agree with Freed and Freed that the joint family has been chosen for its positive qualities; the nuclear family was considered to be a kind of refuge from an unpleasant feature of the joint family life but was generally not valued for its own qualities (1982, p. 199). Instead, we like to emphasise that the nuclear household structure possesses some real advantages which have not been lost sight of even by the staunch supporters of the joint household in the sample.

Still, on the whole respondents agree that if there is a good understanding among the members of the joint household, it will be the best form, the most convenient and pleasure-giving place to live in. But the question is whether this understanding can be achieved in the today's world. What is needed is to make adjustments with and sacrifices for the others, and to have a mentality of tolerance and patience. In the following pages we shall show the views and suggestions of the respondents over this issue.

III

Respondents have expressed their opinion with regard to the future form of our family structure, whether a joint household will survive at all, and under which conditions. Tables 9.4 presents information provided by the respondents in this regard.

As appears from the data, according to the majority of the respondents (even those who at present live in the joint households), joint households will break up in the future for various reasons. Some of these reasons have already been discussed, some more will be presented in the following pages. At the same time, we shall also present, as suggested by the respondents, the conditions which are required to be fulfilled if joint households are to survive.

First, the future form of our family structure. Joint households will break up since the mentality of people at present is not congenial to its continuation. Living in a joint household incurs many inconveniences and nuisances, bearing the burden of the

Table 9.4
Respondents' Opinion about the Future Form of Family Structure

Future Form of Household	*F*
Joint household will	
break up because the mentality of people has changed	116
break up since the environment within which the present generation is brought up does not teach them to obey and respect the others	25
break up since women are being conscious of their rights	39
break up since it is unsuitable to working and career-minded women	4
break up since both spatial and social mobility is increasing	31
break up since economic differentiations among the brothers are increasing	34
break up since today people believe in consumerism and like to live a luxurious life for which joint household is not suitable	20
break up since sons today plan to separate even before their marriage	3
break up since nuclear households are increasing and those who are brought up in such households, particularly those who are 'only child', face a particular adjustment problem in a joint household	8
break up; 'live together' is being the fashion, perhaps family itself won't exist	1
break up due to lack of adequate accommodation in the ancestral home	20
Joint households will survive	
if the daughter-in-law is treated like the daughter	8
since working women in their own interest will try to adjust with their parents-in-law	9
among those who depend on the ancestral property but not among the service-holders	3
in a reduced form (LJ type)	67
when the son is the 'only son' of his parents	13
since Indian sons will never relinquish duties to their parents	11
Joint households will gradually be replaced by nuclear households	31
The present pattern where both types of households exist side by side will continue	23
Structural jointness will decrease, but the spirit of jointness will survive	20

others, which today's people do not like. They have been, instead, selfish, self-centred, impatient, assertive, self-righteous, calculating and jealous. They lack an amiable personality.

Joint household cannot survive under the conditions when people think that catering to others' liabilities is simply unpleasant.

People are today concerned with their spouse and children only. Others are regarded as externals, outsiders and burdens. These people will not show interest in joint households.

People today are very much conscious of their rights, freedom and prestige. While living with the others one has to curtail these things, which the modern generation often does not like.

In the middle class society, people are mostly economically self-sufficient and independent. So there is little urgency to compromise or make sacrifice for the others. Under the circumstances joint households cannot survive. Today, people are always busy and preoccupied with their job and career.

Their circle of friends also has enlarged. So they do not find time to maintain contact with all of their relatives.

Joint households will break up since the present generation of people is grown up in an atmosphere which does not teach them to obey and respect the seniors.

Nowadays, everybody, even the children, have their own opinion which they want to assert. They themselves take decision on their dress, diet, movements, circle of friends, plans, programmes, hobbies and recreation. Youngsters believe that they are culturally advanced, knowledgeable and capable of taking right decisions. To live in a joint household, on the other hand, requires members to abide by and respect the seniors. Hence, nuclear households would suit this generation of people.

Joint households will break up since women are being conscious of their rights. Egalitarian values have attracted them. The age at marriage has risen. Also, education and employment of women have become the current fashion. Today, when women get married, they are sufficiently matured and are not ready to comply with the traditional hierarchy or authority based on age and gender. They now like to come out of the grip of the traditional joint household structure. The chances of the clash of personalities and differences of opinions between the womenfolk of the household have intensified, which would bring more splits in the joint households in the coming days.

Joint households will break up as they are inconvenient to working women. As their number is increasing day-by-day so also the chance of the survival of the joint household diminishes.

"Small family is the happy family" is today's slogan. As a result, in many households, particularly in the middle class, the couple has only one issue. If it is a nuclear household, then this child does not get any chance of interaction with siblings and cousins and hence does not learn the art of adjustment with the peers. Generally s/he is pampered which makes him/her selfish, jealous and assertive. If it is the case of a girl child, it will be difficult for her to adjust with her husband's kin after her marriage. In contrast, girls reared in a joint household atmosphere, know how to behave properly in such contexts and manage the husband's kin.

Joint households will break up under the present circumstances when many people are required to leave their home for job and profession and settle in different places for pursuing their career. Moreover, many more people are now being ambitious and they do not mind to leave their home for fulfilling their motto. With the spread of industrialisation, this trend will augment resulting into the disintegration of the joint household structure.

When the earnings of the brothers in a household vary, disputes over economic matters will increase. Those who earn more will try to upgrade their lifestyle and relinquish others' liabilities. With the march of industrialisation such income differentiation will more and more expand resulting into disintegration of the joint households.

People are now more and more getting attracted towards consumerism and like to pursue a luxurious lifestyle which is not possible when they live in a large household. They believe that only in the nuclear households it is possible to arrange diet, dress, recreation pattern, child-rearing according to one's own will. When people have their independent source of income, they have no compulsion to retain the joint household.

People today require more space to live in. Each member needs a separate room for study, music lessons, entertaining guest and friends. Children of every brother take lessons from separate tutors. Each has a separate circle of friends. Thus, the demand for space is rising, which cannot be accommodated in the ancestral home.

Sons will remain in the stem family for two or three years after their marriage. Then differences of opinion will arise over many matters such as diet, cooking recipe, division of household chores, sharing of the economic liability, and so on. These differences and clashes will aggravate as brothers, one after another, would get married and newly married brides will join the household. Ultimately there will be conflicts and quarrels leading to separation.

Respondents have put several suggestions as well for the survival of the joint household which have been presented below:

Joint households will survive if everybody is responsible and sensible enough and does his/her duty on time, spontaneously and voluntarily. But if others take advantage of one's niceness and shift all major responsibilities to one person, then it is better to be separate. For remaining joint, everybody has to sacrifice, and the head of the household is to sacrifice most. Joint households will survive if the father is solvent and has a personality to command respect from the others. The mother also is required to be physically fit so that she can bear the major burden of the household chores and permits rest and relief to the others.

To continue the joint household it is the parents who are required to take initiative in making adjustment with the other members. They should be liberal and lenient and try to attune with their employed and enlightened daughter-in-law. They should treat her like their daughter. Her imperfections, errors and faults are to be undermined and ignored while her good qualities are to be appreciated. The charge of their son should be handed over to her.

Joint households may be retained by the working women in their own interest. There should be a clear-cut and equitable division of labour and responsibilities. When the earnings of all the brothers are sufficient (affluent households) and there is a parity in the culture, taste and values among the members, living in the joint household is convenient.

Among the respondents there are holders of such opinions as well: The future household structures will be more or less similar to the present ones. Each of the types, as exists today, will be there as each of them has some advantages. Also, there might be people with diverse type of mentalities and personalities. Some are prone to make adjustment, some not. Those who will be able to get along with the others, will do so, while those who will fail, will leave the stem family. Thus, both the processes—the continuation and disintegration of the joint households—will go on.

As today's parents have one or two child(ren), the size of the household will not be large. Unless the son is compelled to settle elsewhere because of his job, he will remain with the parents. Large joint households, however, have little chance to survive.

The LJ type small joint households composed of parents and one son with his wife and children will be the fashion of the coming days. They will gradually replace the large CJ and LCJ types of households.

As today's families are being small having one or at best two children per couple, most children will have no brother/sister of his/her own. Under such circumstance, they will be compelled to maintain interactions, exchanges and contacts with cousins; otherwise children will feel lonely and bored. Also, they will not enjoy the sibling relationship unless their parents maintain contacts with their kin.

Jointness will survive in the mental make-up of the people. They will try to get assembled together, even with their cousins, on various occasions, and, in fact, create such occasions to get the company of their relatives. So though the joint households may structurally disintegrate, the spirit of jointness will never wither away. It is a pleasure to jointly travel, celebrate a festival or ceremony, enjoy a feast. So there will be occasional get-together among the relatives. Co-residence with kin, however, will reduce as joint living leads to clashes and conflicts over many small and trivial matters. It will disturb peace. Then there will be mutual dislike and intolerance. One may suppress these feelings for some time, but ultimately it will not solve the problem. Relationship will then gradually embitter. It is to live apart, occasionally assemble together and cherish the spirit of jointness.

Those respondents who are a bit hopeful about the future of joint household more or less agree that one necessary condition for its continuation would be the solidarity among the members of the household. Being asked to explain their position, they have interpreted 'solidarity' in a variety of ways some of which are presented below. Solidarity indicates:

The habit or mentality of sharing one another's experiences, sorrows and happiness; mutual understanding; the willingness to live together; mutual sympathy, love, affection, responsibility, dutifulness, patience, tolerance, dependence, respect of one another's opinion; free exchange of opinion and elimination of all misunderstandings and disagreements peacefully through mutual discussions; a spirit of helping one another; one should assist the others for the sake of helping, and not taunt for this act afterwards, or not in the expectation of quid pro quo; partial sacrifice of one's own interest for the other; consideration of the others' interest as well. Respect and obey the seniors and love for the juniors.

Non-indulgence in any such concept as the spouses and children constitute a distinct entity (nucleus) within the household; while living in a joint household, one should think for the welfare of all, and not discriminate against the others' kids, or be partial.

Ignore or undermine others' deficiencies and mistakes; to comply with the norm "forgive and forget"; not to be disturbed with or pay attention to or give importance to small trivial matters; abide by the discipline of the home and keep confidence in the same.

It appears that majority of the respondents believe that joint households will disintegrate and gradually they will be replaced by household units composed of the husband, wife and unmarried children. At the best, it may include the parents of the husband. Statements containing these assumptions recur most of the times (Table 9.4). One may then want to know whether the opinion of the rural and urban respondents or of those living in nuclear and joint households vary in this respect. Table 9.5 contains this information.

Table 9.5

Future of the Joint Households, by Residence and Type of Present Household Structure of Respondents (in percentage)

Residence	*Type of household*	*Cat. I*	*Cat. II*	*Cat. III*	*Cat. IV*	*Cat. V*	*Cat. VI*	*Cat. VII*	*Total*	
									%	*F*
Rural	Nu	78.0	4.0	14.0	4.0	-	-	-	100.0	(n=50)
	Joi	60.0	20.0	18.0	2.0	-	-	-	100.0	(n=50)
	Total	69.0	12.0	16.0	3.0	-	-	-	100.0	(n=100)
Urban	Nu	63.4	11.0	11.0	2.4	11.0	1.2	-	100.0	(n=82)
	Joi	40.2	30.4	18.5	6.5	2.2	-	2.2	100.0	(n=92)
	Total	51.2	21.3	14.9	4.6	6.3	.6	1.1	100.0	(n=174)

Note: Cat. I= Joint households will disintegrate/have already disintegrated. Cat. II= Most probably they will disintegrate. Cat.III = Small joint households will replace large ones. Cat.IV= No change in the present condition. Cat. V= Spiritual jointness will exist though structurally joint households will disintegrate. Cat. VI= Jointness with wife's parents will replace that with husband's. Cat. VII= All households will be joint.

As appears from Table 9.5, majority of the respondents are skeptical about the future of joint household and think that it will not exist in the future. The number of proponents of this view is higher in the village than in the town, higher among the residents of nuclear than those of joint households. There are also respondents, though a minority, who believe that the usefulness of the joint household has not completely been lost. Hence, though its incidence or frequency may lessen, it will not totally extinguish.

One point is to be noted here. Urban respondents are more educated, sophisticated and articulate than those from the village. That is why their mode of expression is also more cautious, reserved and precise. It is evident in their answer patterns where there are more varieties and sheds. Unlike the villagers, many of them have avoided categorically saying that joint households will disintegrate. Instead, they have attached many conditions, qualifications and specifications to its future fate.

What may appear to be queer is that why those souls who are at present living in joint household or view that joint household are good, are doubtful about its future. It is understood why residents of the nuclear households are skeptical. But is it not expected that the opinion of the residents of the joint households will be somewhat different?

However, though apparently this may be seen as a mark of contradictory behaviour on the part of the respondents, further inquiry removes this. In the first place, while answering this question, respondents have reported not only their own experiences and inferences, but also those of the others around them—the common and popular conceptions of the society. In other words, they have reported what they have seen and heard in their surroundings. Generally, their attitude is this: "I am in a joint household; my mother-in-law/daughter-in-law/sister-in-law with whom I co-reside also is in a joint household. But we are exceptional species, not typical." A sort of self-eulogisation works here: "Generally, people would not make so much of sacrifices or adjustments as I am doing." Still, another sort of consideration works here: "Though at present I am in a joint household, this may not be so for long. Whenever I shall be able to make any alternative arrangement or the situation will further worsen, I shall seek partition." Or, "It would have been better to remain joint, but circumstances do not permit to do so. Ideally, this might have been good but the reality differs from the ideology." Anyway, to most of these respondents, living in joint households is only a stop-gap, temporary arrangement, and so they cannot be much hopeful about its future.

It seems that majority of the respondents view the joint households as better than nuclear ones (Table 9.3). On the other hand, majority of the respondents are skeptical about its survival (Table 9.5). Any apparent contradiction in these answer patterns can be resolved if one looks the perspectives from which respondents view these issues. They are answering the first question (which household type is better) from a normative point of view, but when they answer the latter question (what will be the future form of household), they are considering the question of feasibility, the reality, their own and others' limitations and helplessness. Hence, there may not be always parity between these two types of answers. That is why even though a respondent thinks that the joint household is good, or herself lives in such a household willingly or under compulsion, may not be hopeful and confident about its future.

While pointing out the advantages of the joint household, respondents also have mentioned that these advantages can be realised only when the relationships among the members are cordial and there is a feeling of solidarity among them and a willingness to stay joint. What appears is that there may not be wrong in the system, but in the behaviour of its participants. And, the problem is that the ideal situation in which the advantages of joint household could be fully realised, is being scarce day-by-day. Why will this be so, has already been stated. Hence, to conclude, the possibility is that under the present circumstances, it will be difficult for the traditional joint households to perpetuate. Either they will shed many of their traditional functions, or their size will be reduced. It means, LJ type households will replace CJ and LCJ types. Other family sociologists also share this view (cf. Kapadia, 1966, p. 305; Madan, 1989, p. 152; Nicholas, 1961; Sengupta, 1958, p.387; Shah, 1998, p.6). Possibly our family structure will be somewhat closer to the modified extended family as has been propounded by Litwak (1962b).

10

Summary and Conclusions

I

This inquiry has been undertaken to understand our family system *as is experienced* in our daily life against its *normative structure*. In other words, it is an attempt to provide a 'field view' of the Indian family in contrast to its 'book view' account which includes the view of a society embodied in the scriptures and in all *a priori* logical models of the society developed by social scientists. A family is more than a structure. It is a vibrant functioning reality, a group of persons living together in intimate continuing relationships. Following Radcliffe-Brown who has observed that human beings are connected by a complex network of social relations and 'social structure' denotes this *network of actually existing social relations*, we assume that for understanding the family structure a dynamic, functional approach of inquiry is the most suitable. And, for this a 'field view' of the family is required.

Family, being a social phenomenon or fact, is required to be investigated from a sociological perspective which assumes that for inquiring into any social fact (by fact we mean any empirically measurable and verifiable phenomenon) one should collect empirical and concrete information. Hence, any inquiry into the family from the sociological perspective should focus on the familial behaviour of our people, the interactions and interrelationships as people commonly pursue within and outside their immediate family circle, and analyse the same logico-empirically. This should be as distinct from a *statistical approach* which merely stresses the relative incidence or frequency of the different types of household structures as evidence of the different familial types, from any *legal approach* which assumes that co-parcenary is the sole or prime evidence of a joint family and all the coparceners are members of a joint family, as from an *Indological approach* which regards that all the persons who are ritually permitted to perform the *shraddha* ritual or offer food (*pinda*) to manes, constitute a joint family, the *only* family structure of the Indian Hindus.

We, therefore, do not agree with such paradigms that believe that joint family is an unchanging, eternal institution, or, that "what breaks up is the co-parcenary unit; ties of kinship are immutable" (Madan, 1962, p.8); or, that the growth of a nuclear family into an extended family is a spontaneous process (ibid); or, that "the motif in West Bengal is thus to form the patrilineal joint family of procreation—presently, eventually or potentially" (Mukherjee, 1977, p.168); or, that "the joint and undivided family used to be accepted as the normal pattern of Hindu family" (Kapadia, 1966, p. 309). We have tried to show in this endeavour to what extent these above suppositions reflect the values of the authors, what these authors think to be the desired and normative structure of the family.

Let us, in contrast, begin with the following suppositions. First, any empirically useful and logically sensible approach of family study should be dynamic in nature. Here we agree with Desai who laments that still our knowledge is inadequate in the field of the possible association between occupational and social mobility and family solidarity, whether residential separation of household units leads to 'effective separation' from the joint family (1955, pp.112-13). However, though we agree with Desai that the jointness of the separated units consists in the 'rights and obligations of the members of different units towards one another and in the feeling of oneness' (p.104), we do not accept his view that co-residence and commensality are neither adequate nor reliable criteria for judging the family jointness (p.103).

Second, family solidarity is not such an unchanging or indivisible entity which either exists or does not exist. Rather, we assume that it varies in terms of both kind and degree. Third, as family solidarity varies, it is a variable and its variations are measurable. Fourth, family solidarity being a complex concept (construct), its depth and extent cannot be adequately perceived in terms of only one, two or three simple criteria like commensality, co-residence or co-parcenary. Hence, side by side checking whether these objective criteria of jointness are fulfilled, one should also note the nature of interrelations and patterns of interactions among the members of the joint family. Fifth, for measuring family solidarity, one should focus on both members' behaviour and opinions; that is, with the inquiry into the interaction patterns and interrelations among the members of the joint family, their opinions towards various family-related issues also should be attended. Sixth, as separation from the stem family in itself does not indicate termination of all sorts of obligations towards it, a mere sharing of a common hearth and residence also does not indicate fulfilment of all rights and obligations towards the members of a stem family. We assume that structural changes are associated with functional changes as well, and therefore, any intensive analysis of the family behaviour of the members must include different types of household structures, e.g., nuclear, joint. Lastly, as splitting up of joint families into nuclear families may be considered as a regular, normal and expected function of the family developmental process and therefore, as is often argued, any separation of a man from his family of orientation does not mean functional disintegration of that family, it is equally probable that all such separations do not mature as the normal or routine process or as the function of the family developmental process. In fact, the developmental process being a social fact, is subject to the pressure of many other factors and forces within the broader social milieu as a result of which not a single, one-dimensional (joint family-nuclear families-joint families) developmental process but several such processes are operative. And these can be explored not from the legal texts or scriptures but from the analysis of the concrete experiences of people.

We, therefore, decided to undertake an empirical inquiry to collect facts, experiences and expectations of people relating and relevant to the above suppositions. In the collection, ordering, analysis and reporting of the facts and information gathered from the respondents, we cared to remain as objective, concrete and explicit as possible. We were concerned with *what it is* and *what it will be* and not *what it should be*. However, whether we liked it or not, some value-loaded issues cropped up in our inquiry. Whenever we had to deal with any such issue, we tried to be explicit, specific and precise in defining those issues and concepts, develop commonly agreed-upon concrete and objective indices for their measurement. It is, however, very difficult to find out such commonly agreed-upon indices for measuring any value-loaded concept, and this is the reason why scientific research does not directly entertain such issues. Values (beliefs and convictions about what is desirable and what is undesirable) simply are not empirically testable. While one group of people may emphasise the inclusion of one set of indices and evidences for the measurement of a concept, another group may focus on a somewhat different set. In our case we had to face this problem. We cannot do away with it and satisfy all the parties. What we can at best do is to faithfully report what we have actually done, which evidences and indices we have actually referred to while measuring any particular value-ridden issue. Whether our treatment is adequate, valid, meaningful and useful is a matter of choice and decision, and we leave it to the judgement of the readers.

Actually, the behaviour and attitudinal traits chosen by us as indicators of functional jointness of the families, or as evidences of the fulfilment/non-fulfilment of mutual rights and obligations towards the family members, may be interpreted as reflecting our values. For example, we decided to include the practice of mealtime discussions as a behavioural trait indicating family jointness; or, allowing one's home as a temporary refuge or shelter for the old, ill, handicapped relatives was included as an evidence of the fulfilment of the mutual rights and obligations among the members of a joint family. A decline in the family solidarity has been inferred from the less frequent occurrences of these events. Now, whether our choice and decision are right is, again, a matter of decision, and definitely, would reflect the dicider's values and belief.

Since the social, economic, demographic and ecological environment of the village and the town is markedly different, we decided to gather data from both these localities. Married women living with their husbands (and others) were the units of observation. To comply with the requirement of the goal of the inquiry, information was to be gathered from people living in different types of household structures. The respondents were selected following the purposive sampling method. Data were collected through the face-to-face interview with the respondents, where issues on which information was sought were decided in advance but respondents were requested to communicate and elucidate their experiences and opinions in their own words and from their own perspectives. Ultimately, we collected data from 274 married women of whom 92 lived in the urban joint, 82 in the urban nuclear, 50 in the rural joint and 50 in the rural nuclear households.

Since there is no systematic base-line data with which we can compare our findings to ascertain whether and to what extent any *change* has occurred in the sphere of functional solidarity of our rural and urban, nuclear and joint households, we discarded any plan to make any 'change study' of our family. But as and when our data permit, we have compared the degree of family solidarity as displayed by the respondents from different household structures in rural and urban areas. At this stage, we place some of these trends which emanate from our findings (details have been presented in the text).

II

Functional ties among a close circle of kin, namely, parents and siblings of the couple, have been found to be active, and these are stronger among the urbanites compared to the residents of the rural households, and among the residents of the joint compared to those of the nuclear households.

People still think it right and proper to help their relatives. They do not always do this in the expectation that they will be paid back from those whom they serve. For example, a person may help his younger brother in finding a decent job. His brother may help his nephews in their education or find a suitable matrimonial match for his nieces. However, the spirit behind this sort of behaviour is just to perform one's duty and obligation to the kindred primarily, and not simply to reciprocate or retort one's aid. Thus, it is not that one must pay back what he has received from a particular kin who obliged him by providing some sort of aid. Within the kindred one person may assist somebody who would help a third person, and so on. Thus, interchange of aid rotates within the circle of kin which cements the kinship ties. The forms and types of aid differ from situation to situation. Among the lower income group people exchange of financial aid is relatively frequent. Among the highly educated, well-placed persons exchange of information, advice, professional skill is more common. Physical help, co-operation, advice, councelling and emotional support are exchanged among people of all categories.

Interchange of aid among the kin is sometimes considered so natural and normal that the respondents do not think it proper to report such behaviour as 'exchange of aid', For example, it is typical that parents should help children in getting established in their life and career; sons (in the absence of sons, daughters) should look after parents when they are ill, infirm and old. A sick relative is to be attended by the others according to their capacity. In solemnising a marriage among the kin circle each should participate and cooperate to perform the ceremony peacefully. If anybody has any influence and connection he should help the relatives in getting a job, bank-loan, license, and so on. A doctor should come to help his sick relatives as and when necessary. Many more examples of this sort can be added.

Nepotism in its naked and disguised forms pervades modern organisations. In both normal times and emergencies, helping relatives is still considered normal and desired. In the absence of adequate social security measures the major and primary responsibilities of looking after the aged, ill, infirm, unemployed, widows and orphans still rest on the relatives. Often such kinship obligations are fulfilled voluntarily, and such reciprocity among the kin constantly refuels and reinforces kinship bonds.

The points to be noted here are: first, day-by-day the circle of kin within which such goods and services are freely, spontaneously and voluntarily exchanged is being narrow. The respondents have generally referred to their and their husbands' parents, sibs and their spouses and children as the kin with whom they normally enter into the exchange relationships; i.e., kin falling within these categories are regarded as 'effective kin' or 'kinsmen of co-operation'. On the other hand, uncles, aunts, cousins are regarded as distant or 'nominal kin' or 'kinsmen of recognition' with whom exchanges occur only on ceremonies and festivals. Beyond this orbit, i.e., interchanges with grandfathers' brother and their children are regarded as exceptional and special events. Here we find a similarity with Parsons' 'onion ring structure'. The greatest number of kin with whom exchange relationship is incurred are in the inner ring composed of the couple's sibs and children's family units. As one moves from the intermediate ring of grandparents' and sibs' children's and grandchildren's family units to the outer ring of cousins' and other relatives' family units, the number of contacted kin declines.

Second, excepting people from the low income group, people in general hesitate to accept financial help even from their sibs, and when they are compelled to take it, it is taken as loan. Such hesitation, however, is less observed in accepting physical, emotional and informative aid. In general, people think it desirable to be self-sufficient in themselves so that less the dependence on the kin, the better.

Third, while helping the kin, a sense of obligation rather than feeling of duty has been found to be stronger. It is true that still parents and children, brothers and sisters interchange aid with one another. But spontaneity, eagerness, voluntariness, inclination, determination are on the wane. As reported by the respondents, filial piety, and respect and obedience to the seniors are declining among the new generation. At the same time, friends, neighbours and work-mates have been competing with kinship groups in winning people's confidence and loyalties.

Fourth, though the bulk of the exchange occurs with the husband's agnatic and consanguineal kin, exchange of aid with kin on the female line is also significant and substantial specially among those living in nuclear households and living below the subsistence level.

Next, those who live in the joint households come to one another's service more frequently and regularly. Indeed, the respondents from such households have not cared to mention many such incidents as 'exchange of aid with relatives' while by

the residents from nuclear households these very acts have been referred to as 'acts of helping others'. For instance, the respondents from joint households think it quite natural that parents-in-law are to be nursed and looked after, the sister-in-law is to be given relief and rest when she is ill, or her husband and children are to be taken care of when she goes out, or a brother-in-law who is financially weak should be granted some relief in sharing the financial burden, and so on. On the other hand, when these very services are provided by the members of nuclear households, they are conscious to point out these events as 'exchange of aid'. When this is so, there is also a latent feeling that these are to be paid back sometime and somehow. When the respondents themselves are the recipients of such 'aid', they would consciously try to minimise such occasions so that one need not remain under obligation to relatives. Like their counterparts in joint households, they do not feel that they have a right to enjoy such 'favours'. It means that with the separation of the hearth, the nature, terms, context and attitude behind the exchange of aid with kin also change. Functional bonds no doubt are still operative, but their recurrence lessens and strength weakens. The data, thus, clearly evince that with structural separation, functional ties also lessen and weaken everywhere and among all segments of the people.

The opinions and activities which more or less bestow the existence of the joint family spirit among the respondents are: exchange of aid and assistance of various kinds among the kin, exchange of gifts, attitude towards approaching and extending aid to kin in crisis and emergency, opinion that the husband should be dutiful to his parents as well, and the influence of the kin in the formation of the political opinion of the members of a lineage. On the other hand, this spirit is somewhat lacking in such matters as absence of the concept of the ancestral home, lack of interest in arranging regular and/or occasional get-togethers of the respondents' husbands' kin, and spontaneous and full-fledged participation of all relatives in marriage ceremonies.

On the whole, joint family ties and solidarity towards the spirit of the joint family are stronger in the urban joint households and weaker in the rural nuclear households, than the other types. It cannot be definitively concluded, however, that urbanites are more faithful to the joint living than ruralites, for in some respects ruralites surpass urbanites in sticking to joint family norms, values, sentiments and behaviours (such as, the opinion expressed by the majority of the rural respondents that men should separate after the death of their parents and marriage of their sisters, or that wives should regard their husbands as their guardians rather than insist on egalitarian relationships between the genders). The study does not find any definitive evidence to draw whether ties with the kin are stronger or weaker among rural nuclear and urban nuclear households, i.e., which ones are deviating more from the norm of fulfilling rights and obligations to the kin.

III

We have inquired to what extent our nuclear households are tied with the respondents' husbands' family of origin, and the rights and obligations of the members of different nuclear units to one another are honoured. At the same time, to what extent our joint households are really joint, i.e., are compact and cohesive functional units, also has been assessed. We have already presented our findings in detail. Now, the major trends only will be discussed.

1. Looking after parents when sons live apart is not yet an immediate and serious problem faced by our society on a large scale generally. Sons make some provisions for their parents in such cases, though that arrangement may not be regarded by the parents as adequate and satisfactory.
2. Though not worried about their wherewithal, parents have grounds to be anxious about the future of their families of procreation since a substantial section of their sons tend to separate in the early stage of the family developmental process.
3. In the village, generally families disintegrate after the death of the father. But since the longevity of the rural men (fathers) is poor, splitting up of families comes here within a few years of the sons' marriage.
4. In both the village and the town, the major single factor behind the split up of a joint household is the members' unwillingness to live in a joint family, selfishness, intolerance

and impatience to one another's problems. In addition, in the village, the early and premature death of the father and disagreement among the malefolk over the share of economic liabilities of the household are the major reasons behind family disintegration. In the town, however, lack of adequate accommodation in the ancestral home and physical and social mobility of the malefolk are important factors causing split of the household.

5. Majority of the rural nuclear households have partitioned their ancestral property too. In the town, this factor is not important since here the amount of property in most of the cases is too meagre to be considered for partition. Here, in most of the cases, separation of the household means separation of the hearth and the dwelling place, and a man seeking partition from the stem family has to arrange his new dwelling place on his own.
6. In the village patri-local residence is the practice, while in the town the trend is towards a neo-local residence. We have not got any indication towards the uxori-local residential pattern, though maintenance of contacts with the wife's relatives is frequent in nuclear households. The increasing trend toward neo-local residential pattern tends to reduce the immediate or close surveillance and control by parents and other kinsfolk.
7. Co-operation with the husband's kin in the matter of performance of rites and rituals is in general poor, and this is more so in the village than in the town.
8. Kin with whom regular and/or frequent contacts and communication are maintained include the parents and siblings of the couple. Contact with such kin as the husband's father's brothers or cousins has become almost a ritual. The problem is more acute in the town than in the village.
9. Households which are joint in terms of sharing a common hearth and residence and holding property in common, mostly do not appear to be economically cohesive units. Husband-wife-children nucleus often maintains its separate and distinct existence within a joint household, and thus often a joint household contains several units whose consumption pattern, style of life, mode of child-bearing and socialisation,

aspirations and ambitions differ. It indicates that there are several decision-making centres each of which is composed of a man, his wife and children. Usually, brothers/sons deposit a portion of their income to a common purse from which some of their expenses are met while the rest are managed on their own according to their individual capacity, taste and standard. Rural and urban households do not differ in this respect.

10. Solidarity of the joint households is equally weak in respect of members' co-operation with each other in the performance of various household chores like shopping, child-rearing, washing of clothes, and so on. Often members do these tasks only for themselves, their spouse and children. Village and urban people show no difference in this respect.
11. Urban people take little interest in mealtime discussions. Instead of taking meal with other members of the joint household, most of them either take it according to their own convenience or with their respective spouses and children. In the village, however, conformity to the traditional norm of the joint family still prevails in this respect to a greater extent.
12. While going out for shopping or any place or recreation and amusement, urban wives generally accompany their husbands. Rural wives go to these places with husbands and husbands' kin as well.
13. On the whole, women of the joint households, in both the village and the town, are in favour of continuing the status quo. Those who live in LCJ type of households, however, do not mostly share this feeling. They have opined that liabilities and costs (surrender of individual freedom, sacrifice of personal interests and comforts) often surpass the benefits and satisfactions derived from living in this type of household, and this is the experience in both the town and the village.
14. The opinion that on the whole joint households are better to live in than nuclear households is held more by the urbanites than by the villagers, and more by the residents of the joint households than by those of the nuclear households. Respondents from 72 per cent of the rural joint, 71 per cent of the urban joint, 34 per cent of the urban nuclear and 20 per cent of the rural nuclear households share this opinion. that

joint household is the *best* form is opined by a higher number of villagers while nuclear household is the *best* form is believed by a higher number of urbanites.

15. At the same time, majority of the respondents are doubtful about the chances of survival of the joint households in the future, and this skepticism has been shared even by those who are at present living in the joint households and accepts its superiority to the nuclear structure. They apprehend that the factors and forces inimical to the survival of the joint households (e.g., occupational and income differentiations among the brothers, people's being more and more assertive of their rights, intolerant and impatient to the others' causes, being selfish, self-centred and ambitious) will aggravate day-by-day leading to the breakdown of the joint households. 'Small family' being the present-day motto, many of the future husbands and wives are the only child of their parents, who would find the atmosphere of the joint household as totally alien and uncongenial to live in.
16. Some of the respondents have opined that the joint household structure may continue but in a reduced size (supplemented nuclear or lineal joint type), or that spiritual jointness among the kindred would replace structural jointness. They, however, find no possibility of patri-local joint households being replaced by matri-local ones.
17. Respondents also suggested that joint households may survive if there is no dispute among the malefolk regarding the share of the economic liabilities. One of the essential conditions for the survival of the LCJ type of households is that there should be an authoritative and impartial head of the household who can effectively control all the members and would not favour one against another. He should also be capable to bear the major expenses of the household on his own. The LJ type of household requires a good understanding between the mother-in-law and the daughter-in-law. The CJ households may continue if the brothers are more or less of the same economic status, their economic status is more or less comfortable, they find living in a joint household convenient and economically rational, and there is no dispute among the sisters-in-law over the distribution of household chores.

18. Our sample, particularly the sample from the village, being geographically and socially not sufficiently mobile either inter-generationally or collaterally, does not offer the chance of testing Parsons' hypotheses regarding the possible impact of mobility on the traditional joint family structure (Parsons however used the term 'classical extended family'). However, the trend noted is that with income, occupational and educational differentiation among the brothers, men tend to separate their residence too. That is, the joint households are more homogeneous in these respects than the nuclear ones. Further, in the town where cases of social mobility is relatively frequent, physical dispersion of the kin is also relatively high.
19. A general tendency noted among all the categories of our sample households is that whether or not people live in the nuclear households, their primary attachment is towards their spouse and children. That is to say, the husband-wife-children nucleus maintains its distinct identity in the structurally joint households as well. This is in consonance with what Parsons (1949) assumed in his concept of the 'relative isolation' of the nuclear families by which he meant, among other things, obligations to one's spouse and children would be stronger than those towards kin outside this nucleus.
20. In the same vein, we have noted some similarity between Goode's (1963) assumptions and our observations in the relevant spheres. Though our families are not of the 'conjugal type', a trend towards the relative exclusion of a wide range of kin from their everyday affairs has been noted.
21. Next, as has been assumed by Goode, our urban nuclear households also show the tendency towards neo-local residence in place of patri-local residence.
22. Goode suggested that the appeal of the conjugal family would be more attractive to those who were suppressed under the previous system, women and youngsters, for example. From our observations also we find that our respondents are more willing and insistent than their husbands on being separated from their husbands' family of origin, and this attitude is more prevalent among the younger respondents than the elderly ones.

IV

Still, we must admit that in our society the appeal of the conjugal family is not yet very attractive. There is no ideological attack on the joint living and no strong values which assert that the joint household *should no longer exist*. It seems that the concept of the joint household at the present moment is not at the verge of extinction. Joint households are a social reality no less than the nuclear households. They have their functions which cannot be realised by nuclear households. These functions, however, are changing, altering and are being modified in diverse ways and respects. The mode of functioning of the joint households—members' consumption patterns, style of life, household authority structure, division of labour, pattern of intra- and extra-familial interactions and inter-relations—is so varied that any generalisation about the mode of functioning of the joint households is difficult. In fact, each household, so far as its functional dimension is concerned, appears as a type. Certainly, only in a few of them members' behaviour comply with the traditional norms and prescriptions. And, this is the relevance of holding empirical inquiries into the functional jointness or solidarity of the joint household rather than taking it as an axiom or 'obvious'. This empirical study has brought to our notice and consideration these varied patterns.

From the inquiry into the functional solidarity of our families a trend toward the emergence of the 'modified extended family' (Litwak, 1960a) can be discerned where emphasis is put on functional ties, affectional bonds, exchange of aid and services among kin, and for this purpose geographical propinquity, occupational homogeneity and hierarchical authority structure are not necessary conditions. This modified extended family deviates in several respects from our ideal type joint family (the features of which have already been presented). This modified extended family is neither incompatible nor an isolated unit in today's India. On the contrary, with its numerous kin ties based on affection and mutual aid it seems to have become a visible unit in the Indian setting as well. And, this trend has been noted in both rural and urban societies, and in all economic and occupational groups.

What to be noted is that though most of the family sociologists analysed the change in the family system and extra-familial kinship interactions in the perspective of the industrialised societies, many of their observations and predictions have been found to be applicable to our society too, both in the town and in the village. Though there are differences in the quantity and pace of changes materialised so far, the dimension and trend of the changes, namely, from structural jointness to emphasis on extra-familial kinship bonds, from ascriptive obligation to personal choice in determining extra-familial kinship interactions, from hierarchical kin structure to diffuse equality, from 'hard' functions to 'soft' functions, and from unilineal to bilineal kinship interactions, are the same.

What we find is that changes are more prominent in the field of behaviour of the respondents than in their values, attitude and opinions. That joint family is a good institution, that it looks good and earns prestige in the eyes of others if married sons live with their parents or if several married brothers co-reside, that joint family has still some important functions to play, services to offer, are not disputed by typical women. But the bone of contention lies in its feasibility in today's context. Many of the behavioural traits of the respondents (mentioned in the text) do not comply with the norm of the ideal type joint family, nor are they hopeful that conformity towards the joint family norms may increase in the coming days; in fact, the situation will deteriorate, the substantial majority of the respondents apprehend.

We, therefore, conclude that our joint household structure is not so much a functionally compact and cohesive unit, nor would it be so in the near future. Though our people generally still do not desire to live in isolation from their kin or do not or cannot refuse their duties and obligations towards their close kin (mainly parents and sibs) or seek participation of relatives in their joys and sorrows, ceremonies and festivals, marriages and cremations, it is not all correct to say that the norms and values of the joint family are intact or that nuclearity is something unknown to the Indian soil. The husband-wife-children nucleus is a social fact, in fact, a more solid and effective unit of operation than the kin group consisting of several married brothers with their wives and children. It means, our society is advancing towards the consensus that one's first and primary attachment and obligation should be towards one's spouse and children compared to the other kin. Law also recognises this fact. For example, in case a person dies, it is his/her spouse who is *automatically* entitled to the compensation and other benefits, if at all available. It is one's spouse who has direct access to one's property. If a man dies, it is his wife who is entitled to enjoy the pension (called family pension). What to be noted is that none of the other kin, even the parents, have any direct and automatic access to these legal securities if the wife is alive. Next to the wife comes the claim of children. Still there is no legal provision in our country which can compel a man to bear the expenses (alimony) of his parents though the same is open to his wife.

Nuclearisation of the family in the sense of complete or total isolation from the kindred, i.e., living in atomised families, possibly is not or cannot be practised in any human society. Nor did Parsons and Goode referred to this interpretation of their concepts. They only insisted on the 'relative' isolation or exclusion. And the degree of this relativity varies from country to country or from one segment of the society to another. Maybe, western families are relatively more isolated than the Indian ones, families of those who are socially and spatially mobile are more than those of the immobile, urban families more than the rural ones, youngsters maybe more detached from the kin than the elderly people, wives may be more detached than the husbands (so far as the attachment to the husband's family is concerned), and so on.

Let us look at the data from yet another perspective. If Indians were committed only to the joint family, there should have been no deviation of people's actual familial behaviour from the normative structure of the ideal type joint family. In that case what should occur is like this:

First, regular and frequent contacts and exchange of goods and services with at least third and fourth degree consanguineal kin of the husband on the paternal line should have been a usual phenomenon. However, what we observe is that most of the transactions and functional ties respondents (and/or their husbands) enter into are limited to their husbands' parents, siblings and siblings' spouses and children. Thus, the circle of 'effective' kin or 'kinsmen of co-operation' is very limited. Kindred beyond this orbit is often referred to as 'nominal' or distant kin or 'kinsmen of recognition' only. Definitely, this does not go in favour of the structure and norms of the joint family (according to the Indological definition).

Second, co-parcenary among kindred of several generations should be a regular phenomenon, for it has been regarded by many of our family sociologists as an evidence of the joint family bonds. What we actually observe is that co-parcenary has not been found to exist beyond two generations. That is, respondents have reported that they do not hold property in common with the brothers of the fathers-in-law or their sons.

Third, mutual rights and obligations were to exist beyond the husband-wife-children nucleus. But the evidences we have collected show that men recognise their 'duty' only towards their parents. Though they have exchanges of aid with other kin (brothers, sisters, etc.) they most often do it out of obligation rather than of duty, or out some calculation of being materially benefited through these exchanges. Thus, exchanges with the kin are not always voluntary or spontaneous. Definitely, it does not indicate the spirit or the joint family. The residents of the joint households are less calculating while they exchange goods and services with the kin, i.e., they accept more obligations to kin than those of the nuclear ones, but their behaviour and attitude also are not disinterested, selfless or self-sacrificing. It shows that even our joint households which are the remnants of the traditional joint family, do not most often work as solid, cohesive units. We have shown to what extent the consumption patterns of different nuclear units (husband-wife-children nucleus) within a joint household vary. Actually, whether or not to remain within a joint household is often decided in terms of the benefits obtained from it, i.e., whether it would be convenient and economic to do so.

Next, ideally joint family being a patrilineal, patri-local institution, intensity of ties with the husband's patri-kin should be closer than that with the relatives in the female line. Our observation, however, shows the emergence of a bilateral kinship system where the ties with the wife's natal kin are sufficiently strong. It goes against the strength and solidarity of the joint family. Desai also accepts this when he says that men displaying thickness with the wife's blood relatives, in effect, leave one family and join another (1955, p.117).

Joint family requires a hierarchical authority structure. Our findings, in contrast, indicate inclination towards the prevalence of egalitarian values and relationships. With the increase in the role and importance of the wife, interactions with her natal kin are bound to increase. This, of course, does not mean that interactions with the husbands' kin will thereby reduce. But, it means that now it is the wife who will decide with which of the kin of the husband how much cordiality or detachment will be maintained.

Further, to make the joint family widely prevalent, men are required to separate at least after their parents' death. But often it does not happen and an early separation has been reported in majority of the cases studied in this sample. Sometimes, it is argued that the poor life span of our men is the reason behind the low incidence of joint households, for after the death of the father there is no ritual bar against separation. But if the spirit of the joint family were really genuine, people should show interest in continuing (in the absence of the father) supplemented CJ and supplemented nuclear types of households, one can reasonably expect. It means, premature death of the parents may be the reason behind the low incidence of LJ and LCJ types of households. But definitely the existence of CJ and SuNu types of households will not be at stake thereby. Many of our respondents, however, are not optimistic about the future of these latter types of households also.

Moreover, though there is no serious ideological attack on the institution of the joint family, the respondents have clearly expressed their verdict in favour of the small joint households, if it is to be practised at all. They do not think that the large three- or four-generational households are feasible or manageable in today's society, though they have spoken in favour of the maintenance of functional bonds and spiritual jointness with the kin. So we can conclude that our society is advancing towards the 'modified extended family'.

The above observations show that in order to adjust itself with the changing circumstances, to meet the demands of the modern way of life, joint households will be reduced to a smaller size (LJ and SuNu types of households). The fact not be lost sight of is that still a substantial section of our respondents consider the joint family as good though not workable. In spite of the existence of friends and work-mates, a substantial portion of interactions of our people, irrespective of whether they live in nuclear or joint households, are embedded within the circle of the kindred. Non-availability of help and support from the government or any other source makes them dependent on the kin, and the dependence and interactions constantly reinforce and revitalise the kinship cohesion. At the same time, this kinship matrix within which aid and assistance are exchanged and the occasions on which such exchanges take place are undergoing modifications and alterations to suit modern environmental needs and pressures.

The foregoing analysis makes it clear that tradition and modernity can co-exist and adjust with one another. The data also display that to accept modern values and behaviour one need not necessarily discard the old ones. In our country where still the same people use magical practices and modern medicine, man-pulled rickshaw and automobile, have faith in both caste and religious dogmas and scientific knowledge and technology, use their democratic rights through casting votes following the dictum of the religious leaders and caste or lineage elders, it is no wonder that diverse types of household structures also co-exist side by side.

Lastly, this is our submission that though this study cannot claim for the *Statistical* validity of its findings, it would open up, we expect, new areas of inquiry into the family behaviour and interactions and would generate far more questions than it has answered.

Bibliography

Agarwala, B.R. 1955, "Caste and Joint Family in a Mobile Commercial Community", *Sociological Bulletin,* Vol. IV (2), September, pp. 138-46.

Axelrod, M. 1956, "Urban Structure and Social Participation", *American Sociological Review*, Vol. 21 (1), February, pp. 13-18.

Babbie, E. 1992, *The Practice of Social Research,* Wadsworth Publishing Company, New York, 6th edn.

Bailey, F.G. 1957, *Caste and the Economic Frontier: A Village in Highland Orissa*, Manchester University Press, Manchester.

— 1960, "The Joint Family in India: A Framework for Discussion", *The Economic Weekly,* February 20, Vol. 12, pp. 345-52.

Bell, C.R. 1968, *Middle Class Families: Social and Geographical Mobility,* RKP, New York.

Bell, W. and Boat, M.D. 1957, "Urban Neighbourhoods and Informal Social Relations", *American Journal of Sociology,* Vol. 62, January, pp. 391-98.

Beteille, A. 1974, *Studies in Agrarian Social Structure,* Oxford University Press, Bombay.

Bhadra, R.K. 1977, "Some Observations in the Study of Family Change in India", *Man in India,* Vol. 57 (1), January-March, pp. 44-59.

Blau, P.M. 1976, *Approaches to the Study of Social Structure,* Open Books Publishing Ltd., London.

Blood, R.O. (Jr.). 1970, "Social Change and Kinship Patterns" in R. Hill and R. Konig (eds.), *Families in East and West*, Mouton, Netherlands.

Bossard, J.H.S. and Boll, E.S. 1966, *The Sociology of Child Development*, A Harper International Edition, Tokyo, 4th edn.

Bott, E. 1957, *Family and Social Network*, Tavistock Publications, London.

Burgess, E.W. et al. 1963, *The Family*, Van Nostrand Reinhold Company, New York, 4th edn.

Chakrabortty, K. 1978, *The Conflicting Worlds of Working Mothers: A Sociological Inquiry*, Progressive Publishers, Calcutta.

— 1982, "A Note on Family Research in India", *Socialist Perspective*, Vol. 10 (3), Calcutta, pp. 155-68.

Chekki, D.A. 1974, *Modernisation and Kin Network*, E.J. Brill. Leiden, Netherlands.

Cohn, B.S. 1961, "Chamar Family in a North Indian Village: A Structural Contingent", *The Economic Weekly*, Spl. Number, July, pp. 1051-1057.

Conklin, G.H. 1968, "The Family Formation Process in India: An Overview", *The Journal of Family Welfare*, Vol. 14 (3), March, pp. 28-37.

— 1969, "Social Change and the Joint Family: The Causes of Research Biases", *Economic and Political Weekly*, Vol. 4, September 6, pp. 1445-1448.

Desai, I.P. 1955, "An Analysis", *Sociological Bulletin*, Vol. IV (2), September, pp. 97-117.

— 1956, "The Joint family in India: An Analysis", *Sociological Bulletin*, Vol. V (2), September, pp. 144-156.

— 1964, *Some Aspects of Family in Mahuva: A Sociological Study of Jointness in a Small Town*, Asia Publishing House, Bombay.

— 1975, "A Note on Family Research" in D. Narain (ed.), *Explorations in the Family and Other Essays*, Thacker & Co. Ltd., Bombay.

Dube, L. 1974, "Sociology of Kinship" in *A Survey of Research in Sociology and Social Anthropology*, Vol. II, I.C.S.S.R., Popular Prakashan, Bombay.

Dube, S.C. 1967, *Indian Village*, Allied Publishers, Bombay (first published in 1955).

Fletcher, R. 1962, *The Family and Marriage in Britain*, Penguin, 3rd edn.

Fortes, M. 1958, "Introduction" in J. Goody (ed.), *The Developmental Cycle in Domestic Groups*, Cambridge University Press, London.

Freed, S.A. and Freed, R.S. 1982, "Changing Family Types in India", *Ethnology*, Vol. 21 (3), July, pp. 189-202.

Goode, W.W. 1963, *World Revolution and Family Patterns*, Free Press of Glencoe, Collier-Macmillan Ltd., London.

— 1965, *The Family*, Prentice-Hall of India (private) Ltd., New Delhi.

Goody, J. (ed.) 1958, *The Developmental Cycle in Domestic Groups*, Cambridge University Press, London.

Hallen, G.C. 1982, *Family Researches in India: Some Strategies*, Rohini Publications, Meerut.

Harris, C.C. 1969, *The Family: An Introduction*, George Allen & Unwin, London.

Homans, G.C. 1951, *The Human Group*, RKP, London.

— 1976, "What Do We Mean by Social 'Structure' " in P.M. Blau (ed.), *Approaches to the Study of Social Structure,* Open Books, London.

Indian Institute of Public Opinion, October, 1955, *Monthly Public Opinion Surveys*, Vol. 1 (3), pp. 6-20.

Ishwaran, K. 1974, "The Interdependence of Elementary and Extended Family" in G. Kurien (ed.), *The Family in India: A Regional View,* Mouton, The Hague.

Kapadia, K.M. 1956, "Rural Family Patterns: A Study in Urban-Rural Relations", *Sociological Bulletin,* Vol. V (2), September, pp. 111-125.

—1959, "The Family in Transition", *Sociological Bulletin*, Vol. VIII(2), September, pp. 68-99.

— 1966, *Marriage and Family in India,* Oxford University Press, Calcutta, 3rd edn.

Karve, I. 1953, *Kinship Organisation in India*, Asia Publishing House Bombay.

Kolenda, P. 1987, *Regional Differences in Family Structure in India*, Rawat Publications, Jaipur.

Kulkarni, M.G. 1960, "Family Patterns in Gokak Taluka", *Sociological Bulletin,* Vol. IX (1), March, pp. 60-81.

Kumar J. 1974, "Family Structure in the Hindu Society of Rural India", in G. Kurien (ed.), *The Family in India,* Mouton, The Hague,

Litwak, E. 1960a, "Occupational Mobility and Extended Family Cohesion", *American Sociological Review,* Vol. 25,pp. 9-21.

— 1960b, "Geographic Mobility and Extended Family Cohesion", *American Sociological Review,* Vol. 25, pp. 385-394.

— 1965, "Extended Kin Relations in an Industrial Democratic Society" in E. Shanas and G.F. Streib (eds.), *Nuclear and Extended Family Relationships: A Normative and Behavioural Analysis,* Prentice-Hall Inc, New Jersey.

Larson, O.P. 1968, "Rural Society" in D.L. Sills (ed.), *International Encyclopaedia of the Social Sciences,* The Macmillan Company and Free Press, New York, pp. 580-589.

Madan, T.N. 1962a, "The Hindu Joint Family", *Man*, Vol. 62, pp. 88-89.

— 1962b, "The Joint Family: A Terminological Clarification", *Indian Journal of Comparative Sociology*, Vol. 3(1), September, pp. 7-16.

— 1989, *Family and Kinship,* Oxford University Press, Delhi, 2nd edn.

— 1993, "The Hindu Family and Development" in P. Uberoi (ed.), *Family, Kinship and Marriage*, Oxford University Press, Delhi.

Mandelbaum, D. 1970, *Society in India*, Popular Prakashan, Bombay.

Mayer, A.C. 1960, *Caste and Kinship in Central India*, RKP, London.

Merchant, K.T. 1935, *Changing Views on Marriage and Family,* B.G. Paul & Co. Publishers, Madras.

Morgan, D.H.J. 1975, *Social Theory and the Family,* RKP, London.

Morrison, W.A. 1959, "Family Types in Badlapur: An Analysis of a Changing Institution in a Maharashtrian Village", *Sociological Bulletin,* Vol. VIII (2), September, pp. 45-67.

Mueller, J.H. and Schuesler, K.F. 1961, *Statistical Reasoning in Sociology,* Oxford & IBH Publishing Co., Calcutta.

Mukherjee, R.K. 1965, *The Sociologist and Social Change in India Today,* Prentice-Hall of India (Pvt.) Ltd., New Delhi.

— 1975, "Family in India" in D. Narain (ed.), *Exploration in the Family and Other Essays*, Thacker & Co. Ltd. Bombay.

— 1977, *The West Bengal Family Structures: 1946-1966*, Macmillan, Delhi.

— 1982, "Family in India: A Perspective" in G.C. Hallen (ed.), *Family Researches in India: Some Strategies,* Rohini Publications, Meerut.

Murdock, G.P. 1949, *Social Structure,* Macmillan, New York.

Nicholas, R.W. 1961, "Economics of Family Types in Two West Bengal Villages", *The Economic Weekly,* July 13, Spl. Number, pp. 1057-1060.

Nimcoff, M.F. 1959. "The Family in India", *Sociological Bulletin*, Vol. VIII (2), September, pp. 32-38.

Nimcoff, M.F. and Middleton, R. 1960, "Types of Family and Types of Economy", *American Journal of Sociology,* Vol. 66 (3), November, pp. 215-225.

Orenstein, H. and Micklin, M. 1966, "The Hindu Joint Family: The Norms and the Numbers", *Pacific Affairs,* Vol. 39 (3 & 4), pp. 314-325.

Parsons, T. 1949, "The Social Structure of the Family" in R.N. Nanda (ed.), *The Family: Its Function and Destiny*, Harper & Brothers Publishers, New York.

Prabhu, P.H. 1963., *Hindu Social Organisation,* Popular Prakashan, Bombay.

Ross, A.D. 1961, *The Hindu Family in its Urban Setting,* Oxford University Press, Delhi.

Sarma, J. 1951, "Formal and Informal Relations in the Hindu Joint Household of Bengal", *Man in India*, Vol. 31(2), pp. 51-71.

— 1964, "The Nuclearisation of Joint Family in West Bengal", *Man in India*, Vol. 44(3), July-September, pp. 193-205.

Sen, L.K. 1965, "Family in Four Indian Villages", *Man in India,* Vol. 45, pp. 1-16.

Sengupta. S. 1958, "Family Organisation in West Bengal: Its Nature and Dynamics", *The Economic Weekly*, Vol. 10, March 15, pp. 384-389.

Shah, A.M. 1964, "Basic Terms and Concepts in the Study of Family in India", *The Indian Economic and Social History Review,* Vol. 1(3), January-March, pp. 1-36.

— 1968, "Change in the Indian Family: An Examination of Some Assumptions", *Economic and Political Weekly*, Vol. 3 (1/2), Annual Number, January, pp. 127-134.

— 1969, "Study of Changes in the Indian Family" in *Trends of Socio-economic Changes in India, 1871-1961,* Indian Institute of Advanced Study, Shimla.

— 1973, *The Household Dimension of Family in India,* Orient Longman Ltd., New Delhi.

— 1998, *The Family in India*, Orient Longman, New Delhi.

Shahani, S. 1961, "The Joint Family: A Case Study", *The Economic Weekly*, Vol. 13 (49), December 9, pp. 1823-1828.

Sinha, R.P. 1977, "Indian Joint Family: An Attempt Toward Taxonomic Refinement", *Man in India*, Vol. 57, (1). January-March. pp. 60-68.

Srinivas, M.N. 1966, *Social Change in Modern India*, Orient Longman Ltd., Pune, Indian edn.

Straus, MA. 1975, "Husband-Wife Interaction in Nuclear and Joint Households" in D. Narain (ed.), *Exploration in the Family and Other Essays*, Thacker & Co. Ltd., Bombay.

Sussman, M.B. 1953, "The Help Pattern in Middle Class Family", *American Soc. Review,* Vol. 18 (1), February, pp. 22-28.

— 1970, 'The Urban Kin Network in the Formulation of Family Theory' in R. Hill and R. Koenig (eds.), *Families in East and West,* Mouton, Netherlands.

Young, M. and Willmott, P. 1957, *Families and Kinship in East London*, RKP.

Index